The Bastard of Fort Stikine

Also by Debra Komar

The Lynching of Peter Wheeler
The Ballad of Jacob Peck

The
BASTARD
of
FORT
STIKINE

The Hudson's Bay Company and
the Murder of John McLoughlin Jr.

DEBRA KOMAR

Edited by Sarah Brohman.
Cover photo of beaver dam by Jason Drury (500px.com/jasondrury).
Firearm photo courtesy of Fredericton Region Museum.
Cover and page design by Chris Tompkins.
Printed in Canada.
10 9 8 7 6 5 4 3 2 1

Library and Archives Canada Cataloguing in Publication

Komar, Debra, 1965-, author
The bastard of Fort Stikine : the Hudson's Bay Company
and the murder of John McLoughlin Jr. / Debra Komar.

Includes bibliographical references and index.
Issued in print and electronic formats.
ISBN 978-0-86492-871-9 (pbk.). — ISBN 978-0-86492-781-1 (epub). —
ISBN 978-0-86492-721-7 (mobi)

1. McLoughlin, John, Jr., died 1842. 2. McLoughlin, John, 1784-1857.
3. Simpson, George, Sir, 1792?-1860. 4. Murder — Alaska — Fort Stikine.
5. Hudson's Bay Company — Employees — Crimes against. 6. Hudson's Bay
Company — Employees — Biography. 7. Fort Stikine (Alaska) — Biography.
8. Hudson's Bay Company — History. I. Title.

HV6533.A53K64 2015   364.152'3097982   C2014-906844-1
                                                      C2014-906845-X

Goose Lane Editions acknowledges the generous support of the Canada Council for the Arts, the Government of Canada through the Canada Book Fund (CBF), and the Government of New Brunswick through the Department of Tourism, Heritage and Culture.

Goose Lane Editions
500 Beaverbrook Court, Suite 330
Fredericton, New Brunswick
CANADA E3B 5X4
www.gooselane.com

RECYCLED
Paper made from
recycled material
FSC
www.fsc.org   FSC® C103567

To my parents,
for never asking how three degrees in anthropology
would help support them in their old age.

CONTENTS

Preface

This book began with one question but ended with another. Initially, I had planned to use modern forensic science to solve an unsolved murder from deep in our nation's past. The impetus for doing so was pure frustration and a dead king.

In 2012, a team of archaeologists found human remains in a car park in Leicester, England. The decedent was a man in his late twenties or early thirties. The grave was centuries old, and although the skeleton was in remarkably good condition, the same could not be said for the individual it represented. The body was stunted in stature, the spine showed marked scoliosis, and there were eight wounds to the skull, clear indications of a bloody and traumatic death. There was no clothing, coffin, or shroud, but the researchers felt certain they knew the man's identity. Five months later, DNA tests confirmed the bones were those of Richard III, the medieval hunchbacked king immortalized in the works of William Shakespeare. The discovery made headlines around the world.

King Richard was just the latest entry in a growing roster of high-profile biohistorical investigations. Biohistory is modern science applied to antiquity, including any form of analysis (such as DNA, radiography, or chemical assays) used on human remains or other biological materials to answer questions regarding historical personages. Although science is all-encompassing, biohistory is not, and the positive identification of putative remains through DNA testing has been the discipline's almost single-minded focus. Such identifications span the globe and the ideological spectrum, and include such diverse personalities as Auschwitz's "Angel of Death," Dr. Josef Mengele, and the apostle Luke.

Forensic scientists have toiled on the fringes of biohistory, and at first glance it seems a logical synthesis of discipline and subject. But the marriage has yet to produce viable offspring, and that is the source of my frustration. Although DNA has opened new lines of inquiry, it is not the panacea many believe it to be. Such testing is invaluable in resolving issues of identity, but DNA contributes nothing to our understanding of *how, when,* and *why* death occurred. Furthermore, subjecting every organic scrap of history to genetic testing only muddies the water, as researchers try to force the technology to answer questions it is incapable of resolving. Most biohistorical studies seem content with simply putting a name to a set of remains, but identifying John or Jane Does is only the first step in the investigative process. DNA testing has its place, but there is more to history than just names. If biohistory is to be a true test of the power of forensic science to illuminate the past, we must move beyond the process of identification and ask more complex questions.

This led me to the first question in this investigation: is it possible to reach back in time and resolve an unsolved murder without relying solely on DNA? Finding an answer required a special test case, and after months of searching I found one in the records of the Hudson's Bay Company (HBC).

The killing of chief trader John McLoughlin Jr. remains one of Canada's most enduring mysteries. The case never saw the inside of a courtroom, and the legal system records no verdict. Understanding what happened at Fort Stikine in the early morning hours of April 21, 1842, became all the more daunting because the crime was never formally investigated: there was no police report, no autopsy was conducted, and no suspect was ever charged or convicted. Still, the truth will out, and history finds myriad ways to freeze a lethal moment in time. Think what you will about the Hudson's Bay Company's tumultuous place in our nation's history, but give them this: they were consummate record keepers.

Solving a murder more than 170 years after it was committed is a challenge, but there is more to this story than a historical whodunit. At its core, the story of John McLoughlin Jr.'s murder is a meditation on the nature of grief and guilt, and how these emotions drove the victim's father, John McLoughlin Sr., to search for justice in all the wrong places. Grief seldom travels alone.

It is inevitably accompanied by feelings of guilt or shame and is laden with the baggage of unresolved issues and troubled relationships.

I saw this grief-generated hunt for justice countless times during the more than twenty years I worked as a medicolegal investigator. Unable to process their pain, survivors shift the focus to an external goal. They believe peace and resolution can only be found in a specific outcome: if only I could find my missing loved one; if only I could bring the perpetrator to account. They begin to fixate on the death and not the life that preceded it. The notion of acceptance or forgiveness becomes incomprehensible to them, and every drop of energy is spent pursuing their objective. The problem, of course, is that solving a murder demands more than just naming the culprit, and prolonged quests for justice do not end suffering. They merely delay it.

I once worked on a case in New Mexico involving the murder of a teenaged girl. For seventeen years, the girl's mother believed the boy next door had killed her daughter, and she dedicated every waking hour to proving his guilt. On the day the boy was finally convicted, the victim's mother looked empty. The conviction did not end her torment but only enhanced it by stripping her of the identity she had created: the mother of a murdered child, fighting for justice. All that remained was for her to mourn her daughter, something she had avoided doing for seventeen years.

Which brings me to my second question: what is justice? How do we define it and, more importantly, how do we achieve it? What are we seeking in the wake of a violent, unnatural death? Advances in forensic science allow us to solve crimes centuries after they occurred, but to what end? Our current system of justice is designed to punish the perpetrator, but how do we right the wrong when there is no one left to penalize?

There has to be more to justice than simple retribution. Years of working on large-scale international investigations of human rights violations and genocide have taught me that our traditional notions of justice are too small to address crimes of real magnitude. Whether it is one murder or thousands, we are defining "success" in our pursuit of criminal justice too narrowly and are therefore condemning ourselves to failure.

Justice is not an end in itself, and what ails us in loss cannot be cured in a courthouse. We need to move beyond the "vengeance equals justice" model that is the essence of our current system of jurisprudence. The goal has to be acceptance and understanding, however and whenever it comes. That message has particular resonance in the case of John McLoughlin Jr., for there can be no legal remedy to a crime so long passed. The objective in solving McLoughlin's murder is not to hold the guilty party accountable or to hang a long-dead criminal in absentia. My intention with this investigation is to understand what happened and glean lessons from the past, for therein lies justice and peace.

§

What follows is a true story. All text in quotes was drawn from historical documents, including depositions, correspondence, and other primary sources. Wherever possible, I have used the words of eyewitnesses to the events. Presenting an exhaustive history of the Hudson's Bay Company is beyond the scope of this book, and those seeking a broad historical accounting can easily find it in the works of Peter C. Newman, W. Kaye Lamb, and Glyndwr Williams, among others. My intention is to reconstruct a specific moment and colour it with sufficient background to anchor it firmly in time and place. What was true of life at Fort Stikine in the early 1840s may not hold true at other junctures in the rich four-hundred-year history of the Honourable Company.

This tale involves two men, a father and son, bearing the same name and similar job titles. To avoid confusion, the murder victim—John McLoughlin Jr., chief trader—will be referred to as McLoughlin, McLoughlin Jr., or Mr. John, the nickname used by his employees. His father—John McLoughlin Sr., chief factor—will be identified as Dr. McLoughlin, McLoughlin Sr., or Dr. John, his Company nickname.

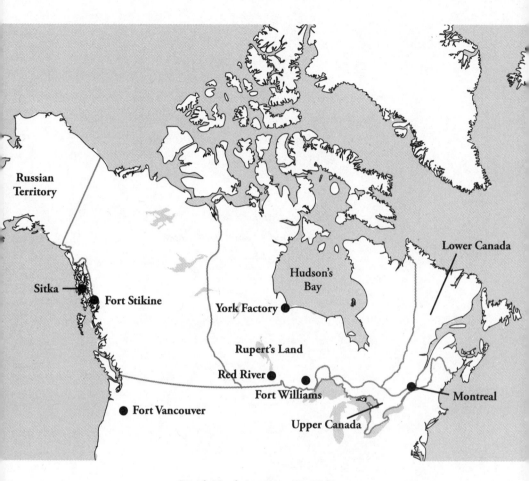

British North America, circa 1840

*It is part of the fascination of the study of history
that we often know more about what went on a hundred years ago
than the men of those times knew themselves.*
William Stewart Wallace, 1932

*I will be glad, if you are writing a history,
if justice could be done to that man.*
J. Quinn Thornton, 1878

Wednesday, April 20, 1842 — Midday
FORT STIKINE

On the last day of his life, John McLoughlin Jr. awoke at noon
to a world that was already going on without him. Beside him
lay his "Indian Wife"; they were coupled *à la façon du pays*,
making her something more than a mistress but less than a
lawfully wedded spouse. Not every man in Fort Stikine was
permitted to keep a woman within its walls, but McLoughlin
was the outpost's chief trader, and rank had its privileges.

History does not record the woman's name. In official
company documents she was simply "Quatkie's daughter" or
"McLoughlin's wife," as though she ceased to exist outside of
her relationships with men. Although nameless, she was still
the daughter of a chief, and McLoughlin was the son of a chief
factor of the Hudson's Bay Company, but what kept them in
bed at so late an hour had nothing to do with their inherited
lustre or even post-coital bliss: it was insomnia, born of paranoia, marbled with fear.

McLoughlin's restlessness had dogged him for months. It
began with his promotion to chief trader, the fort's highest office,
and was exacerbated by the recent loss of his trusted right-hand,
Roderick Finlayson. The departure of Finlayson left the highly
inexperienced McLoughlin in sole and uneasy command. As he
told his colleagues, "I have had all the troubles that a man could
have since I have been alone," adding ominously, "I have had
scarcely any rest, night and day I am up — it is to [*sic*] much for
one and my constitution cannot stand it in such a troublesome
place as this post is."

These laments were no idle boasts or exaggeration. Since
Finlayson's transfer, Fort Stikine had become McLoughlin's
perdition. The outpost — built near what is now the town of
Wrangell in the Alaskan panhandle — was "situated . . . among a
horde of savages." The local people resented the Company's
encroachment on their lands and repeatedly "attempted to scale

the stockade with a view of taking the place." Tensions escalated when the First Nation warriors destroyed the bridge linking the fort to the mainland, which in turn threatened the outpost's water supply. The traders retaliated by taking a local chief hostage and holding him captive until his people repaired the damage.

The threat from outside the fort's stockades, however, paled in comparison to the menace lurking within. Hostile as they were, the aboriginals were no match for the worthless band of miscreants, malcontents, and lost boys that made up the fort's complement. Even the neighbouring tribes knew "Mr. John has bad white men at Stikine."

Some of those men made no secret of their intention to kill their new chief trader; indeed, the assassination plot was an open topic of conversation among Stikine's ranks. In the weeks prior, Company trader Pierre Kannaquassé had gone so far as to shoot at McLoughlin on three separate occasions. Each time the bullet flew shy of its mark, but guns were not the only means at Kannaquassé's disposal. Earlier in March, Kannaquassé approached Nahua, the fort's cook, and urged him "to poison McLoughlin by putting the scrapings of copper in his soup." Horrified, Nahua insisted he "would do no such thing." Nahua later informed McLoughlin of the treachery, and Mr. John gave Kannaquassé a sound thrashing. Still, McLoughlin held off firing his would-be assassin until he received word from his father, the region's chief factor, on how best to deal with the man. It is telling that repeated attempts on the life of one's superior were not automatic grounds for dismissal in the Hudson's Bay Company.

Although the plots were thwarted, McLoughlin knew the threat remained, and he wrote to his supervisor, John Work: "I am still amongst the living of this troublesome post though reports say that I am going to be dispatched to the *Sandy Hills*," a poetic euphemism for the cemetery. McLoughlin put on a brave face, telling Work, "all that does not trouble me much —but it keeps me on my guard."

The demons plaguing John McLoughlin were not all so tangible. He had a history of self-destructive behavior and often suffered from bouts of depression, what he called getting "the Blue devils." His mental darkness always descended at night, when the normal timpani of the fort fell silent, and he often complained, "I do not know what to do in the evening when I cannot sleep."

He did find one nighttime distraction particularly compelling. According to a junior officer, Mr. John "was always trying to catch the Watchmen sleeping, coming by stealth wrapped up in his Blanket." On one occasion, McLoughlin found a guard snoring and beat the man to within an inch of his life. Whether such corporal punishment was a necessary evil to ensure the fort's security or a symptom of the chief trader's declining mental stability was a subject ripe for debate. Curiously, even the man beaten for sleeping on his watch later admitted his harsh discipline was justified.

In between his midnight raids on the watchtowers, McLoughlin spent his twilight hours pacing, his thoughts a choir of despair. As each day drew to a close, his country wife prayed for exhaustion to overtake him. On the evening of April 19, he did not surrender until the light of dawn pierced the cracks of their room. With equal parts resignation and trepidation, McLoughlin pulled himself from his bed. There was work to be done, and if history were any guide, it would not happen without his constant vigilance and firm disciplinary hand. He looked a fright. On his best days, he had more hair than any man had use for, but he had let himself go, and his wild mane and boot-scrape beard did little to foster an image of sanity. He opened his window just a crack, a hedge against the cold and the nebulous threat. He shouted to Nahua to fetch him some food, but his barking was met only by silence.

Low-hanging clouds drained the blue from the sky, and the rain dripped incessantly. The sombre atmosphere matched his décor. Home was little more than a poor man's still life: a timber box on the upper floor of the fort's main house, punctuated with a few meagre possessions. Such was the price owed for the choices he'd made. He was just shy of thirty at a time when men counted themselves lucky to live a decade longer, and he was far from his ancestral home, although this was of no consequence to a peripatetic man like John McLoughlin.

He wasted little time on his morning ablutions, for personal grooming meant nothing in Fort Stikine. He dressed and drank, no doubt cursing the long-lost Nahua for robbing him of his morning meal. Then McLoughlin paused to take his wife's hands, and they shared a few words. The words must have been few indeed, for he spoke only a smattering of her language, and she knew nothing of his. In more public settings, John relied on the services of Hanega Joe, the post's ersatz translator. Joe claimed to have been educated in the United States and spoke "a little English," a triumph of understatement. McLoughlin had already fired Hanega Joe once, only to rehire him almost immediately; desperation breeds forgiveness, and some English was better than none. But here, in the privacy of their room, the couple did what they could to make themselves understood. Even without words, their partings had taken on an air of finality.

It took all he had to leave the room, although his hesitancy had little to do with the menace waiting for him outside the door. Rather, it was a formidable crossbar, recently crafted by the fort's carpenters and blacksmiths, preventing his exit. Call it what you will — a prescient shield against the looming evil or an artifact of his fevered paranoia — but "every night before he went to bed, he used to bar the door on the inside, as if he knew their treacherous intentions." Whether such excessive precaution served to keep evil in or out is the question at the heart of this mystery.

I

"Lamentable Deficiency"

ONE

L'Enfant Terrible

As a child of quiet privilege, much was expected of John McLoughlin Jr., yet he never failed to disappoint. He was labelled "*l'enfant terrible*" from the time he could crawl, and most who knew the boy dismissed him as a good-for-nothing, while the rest were convinced he was not good for much. Thinking poorly of John was a way of life for those cursed with his acquaintance. Even his closest allies felt he had earned such opprobrium, and his life became a litany of squandered opportunities.

John McLoughlin's inability to play well with others was evident almost from birth. He burst forth on August 18, 1812, his tiny fists ready to do battle, and his head topped with a tuft of floss the colour of ravens. His birthdate was recorded for posterity, but the location remains an open question. Most who have given the matter any thought agree that John made his inauspicious debut in the fur trading post of Fort William, nestled in the shadow of the stone formation known as the Sleeping Giant in Thunder Bay, where his father was making a name for himself.

At six foot, four inches, John McLoughlin Sr. was impossible to ignore and wholly unforgettable. Formidable in every sense, he walked with purpose, even when he had nowhere to go. Eternally restless and chronically dissatisfied, he faced the world with the absolute certainty it would bend to his will. HBC governor George Simpson once called the senior McLoughlin a "proud giant," adding that he cut "such a figure as I should not like to meet in a dark Night in one of the by-lanes in the neighbourhood of London." Daughter Eloisa described him with military precision: "Stature tall. Hair white and

The White-Headed Eagle, John McLoughlin Sr., in a photo taken near the end of his life.

partially grey. Eyes dark. Very strong frame. A slightly French accent. Good features." Although his French accent polished off the rough edges, "he had a rapid way of speaking & sputterin" as though his brain and tongue were in a race to the finish. When angered, he lowered his voice in a way that made his displeasure all the more audible. He spoke English and French with equal command and knew at least one aboriginal dialect "tolerably well," giving him "a good deal of influence with Indians." For his efforts, the local tribes dubbed him the White-Headed Eagle, one of several nicknames he accrued in his lifetime, bestowed with respect if not necessarily affection.

What little wit McLoughlin Sr. possessed was gin-dry and seldom displayed. He had a hearty laugh, but his darker side was readily apparent. "My father was very quick tempered," Eloisa recalled, while George Simpson pegged him as a man with an "ungovernable Violent temper and turbulent disposition." Certainly this "stubborn, irascible" man "was well known for his use of physical punishment" and feared by his trading partners. Even Eloisa conceded her father was a stickler for rules, who expected that "what he said must be so." "I think he required those about him to show him proper respect because he was in the Company and was the head man." Mercifully, his surliness was short-lived. "Right off he cooled down when his temper was up, and was quite good hearted," Eloisa recalled, "he was fond of children; very fond of ladies' company; fond of talking and visiting."

Dr. McLoughlin's gregarious nature had served him well in business. He was a fixture of the burgeoning fur trade, one of "the lords of the lakes and the forests" who had inadvertently transformed the pursuit of commerce into the building of a nation and an empire. Heeding the call of the wild, McLoughlin signed up for a life that spit out lesser men without a second thought.

John McLoughlin Sr. was born on October 19, 1784, in Rivière-du-Loup, a crossroads on the southern shore of the St. Lawrence, 120 miles east of Quebec City. He was an earnest child, more interested in science and literature than roughhousing. He began studying medicine at fourteen and soon excelled at his chosen profession. In 1803, just shy of his nineteenth birthday, McLoughlin Sr. petitioned for leave to practise medicine. His application was certified by his tutor, Dr. Fisher, who swore he "behaved honestly, he possesses talents." With that tepid recommendation, McLoughlin Sr. became a licensed physician, and the North West Company (NWC) eventually hired him as an entry-level surgeon.

Legend has it that McLoughlin Sr. only accepted the post to escape an assault charge after he tossed a drunken British soldier into the mud. The soldier had insulted the honour of McLoughlin's female companion, but the military did not look kindly on any affront to the uniform, regardless of the character inhabiting it. The NWC contract saved McLoughlin from jail, and he was dispatched to Kaministikwia, where he took over the fort's medical duties, a period he would recall in his dotage as "his sad Experiment."

While at Kaministikwia, Dr. John's interests were not entirely medical. During his first year he met Marguerite Wadin McKay, the daughter of a Swiss Protestant and his Cree wife. At the time, Marguerite was the country wife of Alexander McKay, a fellow NWC employee. In 1810, McKay joined an expedition, led by Wilson Price Hunt and financed by millionaire magnate John Jacob Astor, which planned to follow in the footsteps of Lewis and Clark and their Corps of Discovery. McKay set sail for the Pacific Coast, leaving behind Marguerite and their young children, but the newly single mother soon found solace in the arms of the outpost's doctor.

When it became clear Alexander McKay was never coming back, Dr. John and Marguerite made their relationship official by exchanging vows in a church ceremony. The nuptials had the added benefit of "giving full legal status to their children," which in the summer of 1812 included a son they christened John.

Whether John McLoughlin Jr.'s childhood was idyllic or hellish is a matter of opinion and degree. He was never a biddable child, and his capacity for mischief grew faster than his bones. Curiously, John never mentioned his mother in his later correspondence, so their adult relationship can only be reconstructed by inference. His earliest years were lonely ones, but he was not alone for long. Sisters Marie Elisabeth and Eloisa joined the family by the time John was five. Brother David followed in 1821, but by then John was gone.

At age eight, young John was sent to study with the Reverend Mr. Glen in Montreal, at the first of what would be many boarding schools. The responsibility for his education fell squarely on his father, but Dr. McLoughlin, now in the employ of the HBC, was travelling constantly for business, leaving him little time for his son. En route to London, McLoughlin Sr. stopped in Montreal long enough to drop the boy on the doorstep of Dr. Simon Fraser, Dr. McLoughlin's favourite uncle. Not to be confused with the famous explorer of the same name, Dr. Simon Fraser (1769-1844) was a major of the Terrebonne Division and a lieutenant of Her Majesty's 42nd (Royal Highland) Regiment. Retired from active service, Dr. Fraser lived in a well-appointed home in one of Montreal's better neighbourhoods.

Dr. McLoughlin had paid good money to place his son with Mr. Glen, but the arrangement was doomed from the start. John found himself alone and homesick in a strange city. His emotions fluctuated wildly and he chattered incessantly. The Reverend Mr. Glen soon sent him packing "on account of the habit [he] had of soiling [his] breeches and remaining in that condition for days." John was dumped back in the lap of his great-uncle Simon, who took the boy to task: "I blamed your mother for this filthy habit. I am now convinced I was wrong, the blame lay solely on your innate perversity." It seems that perversity extended beyond John's scatological protests, for Mr. Glen also alleged John had "corrupted the morals of the other boys," although no specifics were provided.

By this point, John's sole contact with his family consisted of letters from his father, which were few and far between. Although his job required excessive correspondence, many of McLoughlin Sr.'s contemporaries were highly critical of his missives. HBC trader George Roberts spoke for many when he called Dr. McLoughlin "a *very poor* letter writer." His spelling and

The only known photograph of Marguerite Wadin McKay McLoughlin, wife of Dr. McLoughlin, mother of John Jr.

grammar were marginal at best, and his awkward sentence structures left readers struggling to decipher his meaning. John, still in short pants, was equally limited in his literary abilities, and their relationship suffered.

When Dr. McLoughlin returned from Europe, he briefly investigated other schools in Montreal but could find no suitable placement. It was the last time he had a direct hand in his son's education. Frustrated, he once again imposed on his uncle, claiming, "I am so situated that it is impossible for me to attend to my little family concerns." It proved quite an imposition, and Dr. McLoughlin took pains to express his gratitude to Fraser: "I feel very much obliged to you for the Kind attention you have hitherto shown my little Boy. I hope he minds what you say to him."

Dr. McLoughlin's hopes were soon dashed, as his son became a chronic disciplinary problem at school. The father may have been a prolific correspondent with his colleagues, but it seems he had little to say to his son, and the boy struggled with his anger and sense of abandonment. Three years passed without a single written word between them. Alone and ignored, John lashed out at those around him. When his latest headmaster threw up his hands and ordered the lad out, Dr. McLoughlin once again passed his son to Simon Fraser: "You are perfectly at liberty to adopt the plan you chuse in the mode of settling for my Sons Education and I feel certainly under obligation to you for the trouble you have taken."

John was not the only child the senior McLoughlin foisted on his long-suffering uncle. Eventually he pawned off each of his remaining children on Fraser, but the latter three were far less demanding. Accordingly, Dr. McLoughlin had a very different relationship with his youngest children, and he was more openly affectionate, or at least as affectionate as one can be in an annual letter. He expected little of the girls, but Elisabeth, always "a frail child," concerned him. She was sent to the Ursuline convent in Quebec and held under the watchful eye of her aunt, Sister St. Henry, the convent's Mother Superior. Dr. McLoughlin's instructions were quite explicit: "My object is not to give her a splendid Education but a good one—at least a good Education for a Girl."

Fraser's response was a lamentable sign of the times: "The Girl cannot be a nun on account of her birth. I think she ought to be sent to your mother." Dr. McLoughlin did not agree. He valued education highly, even for girls, but his conviction was sorely tested when he received an invoice for £80 to cover Elisabeth's annual tuition. The fee was more than three times what he expected to pay, although less than half the cost of his son's education each year. Still, Dr. McLoughlin was in no position to argue; he sent the money, and Elisabeth remained at the convent.

As for John Jr., help came in the unlikely form of George Simpson, who was then acting governor of overseas operations for the Hudson's Bay Company. Although just days into the post, Simpson was "never at ease with a problem until he had seen its nature for himself," so he implemented a practice that became his administrative trademark: the annual grand tour. The Governor was not content to issue edicts from on high; he wanted to lay hands on every aspect of the operation, although that was more a symptom of his obsessive need for control than an actual management philosophy. Simpson vowed he would visit every one of the Company's outposts, and each tour began and ended near Montreal, a town Simpson dismissed as "a filthy irregular place." This travel itinerary put him in proximity to John's perpetually changing roster of boarding schools.

George Simpson was new to the Company and looking to bank favours with his lieutenants, particularly John McLoughlin Sr. During one of his ceremonial passes through Montreal, Simpson feigned interest in the doctor's children and visited Elisabeth in the Ursuline convent. He even went so far as to offer to "meet any drafts necessary for the children's care," although he later recanted the offer.

Simpson had children of his own, but he never expressed the slightest interest in them. He had left behind two daughters in Scotland: Maria, the eldest, and little Isabella. Simpson played no role in their upbringing and maintained no relationship with either of the mothers. More children by different women were to follow, and one observer noted that Simpson's later offspring had "been taught to be afraid of their own Papa." Family life held no charms for George Simpson, who "was never fully a parent, never a doting father or uncle."

When Simpson paid a perfunctory call on John's latest boarding school, he witnessed an altercation that cemented his impression of the young man, one that would have a direct impact on the events at Fort Stikine almost two decades later. It began with a stern reprimand of John from the headmaster, Dr. Newcombe, for "the offense of absenting himself from the House for a couple of hours on Sunday Evening after dark without accounting for his absence in a satisfactory manner, the night being wet and dark." The scolding was harsh, but it was the boy's reaction that captured Simpson's attention. According to Simpson's own account, the young man "flew into a violent passion, made use of highly improper Language and, providing himself with a bludgeon, threatened the Dr's life." Simpson tried to intervene by grabbing hold of the boy, but "instead of showing the least contrition, he burst out into the most violent gust of rage I ever witnessed, became quite frantic with passing, used the most provoking and unrespectful language to the Schoolmaster and, clenching his fist, threated revenge."

John eventually calmed himself, but the damage was done. He began "to collect his Books and with an Oath declared he would not remain another night in the House." He would get his wish, but the burden of rectifying the situation fell to Simpson, who later recalled that "the poor Schoolmaster was quite horrer [sic] struck and alarmed, begged me to take [John] with me." Simpson declined and tried throwing money at the problem, but it was clear the boy had overstayed his welcome when Dr. Newcombe announced he would not "keep him another Week for £500." Although he did not recognize it at the time, John McLoughlin Jr. had made a lifelong enemy of the powerful and petulant George Simpson.

Simpson deposited John at Simon Fraser's front door and then washed his hands of the situation. The Governor's one-strike policy was evident in a letter he sent to Fraser regarding Dr. McLoughlin's problem child: "Up to the time the first complaint was lodged against him I had a very high opinion of the Young Man; his manners and address were pleasing, his temper appeared even and mild, his disposition good and of promising abilities." Indeed, Simpson's initial impression was so favourable he had considered giving "him a Seat in our Counting House" when the boy came of age. All that evaporated with John's tantrum, forcing Simpson into the rare position of admitting he was wrong: "I have never been so grossly deceived in a Young Man, and regret it exceedingly on account of his Father, for whom I have a very great regard." Simon Fraser's patience had worn thin, and the number of schools in Montreal willing to house the teenaged recidivist had dwindled. John wrote to his father, begging to be allowed to come home. His father's refusal was "full of wise and kind counsel," but it struck John's ears as rejection. Their entire relationship had been reduced to a series of letters and the exchange of money, a literal accounting of a father's affection for his wayward son. Dr. McLoughlin closed his letter with a stern warning: "I expect you to pay particular attention to everything my uncle Desires you, as also your school master, as a complaint from them would Expose you to my Displeasure."

Trawling among the pedagogical bottom-feeders, Fraser finally found a willing tutor—a man by the name of Essom—who agreed to take the boy on for a hefty sum. Mr. Essom provided John with room and board, but he left the lad's instruction to his colleague, Mr. Neagle. John was introduced to the basics of arithmetic and bookkeeping, but soon Neagle "could not go further with him." Simon Fraser wrote to Dr. McLoughlin, admitting defeat: "I cannot complain of your son tho he is not so much advanced in his education as I expected. . . . the truth is I was too sanguine, the development of the human mind requires time. Your son is now come to that period when his mind must expand," although it was painfully obvious to everyone that such expansion would not come through formal education.

Wednesday, April 20, 1842 — Dusk
FORT STIKINE

One by one the men passed through the outpost's side gate, skin drenched and bone weary. Although John McLoughlin Jr.'s day had scarcely begun, the traders had been hard at work since the gates were unlocked at six that morning. Work went on regardless the weather, and the men toiled in rain or shine, frost or swelter, in sickness or in health. The day's labour was as backbreaking as it was monotonous: squaring timber to build a new barracks. There was no need for clocks and little sense of time, for the rhythm of their days followed the course of the sun. Now the darkness spread, signalling an end to the ceaseless cycle of work. The air was crisp and cold, and the afternoon's rain gave way to the promise of a clear moonlit night.

Back in the fort, lumber continued to dominate the conversation. McLoughlin called for Louis Leclaire and gave him the dimensions of the new house to be built. Mr. John asked him to square its logs the next day, but it was an order masquerading as a request, one met with eye-rolling resignation. William Lasserte joined the discussion as measurements were taken, and a work detail was organized to prepare the foundation.

The workday was forgettable but the evening proved otherwise. For the past two days, the outpost had played host to "five Indians from Tako," Stikine's closest neighbour. Governor Simpson had recently decided that Fort Tako, a failure from its inception, would be closed within a year's time. The five visitors arrived bearing letters from Tako's chief trader, Mr. Kennedy, and took up residence in Stikine to await McLoughlin's reply before setting off on their return voyage. No one seemed to be in a hurry to leave.

On their second day at Stikine, one of the Tako contingent got into an altercation with McLoughlin after the visitor said something he "considered improper." A brief dust-up ensued, thanks to Hanega Joe's clumsy efforts at translation, and ended when McLoughlin beat the impertinent delegate with his fists. The misunderstanding was eventually settled, and to make amends for his hasty use of force, McLoughlin ordered some rum be taken out of stores and given to the visitors as a peace offering. The gesture smacked of guilt, but the liquor placated the men from Tako. McLoughlin's token gesture did not sit well with his own men, many of whom had been on the receiving end of the chief trader's fists, with no free booze to show for it.

One such man was the fort's cook, Nahua. That afternoon, the cook "went out of the fort for water and Mr. McLoughlin, suspecting that [he] had gone out for some other purpose, struck [him] upon the head and on the arm, with his fist." Nahua promptly burst into tears, wilting under the assault.McLoughlin never made clear what treasonous offence he suspected Nahua of committing, but then, McLoughlin's beatings rarely came with an explanation. As the night wore on, Nahua milked his injury for all it was worth, telling everyone within earshot of his unwarranted suffering. Word eventually circled back to McLoughlin, who came to check on his histrionic cook. He asked him to join the men for the evening's festivities, but Nahua said he was in too much pain to get up. Long accustomed to the cook's theatrics, McLoughlin told Nahua that the party would go on without him.

The chief trader then made his way to the front room on the lower level of the fort's main building, where he found a ceilidh in full swing. The music was simple, catchy, and repetitive, hammered out on anything capable of holding a beat. Despite the hall's snug dimensions, it was chock-a-block with men and a few of the wives. The gratis liquor was making the rounds, and faces were flushed. A disconcerting number of guns and knives were strewn about, misadventures just waiting to happen. The room was lit by a handful of candles, its furnishings a primitive assortment of filthy tables and chairs. A cloud of blue tobacco smoke momentarily overwhelmed the fort's baseline tang of wet wool, curing animal hides, and overflowing latrines.

Despite Nahua's absence, food still found its way to the table. The evening's repast bore a striking resemblance to that of the night before, and the night before that. Venison was the fort's staple, its ubiquity broken only by the occasional appearance of salmon procured from the local tribesmen. To wash down the game, the men had a choice of "brackish water" or hard spirits mixed with brackish water. They inevitably chose the latter.

Had McLoughlin paid more attention, he would have noticed the free-flowing alcohol greatly exceeded the amount he had authorized, and that the men partaking of it were not all from Fort Tako. One man in particular — Benoni Fleury, McLoughlin's Metis valet and the fort's resident spitfire — had overindulged and was growing increasingly sloppy and belligerent. When Fleury could no longer stand or form sentences, McLoughlin carried him to his room with the help of Antoine Kawannassé and William Lasserte.

Without ceremony they threw him onto the bed, but Fleury did not go quietly. He "became very noisy and troublesome. Mr. John spoke to him kindly and endeavoured to quiet him," whispering to him and calling him "my lad [mon enfans]." Fleury's pickled brain was incapable of registering kindness, and he slapped McLoughlin, locking him in a bear hug and accidentally tearing John's shirt. The tussling continued off and on for almost an hour. Each time Fleury calmed down and the chief trader tried to leave, the shouting would start anew and McLoughlin was sucked into another round of slaps and chokeholds. After five attempts to settle the boisterous drunk, McLoughlin finally conceded defeat and tied Fleury to the bed. Even so, "Mr. John did this without anger and from a kind motive," but Fleury continued to rage. Exhausted and at the end of his tether, McLoughlin slapped him several times across the face.

It was a familiar, dysfunctional dance between the two men. In the fall of 1841, the fort's journal records that Fleury "got intoxicated...by helping himself rather too plentifully without permission out of some spirits remaining in the cupboard, for which he got a few well merited cuffs from Mr. John." The frequently crapulent Fleury had grown accustomed to the back of McLoughlin's hand, but his colleagues wanted none of it. When William Lasserte openly criticized the chief trader for striking a drunken man, McLoughlin slapped Lasserte for his insolence. This too was well-trodden ground. McLoughlin once hit Lasserte for "staring him in the face," demanding to know, "Do you wish to kill me with your eyes?" The room's only other occupant, Antoine Kawannassé, also had a troubled history with McLoughlin. Kawannassé swore that the only time McLoughlin ever beat him was "fore entering his room with my hat on, which I did inadvertently." He stood silent, knowing better than to toy with McLoughlin's hair-trigger, then backed out of the room, hat in hand.

With the last few ticks of a superfluous clock, it became April 21, 1842. The men continued to party through the early morning hours, blissfully unaware of the violence occurring upstairs. In a curious testament to liquor's amnesiac powers, one reveller later recalled: "We spent the evening in the utmost harmony, dancing and singing, without an angry word, all parties being in the best possible humour."

TWO

Reckless Deeds
on Distant Shores

Failure has its own momentum. John McLoughlin Jr. was all of fourteen and had floundered as both a son and a student. He was in dire need of a job, but without family wealth or a proper education, his prospects were limited. Times being what they were, John had little say in his choice of profession as tradition held that a father selected his progeny's career, largely because he was expected to pay for it.

Dr. McLoughlin did not care to throw good money after bad, having already wasted hundreds of pounds trying to educate the boy. He was also forced to admit he knew little of the interests or abilities of the son he had so long ignored. Thoroughly vexed, he told John, "I have written my friends to consider what Business you are qualifi'd for and to place you accordingly," but never paused to ask what John's wishes might be. The elder McLoughlin sought guidance from his uncle Simon, who was the closest thing John Jr. had to a true father figure: "I do not know what to do with my Son — what do you think he is fit for?" Simon Fraser had told McLoughlin Sr. to consider "purchasing an Ensigncy for him. I think he would make a good soldier; he is bold and quick in his motions, a Commission would cost 400£. To make him a Merchant would cost you much more and I think he would not have an equal chance of success."

Other suggestions poured in, although none offered much hope for John's future endeavours. Sister St. Henry cautioned against shipping him off to his grandmother in Rivière-du-Loup, worried that the blind and bedridden Angelique McLoughlin was "too infirm to control the wild youth." When it came to the question of occupation, the most Sister St. Henry could offer was "I do not expect to see J. McLoughlin as a farmer." In truth, she feared "he would fall from excesses to excesses, if he does not have a Master." Dr. Simon Fraser was equally pessimistic: "The best thing that can be done for the young man is to make him an Indian Trader....I do not think he would succeed as a Physician, he would have to go thro a long course of studies. These boys are remarkable for want of steadiness and application tho by no means deficient in understanding." Fraser's derisive use of "these boys" referred to all "boys of mixed blood," and it was clear John's heritage had coloured his great-uncle's opinion of him.

On February 1, 1830, Dr. McLoughlin drafted letters to Simon Fraser and his son announcing his decision regarding John's career options, but he was too late. John had set sail for Paris on October 26, 1829, to become ward to his uncle Dr. David McLoughlin. Fraser, who was tired of evading disaster, made the decision. The situation in Montreal had grown so dire, Fraser later told John, he had no choice, for "young as you were when you went to France, your reputation was such that I could find no situation for you in Canada."

John McLoughlin Sr. did not learn of his son's departure until George Simpson told him almost one year later, but Dr. McLoughlin was not the only one wilfully ignorant of his son. Simon Fraser once freely admitted he "did not know John's age," despite having cared for the boy for six years. It is safe to assume that, when John was a child, his birthdays passed without celebration or notice.

§

Life took a decided upturn for John McLoughlin Jr. as he passed from shore to shore, for his uncle's reputation as a prominent surgeon admitted McLoughlin into the top tier of Parisian society. Young John could scarcely contain his glee as he recounted his adventures to his cousin John Fraser: "I spent the winter very gay. I have been to balls even where the Royal family was and also I had a moment's conversation with the Prince and I hope and wish I shall go to the castle." John's wish was granted less than one year later, and he boasted, "I have been to the Kings Bals [sic] and have been

Portrait of John McLoughlin Jr., likely painted in Quebec
when he was in his late teens.

presented to him." To hear him tell it, he was now rubbing elbows with the French elite: "I am received in the first society in Paris."

John's braggadocio extended to his gaming pursuits, and he told his family, "I have learned to fence and I am reckoned a good fencer." Yet his past indiscretions continued to haunt him: "I have been attacked and called out by a school fellow of mine, but never took notice of him, for there is no use of fighting unless there is great offence... perhaps I should have wounded him and it would have served him very much to have done it." It was this mature and reflective John who wrote, "I shall always endeavour to satisfy everybody, this is if I can. If I fail it will not be by want of hard application.... I regret every moment I lost. I wish I had to begin over again my studies."

Not everyone was impressed by the new and improved John McLoughlin. Simon Fraser cut all ties to his young charge the moment he put him on the boat for France. McLoughlin sent many missives from Paris to Dr. Fraser, but his efforts garnered no reply. After more than two years without a word from his guardian, John faced the matter head-on, asking, "Ah what can be the cause of your long silence to me? Am I the cause of it? If so, tell me on what occasion." The questions were rhetorical, for he already knew the answer: "Alas can I ever cease regretting the loss of your love and regard; no never, I imagine that you must have heard some reports of my conduct."

John's desperation to win Fraser's affection was palpable in his tales of academic accomplishments: "I have passed the examination of Bechelier en lettres and passed it with credit. As soon as I left the room every gentleman said that it was myself that had passed the best of the whole.... I study from ten in the morning till three and then rest till six and from then I study for three hours more." In a heartbreaking addendum, John acknowledged his credibility was shot: "I do not like to say much for myself but you ought to ask my Uncle about it, for you might think that I am not telling the truth or I am praising myself too much." It was a humbling skirmish in a battle long lost.

John began his fourth year in Paris as he had spent the first three: studying anatomy and medicine under the tutelage of his uncle, and soaking up all the exquisite pleasures of the city. Although his letters to Montreal went unanswered, the self-portrait they paint is of a diligent and thoughtful student, eager to adhere to the straight and narrow. And so, in November

1833, the news that David McLoughlin had ordered his nephew to return home — suddenly and without explanation — was met by all with shock, confusion, and a sinking sense of déjà vu.

As usual, John McLoughlin Sr. was the last to know, learning of his son's abrupt banishment in a letter from his brother that complained bitterly of John's profligate ways. Before it was posted, David had shown the letter to John in the hopes of shocking the boy into proper behaviour, but "the gesture angered John and, within four days, he wilfully committed an act of such nature that Dr. David McLoughlin sent him home at once." The nature of that wilful act remains a tantalizing mystery. Although a great deal of latter correspondence referenced the scandal, no one described it in any detail, leaving the imaginations of future historians to run riot.

The tension between the two Paris-based McLoughlins appears to have been financial, namely John Jr.'s sudden extravagant spending. A casual aside, buried deep in a letter John received from his cousin John Fraser, reveals the trigger for this precipitous change. In a missive dated August 1833, Fraser relayed a bit of gossip regarding a voyageur who had recently returned from Fort Vancouver. The man had spent three years working under John McLoughlin Sr. and was telling tales of the doctor's opulent lifestyle. Apparently the senior McLoughlin's property was "very considerable" and everyone could see he was now "*very very* rich." The story came as a shock to John, whose father had always pled poverty in his all-too-rare letters. John took the news of his family's wealth to heart, and he began living in a style to which he felt entitled.

Once he was back in Montreal, McLoughlin's free-spending ways continued. In the early 1800s, "La Métropole" was a city full of temptation. John began to live a little; soon after, he began to spend a lot. Bills for John's expenses quickly piled up at the door of Simon Fraser. The first to arrive was a plea from John's roommate for back rent totalling £30. The next was from a local confectioner, Connet of Montreal, who was owed seven piastres and one shilling, "having been deceived by him as a debt of honor." It was a hefty bill for a bit of candy, but Connet assured Dr. Fraser that "all expenses made by your nephew at my place were for beverage and pastries and sweets." Simon Fraser ignored these petty extortions, firm in his conviction John was no longer his problem.

Dr. John McLoughlin was too embarrassed to address his uncle directly and used his nephew John Fraser to send a back-channel apology: "I was much affected on Learning that John has so Misconducted himself that my Brother has been obliged to send him Back to your father, who certainly at this time of life ought not to be harassed with the care of other people's Children, and what makes it Worse John is no longer a Child and his Errors are the less pardonable."

The doctor used the same dispatch to send a second-hand message to his son: "Is Junior so destitute of feeling or have they been Destroyed by his Misconduct that he is not ashamed at his time of life after so much Money has been spent on his Education and having had the Opportunities that he has had to be unable to Earn his food and to be Indebted for his support to the Labour of Another." Dr. McLoughlin ended his letter with a dramatic postscript: "I respect myself too much to Labour for a person who does not Respect himself." At least one of the olive branches offered by McLoughlin Sr. reached its intended audience. John Fraser wrote to his father to share Dr. McLoughlin's *mea culpa,* but it did little to soften Dr. Fraser's heart. Tired of all the circuitous communications, Fraser took pen in hand and stabbed it directly into the heart of that most "incorrigible" man-child, John McLoughlin Jr. In a scathing communiqué, Fraser told John precisely what he thought of him: "I am convinced you are depraved beyond any hopes of reform.... I have so bad an opinion of you...you appear to me born to disgrace every being who has the misfortunate to be connected with you. If you have any the least affection for your father, mother or brothers, you will retire to some distant far country that you may never more be heard of."

Fraser then cast dire predictions as to John's future in the workforce: "You must know that you are illiterate to the degree that if, by any favour, you should pass an examination for a Physician you would infallibly disgrace the Profession...your invincible indolence and perverse disposition have marred your good qualities.... Your relatives would have no cause to blush for you since your head, thru want of education, is so lamentably deficient. You have nothing left besides being a day labourer in civilized society or a hunter among savages." And with that, Simon Fraser slammed the door shut on young John McLoughlin.

Dr. McLoughlin soon joined Fraser in berating his useless son, for if sides must be chosen, he did not hesitate to pick his uncle over John. Tirades about money and John's flagrant misuse of it became recurring themes in Dr. McLoughlin's subsequent letters to Simon Fraser. His missives grew lumpy with complaints of his son "spending freely for a man who is Dependent on another.... Is he such a fool as to suppose that people will Engage a person...does he think that I undergo privations to Earn Money for him to spend in the Way he seems determined to do."

Money was a major point of contention between father and son, but it soon became a bargaining chip. The first gambit was laid by John, who declared he would "go to Montreal to *resume his studies if a hundred and fifty pounds [we]re given him.*" Dr. McLoughlin was mortified, telling his uncle that "when he made this most impudent demand, I should have sent him at once about his Business and cast him off for ever." Two years later, McLoughlin capitulated and tried to buy his son's compliance. He stipulated that if John "Conducts himself as a Gentleman and if he Endeavours to the Utmost to make up for his past misconduct by applying as Zealously as he possibly can to his Studies," he would reward him by granting him "any sum...under a hundred and fifty pounds" to complete his schooling. John, with no leverage to negotiate, accepted his father's condition-laden offer.

Newly flush, John fully intended to resume his medical training at Montreal's prestigious McGill University, but he needed his transcripts from Paris to secure his enrolment. He wrote to his uncle David, begging for the necessary paperwork, but John had yet to be forgiven. Time and again, David McLoughlin failed to provide the transcripts, and the delays proved costly for John, who lamented that "for my Uncle's negligence, I have lost one year more" of study.

With no coursework to occupy him, and a false sense of financial stability courtesy of his father, John reverted to his prior lavish ways. The fool and his father's money were soon parted, and within months his entire year's allowance was gone. In a letter to his cousin, John admitted to having "squandered" his money and pleaded poverty. On June 15, 1835, he wrote to Simon Fraser, asking for some boots, as "It is certainly very strange that I must go barefoot. Surely you are not without any feeling of humanity. Although I have lost your friendship, it is not the reason why you should leave me go without shoes. Get the boots made in your village, if you will not trust me with the money." Fraser's answer was absolute silence.

John then tried his luck with his cousin John, a historically soft touch. McLoughlin asked his cousin for four or five pounds, begging, "Do not disappoint me, if you cannot send all, send at least half of it." John Fraser acquiesced and John was soon back, looking for another handout. This time, John Fraser was not so easily shaken down. A rebuffed McLoughlin demanded to know "Who is then to pay my washing woman bill?" McLoughlin also tried guilt, telling his cousin, "I think my father himself would not have acted so. I am certain he would have clothed me." John Fraser reluctantly agreed to forward some money for essentials.

He would soon regret his decision. Demands for expenses, all of them "essential," poured in from his destitute cousin. August of that year saw a most peculiar request: "Will you be so kind as to purchase for me a Davier et un deschapain [tooth forceps and gum lancet] in fact a complete set of Instruments for extracting teeth." McLoughlin justified the expenditure by saying it would allow him to "make a little money from my profession so as to enable me to continue my classes."

By the spring of 1836, John had accumulated "such heavy debts that he was arrested by his creditors." In his hour of need, he reached out to his father with a heartfelt plea, but the answer was not what he hoped: "John has written me a Very contrite letter But as he is spending so much More Money…I do not write him." John McLoughlin Jr. had learned a painful lesson: the opposite of love was not hate but indifference. His father's love was conditional, measured in pounds and pence, and doled out as sparingly.

Physically, John was the mirror image of his father, a towering man who commanded attention through sheer mass, but when it came to character, he was a paltry imitation of the great Dr. John. Unable to fill his father's shoes, he had little choice but to follow in his footsteps. The Hudson's Bay Company held no appeal for John and, more importantly, the elder McLoughlin had strong opposition to his son entering the fur trade. Dr. McLoughlin was "concerned about the increasingly limited prospects for men of mixed blood." His fears were well founded and could be traced to a single source: the Company's governor, Sir George Simpson.

As the Scottish-born head of a British monopoly, George Simpson was the quintessential colonial, believing he had been sent by God to "civilize" the indigenous population. No one, least of all Simpson, paused to consider whether those invaded needed civilization. More to the point, he abhorred change and all things foreign, but mostly he despised the people he professed to be helping.

Simpson fancied himself an anthropologist who "made it my study to examine the nature and character of Indians." He did not like what he saw and, true to his colonial bent, he considered it his duty to impose his will upon them: "I am convinced they must be ruled with a rod of Iron to bring and keep them in a proper state of subordination, and the most certain way to effect this is by letting them feel their dependence upon us."

The Governor's "racist attitude toward non-whites" was as sweeping as it was pointed. He believed aboriginal education to be a complete waste of time, because "an enlightened Indian is good for nothing." His contemporaries thought Simpson was a man "a little too much addicted to prejudices" and a little too "prone to act on them," and his bigoted views wormed their way into the Company's hiring policies. Sir George declared all half-breeds to be "thoughtless, dissipated and depraved." Desperation alone necessitated the hiring of mixed-race traders for lowly posts, but it was a practice Simpson detested.

Simpson was blind to his own racist tendencies. He often flattered himself for his handling of the aboriginal peoples, saying, "They look upon me as the greatest man who ever came into the Country." He was convinced the First Nations were stupid and gullible, easy pickings for those white men "qualified to cheat an Indian," and he often bragged of his ability to swindle them.

Simpson's disdain for the First Nations only increased when it came to aboriginal women. He was notoriously libidinous, engaging in a series of dalliances with women he coarsely termed his "bits of brown," "his bit of circulating copper," or his "Japan helpmate."

Simpson's pathological contempt for "half-breeds" was entirely at odds with his fervour for making them. He was a prolific sire; during his first foray into Rupert's Land he fathered a daughter named Maria by his "washer-woman" Betsey at Fort Wedderburn, and a son named Jordie by a woman in Red River. Historian Peter C. Newman once quipped that Simpson's title "Father of the Fur Trade" had more to do with his loins than his legacy.

Bigotry was not Simpson's only vice, as his vanity also knew no bounds. He hired an official chronicler of his journeys into the wild, clear evidence of an ego run amok. Archibald McDonald accompanied Simpson on his earliest voyages, and Simpson got his money's worth when the scribe immortalized him as a man of "rather imposing mien; stout, well knit frame, and of great expanse and fullness of chest, with an eye brightly blue and ever ablaze in peace or war."

Those whose noses were not permanently imbedded in the Governor's backside had an entirely different perspective. In his youth, Simpson was a perpetually hot-faced man, a "red-headed magpie with quivering beak and glittery eye," but he had grown doughy as the years rolled by. His hair was once so orange it caused retinal burns, but age and neglect had reduced the remnants to a greying fringe. Sun-stroked and windswept, he bore the perennially queasy look of an ill-prepared tourist.

His clothes were equally out of step. George Simpson was a zealous adherent to the notion that clothes made the man, and so he dressed for the job he wanted: sovereign monarch. The appearance of wealth and respectability was difficult to amass and expensive to maintain, but by 1833 Simpson's salary had climbed to a staggering £1,800 per annum (excluding expenses). He received a number of exorbitant pay raises throughout his career, and the bulk went to the care and feeding of his wardrobe. He favoured ostentation, including the requisite beaver hats (ferried about in monogrammed carrying cases) and "a gorgeous cloak of red Scottish plaid with a scarlet lining." He was a peacock among seagulls, a preening diva strutting against a ragtag backdrop of "unsung, unlettered and uncouth" voyageurs.

As his annual tour wended through Rupert's Land, the sight of Simpson being carried ashore by rough-and-ready Metis undoubtedly met with awe (and some laughter) at his ports of call. The mocking did not last long. The Governor's greatest weapon was the element of surprise, and no one at the forts knew when he was coming, giving them little opportunity to put their house in order.

The unfortunates who encountered Simpson during his grand tours did what they could to warn those farther afield. It was no easy task, as the Governor had a "penchant for speed" and demanded an unholy pace, forcing his crewmen to begin rowing in the middle of the night and setting records for canoe travel that stand today. Still, the seasoned traders had their ways; news travelled quickly between forts via the "moccasin telegraph," an informal but highly effective aboriginal gossip network.

The Governor was notoriously difficult to please and always found "little to commend and much to reform" at every outpost he visited. He never hesitated to make his displeasure known, nor did he restrict his disdain to infrastructure, for he "had the exact same complaints of many of the HBC employees he met." His contempt for his fellows was matched only by "his caprice, his favouritism, [and] his disregard of merit," leaving the less-favoured in his employ scrambling to keep their jobs.

From day one, Simpson made it known that the HBC was not a democracy and his edicts were final. John McLean, in his bridge-burning treatise detailing twenty-five years of servitude in the Company, claimed that Simpson wrote the minutes of his meetings before they actually took place, as the Governor's lackeys "know better than to offer advice where none would be accepted," and "their assent is all that is expected of them."

Governor Simpson's tyranny, vainglory, and irrational hatred for those of mixed race were cause enough for John McLoughlin Jr. to steer clear of the Hudson's Bay Company, but they were far from the only reasons.

Monday, April 25, 1842 — Nightfall
FORT STIKINE

Under a canopy of stars hung solely for his amusement,
Sir George Simpson stood aboard the deck of the trade
steamer *Cowlitz* as it laboured from Tako to Fort Stikine.
A surprise inspection was in the offing, and though he had
paid a visit to the fort a few months prior, Simpson felt another
cage rattling was in order. When the ship entered the mouth
of the river, the Governor ordered his voyageurs to lower the
canoes and proceed upstream. As they rounded the bend and
were in sight of the outpost, Simpson's impending arrival was
announced with its usual modesty. His personal Highland
bagpiper Colin Fraser (whose retainer was paid by the HBC)
blasted the Governor's melodic signature, a signal for the fort's
complement to roll out the appropriate welcome mat. Having
issued fair warning, Simpson told his crewmen to stop the boat
so that he too might prepare. Before setting foot on shore, he
needed to "don his beaver topper and [give] his paddlers a
moment to spruce up in their best shirts." Only when every
man cut his finest figure did the canoe dock and the procession
begin, swept ashore with a full pipe and drum accompaniment.

On this night, the cavalcade met with deafening silence.
"The stillness that prevailed on shore" was the first indication
something was terribly wrong. The Governor quelled his fanfare
and hurried toward the fort, his mind "filled with apprehension
that all was not right, by observing that both the English and
Russian Flags on the Fort were half mast high, and that Mr.
John McLoughlin, the Gentleman left in charge, did not appear
on the platform."

Thomas McPherson, McLoughlin's assistant, scrambled
onto the dock to greet his distinguished guest, but Simpson was
in no mood to be handled. He careened through the fort at full
speed, and there he found "a scene which no pen can adequately
describe." McPherson had the unenviable task of informing the

Governor that Mr. John had been "hurried into eternity by a gunshot wound from one of his own men." Simpson demanded to know which man had pulled the trigger and soon found fingers pointed in every direction. In a private moment, McPherson whispered that his fellow Canadians tried "to make me believe that it was Indians that shot him," a charge the fort's indigenous population vehemently denied.

The Governor wasted no time in launching what proved to be a "superficial investigation." There were no police to be summoned, no courts to inform. As the HBC's top designate in the Indian Territories, Simpson was within his rights—and fulfilling his obligations—when he convened a panel and deposed the eyewitnesses.

To history's eternal regret, he began with Thomas McPherson.

The Honourable Company

John McLoughlin Jr. stumbled into manhood with no marketable skills, a poor reputation, and a bad attitude. As he contemplated his future with the HBC, his father was haunted by his own past. Fur held remarkably little interest for Dr. McLoughlin; true, it made him a very rich man, but the doctor seemed out of place in an industry devoid of diplomacy or fundamental decency. Medicine remained his first love, but his fateful run-in with an insolent British soldier had tied his fortunes to the North West Company (NWC), a Montreal-based fur trading concern that operated from 1779 to 1821 and "left behind a legacy of alcoholism, syphilis, [and] Mixed Blood babies."

From its inception, the NWC was the chief rival and existential bane of the Hudson's Bay Company. The HBC was bigger and had been in the game longer; the Company was granted its charter by King Charles II in 1670. The royal decree gave the firm monopoly over all land drained by the waters flowing into Hudson Bay, a region dubbed Rupert's Land after the Company's first governor. Prince Rupert was "a man of intense loyalties but few friends," a description which proved equally applicable to the post's later occupant, George Simpson.

From 1783 to 1820, the North West Company repeatedly challenged the supremacy of the Hudson's Bay Company. Although the Nor'Westers initially concentrated their efforts in the United States, the War of 1812 forced the company north of the border, where it clashed with the HBC. The rivalry intensified as the years wore on, leading to some rather shady business practices.

Both the HBC and NWC used liquor and trade goods to curry favour with the indigenous peoples in an effort to secure the choicest furs. When booze and baubles weren't enough, NWC traders began telling the aboriginals the HBC planned to exterminate them, and a few scoundrels even whispered that the Company's clerks mixed their trading tobacco with poison.

Despite the NWC's questionable policies, Dr. McLoughlin enjoyed a cordial relationship with the First Nations at Kaministikwia. Indeed, he was "proud of having so many Indians employed and always held out to the missionaries that that was the way to civilize them, to teach them to work." Those interactions had dire consequences, however, as European-derived diseases "scourged the poor Indians dreadfully." Dr. McLoughlin soon realized the timing of outbreaks coincided with the arrival of the annual supply ships from London. Although the prophylactics available were limited and often suspect, he saw to it "all the Indians that could be got at were vaccinated."

Dr. McLoughlin had witnessed first-hand the devastation wrought by the fur trade, and he wanted no part of it. He quietly put out feelers and was soon being courted by banking and other less offensive industries. On October 5, 1818, he ended a letter to Simon Fraser with a cryptic postscript: "Between you and me I have an offer to enter into Business in the civilized world—if I do not accept the proposal—it will be from want of capital. This is between us—no one else must know it." McLoughlin and Fraser held true to their oath of secrecy, for no record survives as to the source of the offer. Given that Dr. McLoughlin remained in the employ of the North West Company, it is safe to assume he never acquired the necessary capital to fund his return to civilization.

As Dr. McLoughlin struggled to secure a brighter future, his employer was hitting hard times. The competition for control over the North American fur grounds had driven both the HBC and the NWC to the brink of bankruptcy. Although the HBC was larger and better funded, the NWC had two significant advantages: "sheer manpower," and the "ability to make decisions on the spot," rather than waiting for dictates from London. To save both organizations from fiscal destruction, a merger was proposed, and in 1821 both companies sent representatives to London to negotiate the terms. McLoughlin (then an NWC wintering partner at Fort William) agreed to serve as his company's delegate at the conference. He quickly learned he was to be a decorative placeholder; he contributed nothing to the final negotiations, and the meeting ended with the Hudson's Bay Company in full control of the Canadian fur trade. Disgusted, McLoughlin elected to spend the winter with his brother David in France. The siblings' bond was "one of real affection," the only truly equitable relationship in McLoughlin's life, and he used the time to re-evaluate his priorities.

McLoughlin Sr. returned to Canada in January 1822, uncertain what the future held. When the Company restructured post-amalgamation, it allocated forty percent of the profits to its field traders, namely former HBC field officers and NWC wintering partners. McLoughlin was made an HBC chief factor, transforming him overnight from a salaried employee into a wealthy shareholder, and his first assignment under the new umbrella corporation was at Lac La Pluie.

The posting did not last long. The region was quickly trapped clean and, as the Company expanded westward, Dr. McLoughlin was transferred to Fort George on November 8, 1824. The change of scenery was not to the doctor's liking. The local tribes were extremely hostile to Company operatives encroaching on their lands, and he was certain "the country was not worth a war."

Despite the hardships, Dr. McLoughlin ruled over Fort George "with unorthodox methods and astounding results." His love of innovation and refusal to toe the party line won him admirers and critics alike, and many of his underlings were convinced the doctor believed "too firmly in his own incorruptibility." Governor Simpson argued both sides when he described McLoughlin Sr. as "very Zealous in the discharge of his public duties and a man of strict honour and integrity but a great stickler for rights and privileges [who] sets himself up for a righter of Wrongs." Daughter Eloisa was equally conflicted: "I always heard that my Father had a good head. He was quick in trading with the Indians and could get on well with them." Of course, it was to his benefit that his aboriginal colleagues "were afraid of him.... He was very large and strong, a straight and fine looking man and they were afraid of him."

The Governor continued to have strong reservations, viewing McLoughlin as "a very bustling active man who can go through a great deal of business but is wanting in system and regularity, and has not the talent of managing the few associates & clerks under his authority." Simpson also vacillated on the man's character, as he found Dr. McLoughlin to be "a disagreeable man to do business with, as it is impossible to go with him in all things and a difference of opinion almost amounts to a declaration of hostilities, yet a good hearted man and a pleasant companion."

Meanwhile, the seasons came and went as Dr. McLoughlin completed work on an outpost of his own design, later christened Fort Vancouver. It was a formidable presence, "an island of luxury in the wilderness," dominating the north bank of the Columbia River. When she first laid eyes on the fort's towering palisades, missionary Narcissa Whitman dubbed it "the New York of the Pacific."

Dr. McLoughlin governed his creation with a mirthless, inflexible fist: "There was no society. The clerks just came in when the bell rung. After that they went right away to their business. And so with the men in the field. The bell was rung at twelve for dinner and at one o'clock for work; and they all kept regular hours, like clock-work." According to fort inhabitant George Roberts, Dr. McLoughlin did what the politicians in London could not: "One thing occurs to me that has been little noticed & that was the good order & discipline that was maintained by the Company. No organized govt could have maintained better order."

Despite his legendary inflexibility, McLoughlin's views on business were surprisingly progressive. HBC policy held "that this country should not be inhabited by an agricultural population; they wished to keep it for hunting & trapping purposes. They were influenced purely by a mercantile spirit." Despite his employer's singular focus on the bottom line, the doctor knew beaver skins were a finite resource, and he kept one eye on the horizon. He set about making the fort self-sufficient, ordering the construction of grist and lumber mills, the large-scale cultivation of all arable lands, and the tending of livestock. Dr. McLoughlin also encouraged the clerks to fish and harvest the region's plentiful natural resources, and the result was the Company's only truly autonomous outpost, offering comforts and amenities rarely found in such remote locations.

It was not all work at Fort Vancouver. A portion of every man's salary was paid in liquor, although the doctor never drank anything stronger than wine. McLoughlin's temperance was born of a teetotal mother and a religious indoctrination that left no room for sinning and little tolerance for sinners.

Dr. McLoughlin was "a convert to Catholicism, with all the zeal that this involved," and at his bidding "they kept Sundays" at Fort Vancouver. No trade was permitted on the Sabbath; instead, the chief factor and his clerks read the Bible. His campaign of forced spiritual conversion also included the aboriginal tribes of the Columbia region. McLoughlin was a brilliant man of two minds. He was, first and foremost, "a British subject with British prejudices & British Characteristics," predisposed to believe in the absolute superiority of the English and, by extension, the inferiority of those they sought to colonize. But McLoughlin was also "a gentleman of large heart & catholic spirit, benevolent in his feeling." He fervently believed the road to civilization ran straight through the Catholic Church, and he was supported in his thinking by a much higher power.

The HBC's charter mandates included a call to bring Christianity to the country's aboriginal masses, yet many perceived the Company's efforts in this regard to be a resounding failure. One trader claimed the natives were "neither more enlightened, nor more civilized, by our endeavours than if we had never appeared among them." Even First Nation members employed by the HBC remained "as ignorant of Christianity as the rudest savages who have never seen the face of a white man."

Dr. McLoughlin used the lure of trade to impose his own moral code on everyone within the sound of his voice. He broke with HBC custom and allowed aboriginal hunters to enter Fort Vancouver. Eloisa believed the aboriginals welcomed her father's brand of frontier justice: "The Indians came and asked what is right to be done, and my father told them what was right and what was not right—whether they should kill such a man for doing so and so. My father said 'No, you must not do it, it is wrong' and it would all stop."

In a land without police or courts, the Hudson's Bay Company appointed itself as judge, jury, and (if need be) executioner in all criminal matters relating to trade or employees. The genesis of such notions was legitimate—in the rural outposts, there were no social structures in place to administer justice—but the HBC leadership took this lack of regulation to lengths that were often extreme and sometimes downright illegal. In clashes between the First Nations and traders, "the HBC settled such incidents by the adoption of a 'blood for blood' policy against the immediate wrongdoers." Things grew far more ruthless when events involved traders alone, for the Company viewed such transgressions "as matters of corporate discipline," to be handled entirely in-house. That unwavering sense of judicial entitlement sprang from the head of George Simpson and trickled down to senior management, including the chief factor for Columbia District. West of the Rockies, Dr. McLoughlin's word was gospel and his rule was absolute.

Dr. McLoughlin kept the peace through a volatile mix of civility, sobriety, incarceration, despotism, and unflinching brutality. Many of the men under his command marvelled at the results: "It is strange that without police or military the good order we had could be maintained. It is perhaps owing partly to the diverse people... & partly to there being no liquor & partly to the good management of the Company's officers. They never used bad or ribald language."

Dr. McLoughlin also refused to hear dissenting views from his subordinates. "You see the Co.'s chiefs in my mind were not at all influenced by any passions or prejudices entertained by men less capable than themselves," one underling later recalled, "they were very independent in that way, *no government from below.*"

John McLoughlin Sr.'s disregard for his subordinates came back to haunt him when he was posted in the Red River valley in 1824. One day, an aboriginal boy approached him with a disturbing story. He said some white men from the fort had tried to convince him to kill McLoughlin with his own gun. The doctor was outraged and summoned the men immediately. He dragged the boy before the company and demanded he repeat his accusation. The terrified youngster stammered out his account, but the allegation met with vehement denials. The boy insisted the men were lying, but again they denied it. At a stalemate, McLoughlin told the boy to go home. Eloisa McLoughlin, an eyewitness to the strange event, picked up the tale: "My father's method in such cases was to iron the men and keep them in a private room and separate them. The men finally admitted that they said so, but they said they were joking with the boy." McLoughlin was not amused. The treacherous conspirators were shackled—"the punishment was always putting them in irons"—and thrown in a cell indefinitely, without due process or appeal. Dr. John was the first McLoughlin to have his life threatened by his own men, but he would not be the last.

§

Although he ruled Fort Vancouver with impunity, Dr. McLoughlin had been on the wrong side of the law. His dust-up with the British soldier was a youthful indiscretion, but in 1816 the fur industry's brand of justice collided head-on with the laws of the land, and McLoughlin found himself accused of a heinous crime: the murders of twenty-one men during the "Seven Oaks Massacre," the horrifying climax of an ongoing campaign to settle the Red River valley.

The campaign was waged by Thomas Douglas, the fifth Earl of Selkirk. In 1810, Selkirk received a land grant of 116,000 square miles of the Red River valley from the Hudson's Bay Company, in which he was a major shareholder. The North West Company counted the valley among its holdings, and the slight was not soon forgotten.

Selkirk paid only one visit to Red River, and he did not stay long. Upon his return to the British Isles, he began recruiting settlers from across Scotland with exorbitant promises of prosperity and transported them to Red River. They arrived in 1812 woefully ill-equipped, wielding hoes and spades against the granite-like soil of the prairies. During their first year in-country, the settlers endured extreme hardships: predators feasted on their livestock, floods washed away seedlings, and punishing weather and plagues of insects destroyed what few crops survived.

When the end came for the settlement, it came from within. Miles Macdonell, the newly appointed governor of Selkirk's lands, issued two fatal proclamations. The first prohibited the export of pemmican, a noisome blend of dried meat, berries, and fat that was a mainstay of Metis voyageurs. In his second declaration, Macdonell ordered the evacuation of all North West Company posts in the area. Both pronouncements caused resentment among the company's traders, and they retaliated by marshalling the aboriginal and Metis people — who also laid prior claim to the land settled by Selkirk's pioneers — to run out the homesteaders.

So began the Pemmican War. The militia organized under the leadership of Cuthbert Grant, and they arrested Macdonell, charging him with illegally seizing their foodstuffs. He was dispatched to Montreal to stand trial, leaving Selkirk's followers without a leader. Terrified and unprotected, many fled for their lives, and by the fall of 1815 only thirteen of the original settler families remained in Red River.

A new governor was hastily appointed. Robert Semple was a steely-eyed, hawk-nosed Loyalist who had been a popular travel writer in his native England before making his way west with the second wave of Scottish emigrants. Semple, blessed with an "overburden of self-importance," gathered up the last few survivors and his fresh recruits and returned to Red River in hopes of salvaging the harvest. Cursed with equal parts naivety and arrogance, Semple refused to learn from the mistakes of his predecessor. In June he ordered the destruction of the NWC outpost Fort Gibraltar, which was burned to the ground as its occupants looked on in disgust. The sacking of Gibraltar became the rallying cry for Grant and his ragtag band of Metis, who began targeting the region's settlers, as well as the HBC's five newly established but poorly fortified outposts.

Hubris proved the undoing of Robert Semple. He believed his pen to be mightier than any sword, and he drafted "a stern proclamation forbidding Metis" from acts of violence. Governor Semple sent word to Cuthbert Grant demanding a meeting so he might recite his edict in person. Grant agreed, and Semple ordered two dozen men to accompany him to the rendezvous.

Semple and his men rode to an area known as Seven Oaks, delivering themselves into a perfectly orchestrated ambush. Semple's cohort was instantly surrounded, and they were told to lay down their weapons or be shot. Grant kept his own gun trained on Semple, who foolishly entered into a war of words with his enemies. One Metis, Francois Firmin Boucher, called Semple a "damned rascal" for burning Gibraltar. Semple took offence and grabbed for Boucher's gun, at which point Cuthbert Grant shot Semple in the thigh, igniting the massacre.

The battle lasted fifteen minutes. When the smoke cleared, Semple and twenty of his men lay dead alongside the lone Metis who fell that day, but an even greater atrocity was yet to come. There, in the shade of the seven oaks, "the dead were stripped and dismembered in an orgy of mutilation."

Word of the slaughter soon reached Lord Selkirk, who was marching toward Red River, backed by his personal army. Selkirk pointed his cannons at the NWC stronghold of Fort William, and after a brief, lopsided battle he planted his flag and claimed his spoils. He also ordered the arrest of the fort's senior officers.

Among those charged with treason was William McGillivray, who refused to go quietly. He demanded a meeting with the earl, who had taken to strutting about the fort "like a kilted messiah." McGillivray asked two other NWC officers — Dr. John McLoughlin and Kenneth McKenzie — to accompany him to the meeting, but it did not end well. McGillivray called Selkirk a "piddling lord," and a foot-stamping Selkirk had the men arrested. The earl then decided anyone representing the NWC was guilty of murdering twenty-one of his men. The charges laid against Dr. McLoughlin included "receiving, relieving, comforting or assisting the felons to escape," as well as the capital offence of accessory to murder.

Dr. McLoughlin and his fellow Nor'Westers waited for their day in court in the outpost's mess hall, mere feet from the quarters he shared with his wife and John Jr. The earl tried repeatedly to extract confessions from his hostages but they refused to yield, even burning incriminating documents in the kitchen stove. Selkirk then ordered them to be sent to Upper Canada to face trial.

Selkirk had legal problems of his own, including countercharges stemming from his unlawful occupation of Fort William. He was also riddled with tuberculosis and had little fight left, having exhausted his fortune to sustain the settlement and his army. The earl was detained by NWC traders and soon found himself headed for Upper Canada to await justice beside his former prisoners.

It was a fateful voyage to the courthouse. Dr. McLoughlin's canoe tipped in rough seas near Sault Ste. Marie, and nine of the twenty-nine passengers onboard were drowned. McLoughlin Sr. "was taken lifeless to the shore, and it was long before he was restored." From that day on, he was plagued by "a haunting fear of death."

Dr. McLoughlin eventually landed in Upper Canada, only to spend months awaiting his turn to answer the indictment against him. McLoughlin had never set foot in Seven Oaks, yet he still faced the death penalty if convicted. The trial was a showcase for the chronic ineptitude of the legal system, lasting less than two days. McLoughlin and his co-defendants never testified, the jury deliberated a mere forty-five minutes, and on October 31, 1818, he was discharged as "not guilty." Dr. McLoughlin, scarred by his near drowning, nervously took his place in the canoe and paddled home to Fort William, arriving just in time for John Jr.'s seventh birthday.

The Seven Oaks debacle instilled a healthy respect for the rule of law in Dr. McLoughlin, but when the NWC joined the HBC, he immediately returned to the fur trade model of autonomous justice. In 1828, Clallam hunters in Puget Sound killed a young clerk named Alexander McKenzie. The senseless violence enraged Dr. McLoughlin, and he sent his men on a series of retaliatory raids. His henchmen killed twenty-three members of the local tribe before burning two of their camps to ashes, all with McLoughlin's blessing. His message was clear: attack the Hudson's Bay Company at your peril. The family of McKenzie's killers took the warning to heart, and those responsible were executed by their own kin in a shocking effort to "placate the Company's death squads." In an eerie corollary to the Seven Oaks massacre, Dr. McLoughlin had not pulled the trigger, but his hands bore blood all the same.

The HBC's motto — *Pro Pelle Cutem* — translates to "a skin for a skin." The slogan was meant to reflect their trading philosophy, but Dr. McLoughlin had recast it as the basis for a system of jurisprudence, in which the senseless deaths of twenty-three people was fair compensation for the murder of one clerk.

John McLoughlin Sr. had been accused of a massacre he did not commit and saddled with the weight of a bloodbath executed on his command. It was not the life of peace and healing he had planned for himself, nor was it a life he wanted for his son.

The fur trade had been a bad fit for Dr. McLoughlin from the start, and he feared his son would prove an even worse match. After years of faithful service, McLoughlin Sr. had grown weary of the Hudson's Bay Company. He was at odds with the Company's policies, and he knew all too well the lawless nature of the business. His experiences were enough to give any man pause, but Dr. McLoughlin could sum up his strongest reservations about the Honourable Company in two words: George Simpson.

History has not been kind to Sir George, but since he never gave a tinker's damn about kindness, let's call it a wash. To be kind was to be

Portrait of Sir George Simpson, taken in the last years of his life.

weak, at least as Simpson saw it, and he abhorred weakness, as well as indolence, drunkenness, stupidity, and anyone with the temerity to disagree with him. Sir George also had a penchant for name-calling. Early in his career, Simpson created his "Character Book," a leather-bound, no-holds-barred accounting of his thoughts on his colleagues. The tome was "a *tour de force*," a hymnal of indiscretion, which Simpson kept under lock and key, his victims identified only by number.

Simpson fancied himself something of an armchair alienist, able to diagnose any man's mental ills simply by looking at him. He displayed "a readiness, almost an eagerness, to pass judgement on his fellows." Few others agreed with his perspicacity, although the Governor's ability to call them as he saw them impressed at least one powerful ally. Lord Selkirk believed Simpson "has such tact in seeing people's characters that there is not a man in the country that he cannot lay down on paper at once, and tell what they are good for." With few exceptions, Simpson thought his colleagues weren't good for anything, and he felt most would benefit from a sound "Damning & Bitching."

Simpson's Character Book reads more like an unintentional autobiography than a searing exposé of others. Simpson's lifelong tendency to tar others with a brush best suited to himself is well-represented in the historical record, leading scholar Alan Cooke to posit the Governor was "an outstanding example of an immature ego possessed by personal complexes, which he projected onto his colleagues."

The most telling projection of all was Simpson's denouncement of Francis Heron as "a perfect Hypocrite." The Governor should have engraved the words "hypocrisy" and "inconsistency" on his letterhead, for they seemed to be the watchwords of his administration. His cousin Thomas felt Simpson's "firmness and decision of mind are much impaired," and his tendency to shift with the winds reduced him to "a weathercock."

Like all clueless egotists, Simpson was easily manipulated, provided one knew how. HBC employee John Stuart once advised a junior man that, when it came to Simpson, "it is his foible to exact not only strict obedience, but deference to the point of humility. As long as you pay him in that coin, you will quickly get on his sunny side." Complexity and vanity are mutually exclusive in the human psyche, and, thanks to the Governor's excess of ego, the portrait limned by his contemporaries bordered on caricature. Perhaps the most generous assessment of his personality ever offered was that Simpson "had unrivalled opportunities for personal growth but did not seize them."

Those on the receiving end of Simpson's scorn reciprocated, for however lowly he held his fellows, his contemporaries thought even less of him. He had earned his place as "one of the best-hated men in North America." He was "despised" by his closest relations; the kindest thoughts they could muster were that he was "plausible and full of animal spirits." His cousin Thomas declared the Governor to be a "severe and most repulsive master" who was "guilty of many little meannesses... quite beneath a Gentleman, and... are indicative of his birth."

George Simpson came by his dysfunction honestly, for he was quite literally "a bastard by birth and by persuasion." He was born the unintended by-product of a "non-conjugal relationship" between an eponymously named Scottish lawyer and an unknown mother and was left to be raised by his aunt Mary.

While still in his teens, he was sent to apprentice at the London brokerage firm of his uncle Geddes, "where his talents soon advanced him to the first seat at the desk." The firm dealt in sugar, one of the top commodities of the day, but it was all the same to young Master Simpson.

The first requirement of any social climber is a good toehold, and he found sure footing in Andrew Colvile, one of the partners in his uncle's firm. Simpson possessed plenty of derring-do, and Colvile was taken by the young man's "sufficient promptness and determination." Colvile also held a seat on the Committee of the Hudson's Bay Company, an institution then mired in turmoil thanks to the feisty antics of its overseas governor, William Williams. The sitting governor had been "chosen for his courage rather than his business acumen or his good judgment," and his unique brand of rash diplomacy had landed him in hot water with the Company's competitors. Arrest warrants were issued for Williams following his attack on North West Company employees in Grand Rapids, and the Company feared he would soon be captured. HBC leaders were quietly on the hunt for an acting governor for Rupert's Land, and Colvile nominated the red-headed spitfire with the impenetrable Scottish brogue, George Simpson. It bears noting Andrew Colvile "did not allow consideration of personality to intrude into his business affairs."

Simpson thought himself the perfect candidate and felt his nomination deserved serious consideration despite his having "no background... or demonstrable skills." What Simpson had was "an authority combining the despotism of military rule with the strict surveillance and mean parsimony of the avaricious trader." The rest he could learn, as, thankfully, "the North-West Company had previously reduced the business to a perfect system, which he had only to follow." The HBC's London Committee clearly agreed, and Simpson became the "heir apparent to the HBC's overseas operations" in 1820. His notice of appointment explicitly stated his powers were limited and temporary at best, but Simpson overlooked such conditions.

The HBC were "the ultimate absentee landlords," and Simpson was their new superintendent, although he acted as if he owned the place. He landed with a resounding thud on the shores of British North America, teeming "with the lordly hauteur of a man in charge of his private universe." According to one employee firmly under the jackboot of an increasingly "despotic" Simpson, the little emperor treated his underlings "as if we had been so many cattle," and saw himself "clothed with a power so unlimited, it is not to be wondered at that a man who rose from a humble situation should in the end forget what he was and play the tyrant."

His unwelcome habit of "acting as uncrowned king" was brought to the fore in his first meeting with William Williams. The sitting governor's days as a free man were numbered and, under duress, he agreed to step down and let Simpson take charge. Luck and timing continued to be on Simpson's side; in less than one year, an unknown, unskilled sugar clerk had gone from *locum tenens* to the overseas governor of one of the most powerful monopolies on the planet. With the nod of the outgoing governor and the stroke of a pen, Simpson's rule was now "more absolute than that of any governor under the British Crown."

Simpson found himself in the enviable position of answering only to the HBC's London-based governor Sir John Henry Pelly and his committee. Simpson considered "his role in Hudson's Bay Company as proxy for the British government in North America," a self-serving interpretation that was equal parts ego and truth. He was a master of misdirection and exaggeration, but Simpson's true font of power was "the slowness of the communications system with London." In an age before transatlantic telegraphy, correspondence travelled by ship and often took a year to reach its destination. Simpson always did Governor Pelly the courtesy of writing a letter, ostensibly seeking permission, only to then do as he pleased, safe in the knowledge it would be a year or more before he would be called to account, by which time the damage was inevitably done.

Buoyed by his mercurial rise through the ranks, Simpson transformed overnight from insufferable to unbearable. He introduced sweeping policy changes and imposed cost-cutting measures he called "Œconomy." He slashed wages, eliminated "old and useless men," and denied pension benefits to widows and dependents. His belt-tightening was seen by those affected as "parsimony of a very questionable and impolitic kind." It became an issue of character, as many employees felt "economy so ill-timed argued as little in favour of the Governor's judgement as of his humanity." It was the worst kind of micromanaging, but it fattened the bottom line, and that was all the proof Simpson needed to show he was steering the Company in the right direction. The shareholders in London appreciated his efforts, but the men in the field were not impressed. They labelled him *"mangeur du lard"*—a "pork-eater," untutored in the ways of the trade. They had a point, and Simpson had a morale problem.

In his first act as governor of the northern department, Simpson called a meeting of the Company's chief factors, summoning Dr. McLoughlin and his peers to York Factory. The host and his skeptics were led to the dining hall, where a sumptuous banquet awaited. Wine, port, and spirits flowed freely, loosening the tongues and tempers of those assembled. By sun-up, the Governor had won over his critics, save for Dr. McLoughlin. Simpson was a master "in the art of getting his way," and McLoughlin soon had a very large target on his back.

Company regulations required Simpson to meet with a full council of his factors once a year, but the Governor detested both regulations and the chief factors. He weaned them off the mandate by holding "sham" councils, which were nothing more than a recitation of *fait accompli* edicts from London, reducing the factors from full shareholders to glorified errand boys. Dr. McLoughlin rebelled, but Simpson remained confident in his shameless power grab, gloating the factors "could outvote me, but it has never been so."

Governor Simpson had become that most loathsome of creatures: a narcissist with actual power. His bosses in London swore by Simpson just as the men in the field swore at him, though rarely to his face. His detractors tried to warn the home office: "The Committee received several hints of the Governor's 'strange management' but they only smiled at the insinuations."

Dr. McLoughlin saw through Simpson's carefully crafted façade and hated him for the same reason the HBC loved him: his ruthlessly inhumane approach to business. The animosity between the two men had been instantaneous. Simpson and McLoughlin Sr. first crossed swords on July 26, 1824, when the newly appointed governor transferred the doctor to Fort Astoria. Simpson agreed to meet him there, leaving several weeks after the chief factor was dispatched. The journey from Fort William required both men to make a series of lengthy portages, and what began as business travel soon escalated into a cross-country grudge match.

Dr. McLoughlin had a twenty-day lead but Simpson, driving his voyageurs to the point of exhaustion, soon caught up, and McLoughlin never heard the end of it. Throughout the journey, Simpson had dined on "tidbits and wine" served to him on china by his manservant in between naps, all while his rugged *engagés* chased their daily allotment of pemmican with another six hours of hard paddling. Those in the trenches were painfully familiar with meals consisting of nothing but "Hudson's Bay sauce"—a euphemism for hunger and privation—and while such class disparity undoubtedly caused resentment, the crewmen knew the temper of their captain well enough to keep their displeasure to themselves.

After weeks of arduous travel, Dr. McLoughlin was dressed in "Clothes that had once been fashionable but [were] now covered with a thousand patches of different Colours, his beard would do honor to the chin of a Grizzly Bear, his face and hands evidently Shewing that he had not lost much time on his Toilette, loaded with Arms and his own Herculean dimensions for a *tout ensemble* that would convey a good idea of the highwaymen of former Days." The Governor, meanwhile, was playing dress-up. Simpson had temporarily eschewed his usual finery in favour of the checked chemise, green blanket coat, moccasins, and unkempt beard of a voyageur.

Such adventures can lead to the sort of bond forged in foxholes, but their competitive natures, and mutual distrust, drove a wedge between the Governor and the doctor. The demands of work forced the men to broker a fragile détente once the competing teams arrived in the Columbia District, but the brittle truce did not hold for long. The Governor dismissed Dr. McLoughlin as "a Radical" who "would be a troublesome man to the Company if he had sufficient influence to form and tact to manage a party." He thought Simpson was arrogant, ridiculous, and dangerously short-sighted.

Simpson and McLoughlin Sr. continued to square off on matters great and small over the next three decades. The two were more alike than either man cared to admit, yet on one topic they were in complete agreement: the Hudson's Bay Company was no place for John McLoughlin Jr. For Dr. McLoughlin, his hesitation was born of parental concern. He wanted to protect his son from the so-called Honourable Company and its tyrannical leader, although pride and the likelihood John Jr. would reflect poorly on him may also have coloured his thinking. Simpson, on the other hand, was driven by his disdain for those of mixed race in general, and for John Jr. in particular, thanks to the boy's tantrum in a Montreal boarding school sixteen years prior. Whatever their respective motivation, the net result was the same: John Jr.'s future did not rest in the Canadian fur trade. His application was summarily rejected.

It was official: John McLoughlin Jr. was unemployable. Even a company that routinely hired criminals and deviants did not want him, and his desperation was about to lead him into strange and dangerous territory.

Thursday, April 21, 1842 — Midnight
FORT STIKINE

As recounted by Thomas McPherson.

It began with Benoni Fleury, pie-eyed and slobbering in the arms of John McLoughlin, who was himself "half-seas over," an era-specific euphemism for drunkenness. William Lasserte lingered like a useless prop as McLoughlin fought to tuck his servant in for the night, but things soon got out of hand. To hear Fleury tell it: "I fell to bed, in doing which a scuffle took place between us and I unfortunately tore the sleeve of his shirt." The rent was accidental but McLoughlin "became outraged and thrashed [Fleury] unmercifully, so much so that Lasserte requested leave to desist." The boldfaced challenge to his authority inflamed McLoughlin, who "flew at Lasserte and struck him repeatedly." Lasserte had no choice but to turn tail and run, with McLoughlin on his heels. At one point, McLoughlin managed to grab hold of Lasserte and smacked him again for good measure. Lasserte wrenched free and fled, with McLoughlin staggering in pursuit. Lasserte made for the staircase, leaving McLoughlin listing in his wake. Step by step, McLoughlin pulled himself halfway up the flight of stairs before finally giving up the chase. He then stormed into Belanger's room, where he found Simon Aneuharazie, Francois Pressé, Urbain Heroux, and Charles Belanger drinking to excess. McLoughlin grabbed Aneuharazie by the throat, mistaking him for Lasserte. A terrified Aneuharazie gulped for air as he told his master he had the wrong man. McLoughlin relinquished his death grip and lurched from the room, leaving the men bewildered.

Lasserte waited for McLoughlin to leave, then headed into the room where Aneuharazie sat rubbing his swollen throat. Lasserte tried to rally his colleagues with tales of the master's abuse, but to no avail. He then proposed a plan that bordered on mutiny, suggesting they capture and bind McLoughlin if he once again "became outrageous." Aneuharazie was still smarting from the last drubbing, and Lasserte could find no takers among the drunken cohort, save for Urbain Heroux.

It was a fateful meeting of unsound minds. Heroux had imbibed heavily for the past eight hours and was exhausted, having not slept in many nights. Illiterate and uneducated, Heroux was a profoundly superstitious man. He was frightened of the dark and terrified to be alone at night, certain that "there is a danger near me." His fears were well-founded, for McLoughlin "appeared particularly irritated against Heroux."

Lasserte's treacherous pleas found a receptive audience in Heroux. He took up the cause and "Urbain made his escape through the door, calling out 'take care of yourselves, [McLoughlin] is maltreating Fleury.'" In truth, the mistreatment had ended the moment Fleury passed out cold, but Heroux's warning finally roused the men to action.

Meanwhile, McLoughlin continued storming through the halls of the outpost. Drawn by the commotion, Francois Pressé stood peering out the door of the big house when he heard McLoughlin cry, "They have wounded me. I must kill some of them." McLoughlin then ran to where the Kanakas lay sleeping and tried to marshal his troops by shouting "Aux arms, aux arms!" Pressé was a little drunk and still did not know what all the fuss was about, but he heeded his master's call. He ran to his quarters and grabbed his rifle, only to come face to face with a raging John McLoughlin.

Despite his recent call to arms, there was something about the sight of Pressé with a gun that made McLoughlin uneasy. Paranoia tightened its grip, and McLoughlin turned on Pressé, whispering, "You also want to kill me." He confiscated Pressé's gun and ordered those within earshot to place him in irons. Pressé did not resist, later saying he had only been following orders and knew better than to challenge McLoughlin when he was so far gone. Despite the chief's call for shackles, Antoine Kawannassé refused to comply. Pressé had done nothing wrong, and Kawannassé saw no indication the man had "any bad intention." Outraged at again being defied, McLoughlin grabbed hold of Pressé's shirt collar and bum-rushed him toward the holding cell. The awkward motion, mixed with spirits, caused McLoughlin to trip, and "his rifle fell and went off." Startled by the noise, McLoughlin righted himself and slapped the cuffs on Pressé, locking him in the outpost's makeshift cell.

McLoughlin, shaken and shaking, then headed upstairs to hide in McPherson's room. Fortunately for Pressé, McLoughlin had been too drunk to secure the chains properly, and Pressé "succeeded in extricating [himself] from the irons." Locked in a room with no hope of escape, Pressé was "in dread for my life," horrified by the ruckus emanating from the other side of the wall. He pressed his ear to the door and his hair stood on end as he overheard McLoughlin give Antoine Kawannassé a final chilling directive: "The first Canadian you see, shoot him."

Outside Pressé's locked cell, bedlam reigned. The fort's complement was now heavily armed thanks to the competing war cries of Heroux and McLoughlin. Just then, Pressé heard seven or eight shots fired in rapid succession. He became "seriously alarmed" and hurled himself against the door, frantic to break free.

Although many had taken up arms, not everyone joined in the fray. When the call went out to shoot any Canadian on sight, everyone fitting that description went into hiding. Charles Belanger gathered up several of the wives and led them to the carpentry shop, where they huddled like frightened children. Louis Leclaire was too proud to cower with the women but he found similar sanctuary beneath the bench in the blacksmith's shop. George Heron cast dignity aside and hid in the latrine, hoping its rancid vapours would deter all comers. Even the fort's resident idiot, Oliver Martineau, knew better than to make himself a target. He bolted for the southeast bastion, where he promptly lay down and fell asleep.

McLoughlin remained upstairs, hunkered down with Antoine Kawannassé and Thomas McPherson. The lone thought rattling in his well-oiled brain was to arm himself, and McPherson watched helplessly as McLoughlin "was walking about the floor trying to load his rifle. He gave it to me to load as he could not do it himself, being too tipsy." That was the last thing McPherson needed.

Thomas McPherson was already having a rough night, made all the more unbearable for being the only sober man left in the rogue's gallery. He had spent the evening fetching liquor for his boss: "About 9 P.M., [McLoughlin] called in the Canadians and Iroquois and sent me into the Store for 3 Bottles of Rum, those 3 Bottles were filled 4 times in the course of the Night." By then, McLoughlin was so wasted he "thought he saw a person in a white dress in front of the men's house." Unable to stand, he dispatched Kawannassé and McPherson "to see who it was, but [they] could neither see nor find any one." McPherson had seen McLoughlin soused on many occasions, and experience had taught him that when McLoughlin drank, there was always hell to pay. In between rum runs, McPherson barricaded himself in his room, "apprehensive of Mr. McLoughlin's violence."

McPherson heard what followed through the floor in his room. Having guzzled "1½ Gallons of pure Spirits," the chief trader and his men "began to fight." As the shouting escalated, Heroux and Lasserte "ran out of the House with their Guns and [McLoughlin] sent all hands out after them." McPherson would have remained locked in his room were it not for "Mr. McLoughlin, who had come for his Rifle on account [of] Heroux & Lasserte's threatening him."

McLoughlin ordered McPherson to take up his lantern and accompany him in "search of Urbain and Lasserte, who had secreted themselves." McPherson thought the chief trader was simply paranoid, but he could not disobey a direct order. Holding aloft their lone source of light, he trailed McLoughlin as he hunted under the beds, although "for what object I cannot say." McLoughlin then "went around in the Gallery and searched the

Bastions but could not find Urbain and Lasserte." As McPherson made his way into the southeast bastion, McLoughlin "ran down into the Area of the Fort, calling out 'Fire, Fire,'" pleading with his loyal followers to commence shooting.

A hail of gunfire ensued, filling the night air with lead and the acrid smell of spent powder. A strange metered lull ensued as each man struggled to reload. Then, according to McPherson, "3 shots were fired near Fleury's house and one from the Gallery." From his hideout inside the carpenter's workshop, Belanger heard one shot, followed almost immediately by another, "the ball passing through the door where I was standing." Moments later, when the smoke finally cleared, McPherson learned that "one of those Shots took effect."

Moonlight etched the scene in stark relief. The body of John McLoughlin lay crumpled in a pool of blood at the door of Urbain Heroux's house. Leaving the safety of the carpentry shop, Charles Belanger saw McLoughlin "lying on his face, his rifle under his arm, quite dead." He had been shot through the chest. The wound proved instantly fatal; there were no final words, no last desperate gasps—"he did not even say, 'I am killed.'"

Almost immediately, the men began to speculate as to who had fired the lethal shot. Belanger posed the question to the growing crowd but his query met with stony silence and averted eyes. When pressed, several of the Canadians insisted, "We do not know, perhaps it was the Indians [from Tako]." When he asked the Kanakas, "some said it was Urbain and others said it was Antoine." McPherson, having inherited the mantle of command by default, immediately sat down and drafted a letter to the Company, writing: "I do not know the very man that have done it, but some of the Islanders were on the Gallery...and they saw two men firing, who were Lasserte and Urbain."

The debate raged on through the night, and by morning all agreed "the fatal shot had been fired by one Urbain Heroux."

FOUR

Dickson's Folly

As 1835 drew to a close, "General" James Dickson materialized from thin air, devoid of biography or pedigree. He stepped onto history's stage first in Washington and later New York, although it was Rupert's Land where he staked his claim and cemented his infamy.

In the absence of hard facts, speculation ran rampant. Dickson had money, although its source remained elusive, and he was clearly educated. His bearing and "air of command led to rumours of a distinguished lineage...English, Scottish or possibly Indian." He certainly looked the part; he was a well-knit specimen, rugged and ruddy, more ropey than muscular. George Simpson once described Dickson's face as "covered with huge whiskers and mustachios and seamed with sabre wounds," vestiges of a life hard lived. He claimed a vague prior association with Texas and the acquaintance of a number of well-regarded American military men who, in all likelihood, would not have known Dickson had they tripped over him.

As for the rank of general, it was a self-appointed commission. He commanded no troops, carried no colours, and bore no insignia. His uniform was entirely of his own design, as much a part of his spurious trappings as his blade-ravaged face. He was a man without country or conscience, but that was of little consequence to a visionary like James Dickson.

The general's vision was every bit as grandiose as the man who conceived it. He dreamt of establishing an independent "Indian" state encompassing all of Rupert's Land and extending as far south as Texas and California. He intended to raise an army of mercenaries and volunteers and launch an attack on Santa Fe, a New Mexican stronghold he assumed would collapse upon his approach. The fort's capture would then pave his way into California, where he would create—and rule—a Native American utopia far from the meddlesome influence of European authorities.

To achieve his objectives, Dickson placed some misleading advertisements for recruits "to aid the cause of Texas." He hoped to build a fighting force two hundred strong, but when he assembled his newly named Indian Liberating Army in Buffalo, New York, during the summer of 1836, the rank and file numbered only sixty. The majority were "half-breeds," the unwanted sons of HBC traders and their aboriginal wives. One of the first to enlist was "Major" Martin McLeod, a would-be poet who kept a journal of his "*Quixotic career*," peppered with quotations from Byron and other lyrical flights of fancy. He described his commander as "quite sanguine of success. As yet I know little of the man, but if I may judge from so short an acquaintance, he is somewhat visionary in his views." Although he admired his chosen messiah, McLeod acknowledged that Dickson's "movements at Buffalo [were] being looked upon with suspicion by the Americans." McLeod would have done well to heed their skepticism.

The general's disappointing recruitment drive left him no choice but to head north in search of more forgotten sons of the Honourable Company. One of his first ports of call was a bustling harbour town on the shores of Lake Ontario. McLeod captured the scene for posterity: "Remained one day at Toronto, do not like the place.... People kind enough apparently, but I think somewhat pompous. Why? God only knows. What have they to bost [*sic*] of. Their town or city (as I believe it is call'd) is a muddy hole." Still, even mudhole dwellers knew crazy when they saw it, and Dickson garnered only a handful of new recruits. Hoping for better luck in a bigger city, the crew headed east.

During Dickson's sweep through Montreal, John McLoughlin Jr. signed on without a moment's hesitation. His enlistment was not politically motivated, for he did not identify as "Indian" and cared little for their plight. Rather, he saw Dickson's campaign as the perfect opportunity to prove to his father, Simpson, and all his detractors that he could succeed at some occupation. More to the point, Junior was flat broke and solvency was an alluring mirage.

At McLoughlin's side was John George McKenzie, the son of Emperor Alexander McKenzie of the Athabasca and another chronic failure in his family's eyes. Young McKenzie had accomplished little, but his father's exalted status quickly earned him a place of honour among Dickson's recruits. He was named "Secretary of State" and "Brigadier General," ranks as heady as they were meaningless. Sadly, McKenzie was a very sick man; he lasted only as far as Sault Ste. Marie, where his failing health forced him to retreat to Berthier to spend the winter with his sister. There, McKenzie took a final turn for the worse and died in 1838.

Having lost his friend and Brigadier General, McLoughlin soon found another role model among Dickson's ranks, a fellow Metis by the name of McBean. The two men "encountered many interesting anecdotes" as the liberation army made its way into the heart of Rupert's Land in search of recruits. The voyage was circuitous and haphazard, a random itinerary of cities visited and revisited in the hopes of finding fresh recruits, and it proved more treacherous than expected once they reached the Sault. McLoughlin recalled, "Crossing the lakes Erie and Huron...took us at least one month, and we who expected to make it in fifteen days....I was in command of one of our vessels." Strong winds nearly capsized the boat, and it was only through "courage and resourcefulness that I was able to save the life of my men. The water was entering my vessel by tons. I was able to beach it on the beach and to save all my men with my small boat." McBean showed similar grace under fire, and the two men were amply rewarded, as McLoughlin boasted to the folks back home: "For the devotion which I have shown, as well as McBean, the commander has given us the commission of Major in the cavalry. I am naturally satisfied with my rank as it increases my pay. We are very much liked by our general and by the other officers."

Not everyone shared Dickson's high opinion of the newly minted Major. Fellow libertine Martin McLeod saw things differently and made note in his diary, which now stands as the best account of Dickson's ill-conceived march toward glory. McLeod recalled that during the near shipwreck, "McLoughlin and his men saved themselves at the expense of a good wetting but some of our luggage (which was carelessly left in the boat) was lost....No lives lost fortunately."

McLoughlin and McBean continued to bask in Dickson's good graces. The general and his majors even vacationed together, enjoying a short foray to Detroit, where they raised some eyebrows among the local populace: "Rambled through Detroit. Think it a pleasant place enough. Increasing rapidly, like all the American towns. People inquisitive and rude. Much speculation as to who we are." Five days later, the party still awaited the arrival of their schooner, and their impressions of the city soured after they "saw some of its curiosities and went to the menagerie, saw a variety of large snakes, birds, Monkeys and other beasts, besides some beastly spectators *half seas over, chewing tobacco* as if for a wager."

Curiosities aside, Detroit proved pivotal for an altogether different reason. When the long-awaited schooner finally hauled anchor two days later, the city's sheriff and his posse—whom McLeod called "his unwashed followers"—commandeered a boat and proceeded to hunt down Dickson and his mercenaries. It seems that, in addition to dining and taking in the sights, a number of Dickson's men engaged in some rather nefarious pursuits, including killing livestock and other light pillage and plunder. Whether McLoughlin was counted in that number remains unclear. The sheriff's boat quickly overtook Dickson's schooner, and the lawman declared he was charging the crew with killing some oxen, valued at $150. McLeod thought the sheriff was "an ignorant brute and I longed to kick him." McLeod dismissed this furor over cows as much ado about nothing and declared that "the person who talk[s] about it should be set down as a fool, and those who would believe accommodated with rooms in Bedlam."

Dickson and his officers erroneously believed their militia was covered by the same wartime statutes that allowed advancing armies to take necessary provisions from civilians without compensation. The general was a zealous advocate of the ends justifying the means, a mindset that led to some contrary policies. For men looking to liberate the aboriginal populace, the army certainly never hesitated to exploit them, such as when they beguiled a Huron warrior and "his squaw" into handing over "some excellent Salmon trout in exchange for a couple of handkerchiefs."

Like George Simpson, Dickson and his militia fancied themselves liberators, but they held in contempt those they sought to free. Throughout his journal, Martin McLeod disparaged the very people he claimed to be fighting for, referring to them as "Some savages" and far worse. In his more contemplative moments, he even wondered if they were doing the right thing: "Such is the manner of these simple but happy people...I could not but envy their happiness yet upon reflection, to me, they appear miserable.

How noble and truly philanthropic the attempt of regenerating these people. The[y] are, I feel confident, susceptible of all the refinements of civilized life. Still, perhaps, they would not be so happy."

The refinements of civilized life included the sartorial, at least in Dickson's army. To celebrate his new commission, McLoughlin wanted a uniform befitting his rank. He wrote to John Fraser in Montreal, asking to have one tailored: "The coat must be red worked with silver lace on the chest and collar with large silver epauletts [*sic*] and two pair of pantaloons, one black and the other...with gold lace on the sides.... do not be afraid of the Expense. I shall pay for it." The garish design was not his own. The company's roster included Hy Hartnell, a doctor who enlisted in Dickson's brigade purely in search of adventure. Hartnell reported for duty resplendent in full regalia, having "already prepared a sort of 'horse marine' uniform in addition to a famous *pair* of moustaches and hessian boots." The doctor's self-styled livery quickly became the envy of the complement, and those with means rushed to have their own suits fashioned.

Having reached the Sault as winter fell, Dickson foolishly pushed his troops ever northward. Their local guides abandoned them during their trek in the freezing wilderness with few provisions. Dissension in the ranks grew as many begged to overwinter in the protective confines of the city. Even Dickson's once-favoured sons McLoughlin and McBean "endeavoured to persuade a number of the men to return with them by pointing out the great dangers they were exposing themselves to—Such as starving or freezing to death." At one point it seemed inevitable that the men would resort to "*casting lots to eat each other*." It never quite came to cannibalism, but man's best friend was soon on the menu: "Out of Provisions, obliged to kill one of our dogs." Much to his delight, McLeod found "Dog's meat excellent eating."

Unable to convince his comrades to retreat, McLoughlin soldiered on with his men. He recounted his struggles to John Fraser: "Since I last wrote you I have met with many hardships in the way of traveling and starvation—The whole winter I did not sleep in a house, always travelled and still I am not at the end of my journey." McLoughlin was initially horrified at the prospect of eating dog but later recalled the delicacy with fondness, having been reduced to "long living on corn and pork (and not of the very best, exposed to cold)....I anticipate more yet which will be worse." Privations notwithstanding, McLoughlin's lowest point came when he lost all faith in Dickson, telling Fraser, "The more I think on the subject, the more I see my folly."

John Fraser knew his cousin had made a fateful mistake, and he did not hesitate to tell him so, counselling McLoughlin that "a man such as your Dixon [*sic*], who is a self created General without either sufficient money or influence, a man without any principles, as he well denoted by your landing on the Island Huron to commit plunder...why such a man ought to have been hung on the spot, he must be a worthless villain...a degraded vagabond, one whom the world abhors and despises." McLoughlin shamefully concurred but he had no other vocational options. Fraser, his most loyal and trusted adviser, entreated him to "join your Honorable Father who waits anxiously for his lost son....he will receive you with his arms open, he will soothe the pain and suffering you are feeling, he will restore you to yourself and make a new man of you."

Even in the worst of times, father and son were unable to communicate directly. After hearing second-hand tales of his son's descent into paramilitary purgatory, Dr. McLoughlin softened his stance and once again used John Fraser as a back-channel emissary. McLoughlin Sr. offered to let his son come home, but John Jr. possessed too much pride to beg his father for help. Furthermore, he knew full well George Simpson hated him, and nothing shy of a miracle would compel the Governor to offer him a place in the Hudson's Bay Company. Miserable but resigned, McLoughlin kept his word to Dickson and continued to march northward into the snow-covered heart of Rupert's Land.

There was only one problem: Dickson did not have permission from the Hudson's Bay Company to enter their territory, nor was he likely to get it. The general's rabble-rousing had outraged and unnerved Simpson. Although the messenger was insane, his message was not, and Dickson's proposal found strong support among the aboriginal populations, particularly the disavowed progeny of the HBC. The general's credibility was negligible but his timing could not have been better. His campaign took full advantage of the escalating misery and public resentment arising from President Andrew Jackson's disastrous Indian Removal Act of 1830. The government's push to open the American west for white settlement had culminated in the

"Trail of Tears" and the forced expulsion of Cherokee and other "civilized tribes" from their ancestral lands. The Honourable Company had become a despised and often ridiculed monopoly, and it could ill-afford such a wholesale public relations disaster.

To break Dickson's lingering hold on his troops, Governor Simpson devised a plan that was as devious as it was simple: he offered several key Liberating Army officers jobs with the Hudson's Bay Company. "By detaching them you will have less difficulty in managing the others," Simpson told the higher-ups in London. McLoughlin could scarcely contain his shock when he "got a letter from Gov. Simpson informing me that he had a place for me if I wanted to accept of it." The timing of the offer was serendipitous, for Dickson's army was bivouacked at death's door, and McLoughlin had finally come to his senses.

The prospect of life in the HBC no longer felt so repugnant, and having mortgaged his future to a madman like Dickson, the thought of pledging allegiance to George Simpson seemed the lesser of two evils. To his family's surprise, John Jr. accepted Simpson's duplicitous offer and became an HBC junior clerk and surgeon. He was engaged for three years at the modest rate of £100 per annum; the salary was an insult, but at least the HBC was good for the money. McLoughlin had not seen one penny from Dickson during his year-long ordeal, despite the general's repeated promises.

Simpson initially assigned John Jr. to Fort McLoughlin, but his father "chose to keep him closer at hand, at Fort Vancouver." When McLoughlin arrived on the west coast, he was reunited with his parents and his younger brother, David, whom he knew only through the occasional exchange of letters. Though brief, it was the best of times for the McLoughlin clan.

As for the general and his quest to liberate the aboriginals from their Occidental oppressors, the dream died in the spring of 1837. Thanks to Simpson's machinations, Dickson's officers began deserting at an alarming rate. The general and his last holdouts finally headed south for Santa Fe, but the men were exhausted, ill, and unpaid. Just south of the border, the troops refused to go on. Unable to marshal his forces, "Dickson's disordered mind" finally came undone and, in keeping with his oeuvre, "the invasion ended in the fashion of an *opera bouffe*." The general, dressed in his full regimental finest, ordered his army to stand at attention. As a handful of bedraggled tin soldiers looked on, Dickson "made a laudatory speech, removed his epaulets, fastened them on Grant's shoulders, handed him his sword, mounted, and disappeared in the wilderness." He was never heard from again.

It had taken a lunatic's quixotic war to accomplish what many thought impossible: Governor Simpson had reversed his own dictate and invited John McLoughlin Jr. to join the Hudson's Bay Company. Let the record show that in June 1837, hell froze over.

Monday, April 25, 1842 — Full Dark
FORT STIKINE

Simpson sat poker-faced, digesting Thomas McPherson's
account of McLoughlin's untimely demise, for that was how
the Governor thought of it: as a death, an unfortunate accident
perhaps, but certainly not a murder. McPherson had not
witnessed the actual shooting — he had been in the southeast
bastion at the moment McLoughlin fell — but Simpson had
little interest in the death itself. It was the story McPherson told
of McLoughlin's behaviour leading up to the shooting that
captured Sir George's attention. He wanted to hear more of
McPherson's sordid tale of debauchery, and so, at the Governor's
urging, McPherson began cataloguing McLoughlin's all-too-
human failings: "Mr. McLoughlin was in the habit of drinking
Grog after dinner.... McLoughlin became very much addicted
to liquor, frequently getting drunk as early as 1 and 2 O'Clock
in the afternoon... more so even to madness before evening."
The slander struck the perfect discordant note, for Simpson had
little patience for those "addicted to the Bottle."

Being a lowdown drunk was bad enough, but McPherson
insisted that when McLoughlin was in his cups, he "was
exceedingly violent, beating the People with his Fist and
Bludgeons, inflicting wounds, tying them and flogging them
on the bare back with a cat even till Blood Streamed down."
McPherson could never be mistaken for a wordsmith, but he
limned a visceral and brutal image of the young McLoughlin,
and Simpson embraced that vision wholeheartedly. He had
believed McLouglin capable of great savagery since witnessing
the boy's rage at his Montreal boarding school. Sir George also
knew McLouglin had made overt threats to his subordinates in
the past. While serving in Dickson's Liberating Army,
McLoughlin held command of a small band of men he described as "the worst of all those living under the face of
Heaven." In a letter to John Fraser, McLoughlin confessed he

"could not get them to work without hard treatment."
McLouglin then assured his cousin: "before I get to red river I shall break some of their bones, and I will do it with the greatest pleasure for they deserve it, they give me more trouble than they are worth." Fraser recounted his cousin's disciplinary tactics to Dr. McLoughlin and Governor Simpson, who mentally filed them away for future use.

McPherson's litany of abuses ended with a blanket indictment of the chief trader's shortcomings as a boss and as a man: "McLoughlin in other respects led a very irregular life, generally keeping 3 women at the same time in the Fort, Sleeping the greater part of the forenoon and paying little or no attention to the Business." Simpson lacked the moral authority to judge another man's conduct with women, but that had never stopped him before. McLoughlin's tendency to sleep the morning away also stuck in the Governor's craw, as it was not in keeping with "Simpson's penchant for early starts." It was McPherson's final charge, however, that Simpson found most objectionable. Based solely on McPherson's word, the Governor declared, "The business of the post seems to have been very badly conducted. . . . the accounts, I fear, are in a very irregular state."

To a Company man, this was inexcusable, even if Simpson himself had occasionally fiddled with the books in the past. "Ledger books and post journals, Simpson knew in his bones, could cover as many sins as they could reveal,"and Simpson was certain McLoughlin's books would disclose myriad indiscretions. So certain was Simpson that, without so much as cracking a single spine or reading a single inventory, he declared Stikine's books to be in complete disarray, conclusive proof of McLoughlin's incompetence, corruption, and malfeasance. Sir George's mind was made up, and hard evidence was neither necessary nor welcome.

For the sake of appearances, Simpson deposed four other men: Canadians Phillip Smith and Benoni Fleury, and two Kanakas, Kakepé and Captain Cole. During each interview, he asked no questions and challenged no accounts, even when the witnesses openly contradicted themselves or one another. It was only so much legal theatre, for Simpson had reached his verdict the moment McPherson stopped talking.

The Governor believed what the men told him "because it confirmed his views of the case," and his credulity flowed from the wellspring of his studied cynicism. He quickly developed a theory of the crime: McLoughlin "had simply reverted to type." Accordingly, Simpson determined that "this dreadful act [was] done, I firmly believe, under the influence of terror, as a measure of self preservation."

As for who had acted in self-defence, Simpson settled on one man: "I have no Doubt on my mind that Urbain Heroux fired the fatal shot But I think it better not to bring it home to him." The Governor's sympathies for the perpetrator stood in sharp contrast to his growing indifference for the victim. Dealing with Heroux meant more headaches for the Governor, and Simpson's concerns for his own well-being always eclipsed the misfortunes of others, even those of the newly deceased John McLoughlin Jr.

It was not the first time Simpson had been so forgiving. Years before, HBC trader John Siveright had "shot a man in cold blood ... and although little is now said about it, he is still looked upon as a Murderer by many of his colleagues." Homicide, however, was not grounds for dismissal in Simpson's world, and Siveright went on to have a stellar career with the Honourable Company, rising to the rank of chief factor before retiring with a comfortable pension. Siveright was ultimately acquitted of the killing because Simpson believed "he was more influenced by personal fear and want of Nerve than by any worse feeling."

With Siveright, and now with Heroux, Simpson had little motivation to cull the truth from the innuendo. He was the quintessential Company man, this was a Company problem, and, as such, all misadventures would be handled in-house. That the crime was committed "in self defence, might, under such circumstances, prove convenient," for any public inquiry would bring McLoughlin's demons to light and "attract much unfavourable attention to the Hudson's Bay Company," a situation Simpson wanted to avoid.

In truth, McLoughlin's reputation was the furthest thing from Simpson's mind. His only thought was to protect the Company from a trial that would expose his questionable labour practices — including hiring ex-convicts and retaining problem employees — to public scrutiny. The Governor had gone to great lengths to promote the erroneous impression "he had access to a real labor market," for in the world of commerce, "perception was everything and no one knew that better than George Simpson." From the Company's perspective, the timing of this corporate glitch could not have been worse.

Simpson sat at the dead man's desk and, in a letter to his overlords on the London Committee, offered a master class in corporate weaseldom: "In the whole case our aim has been to assume as little responsibility as possible and at the same time to facilitate the prosecution by every means not incompatible with the rights and feelings of innocent parties." Ethics aside, Simpson knew his efforts at spin doctoring were futile, and he cautioned, "Neither by this course, nor by any other practicable course, can the Hudson's Bay Company expect to avoid popular censure in this most untoward business."

In closing, the Governor offered a crafty yet simple solution: make McLoughlin's death Russia's problem. After all, the event had occurred on Russian territory, albeit on land under HBC control. Simpson conveniently glossed over a number of confounding factors, most notably that both the shooter and victim were Canadian and therefore British subjects. Still, he assured the Committee, he was certain such minor details could be resolved in the fullness of time. Simpson then congratulated himself on his "conveniently antiseptic solution of conceding jurisdiction" to Russian authorities and set about taking care of business.

To that end, he made a number of key staff changes. The first was to place "Mr. [Charles] Dodd, chief Mate of the

Cowlitz in charge of the Fort, for which he appears well qualified." He also ordered "a respectable young man, George Blenkinsop, one of the Sailors, to act in the capacity of assistant." The Governor left Dodd and Blenkinsop a series of written instructions, as well as some paternal words of wisdom: "Notwithstanding the melancholy event which has lately occurred, the people of the establishment are upon the whole a well conducted body of men. With firmness and kind treatment you will have no difficulty in managing them and I have to beg that no violence be used either towards men or Indians unless such should become absolutely necessary as a measure of self preservation." In addition to Blenkinsop, Sir George counselled Dodd to rely on "McPherson and Smith, who are trusty and confidential."

There remained one very real threat facing Stikine. As Simpson struggled to solve his personnel problems, "the Indians, who are collected to the number of about 2000 in the neighbourhood . . . were talking of attacking the Fort, which . . . they thought would be an easy capture." The Governor's recommendation to Dodd was a triumph of effect over effectiveness, and showed just how poorly he understood the situation: "The indian interpreter Hanaga Joe I think ought to be removed to outside the Fort as it is not fit that any Indian should have an opportunity of knowing your weak points." Banishing Hanega Joe was a meaningless gesture, but Simpson had given an order, which, to his mind, meant the problem was solved.

That left the sticky question of what to do with those responsible. To begin, Simpson fired Pierre Kannaquassé because "he had been guilty of an earlier attempt to shoot John McLoughlin, Jr." The Governor also decided Kannaquassé should be sent in irons to Fort Vancouver, "to be forwarded to Canada, as a worthless character and not to be re-admitted to the Service." As for Heroux, the alleged triggerman, Simpson ordered that he be shackled and secured aboard the *Cowlitz,* so that he could be transported to Sitka and handed over to

Russian authorities for assessment. With that, Simpson felt certain he "had done all that was necessary or expedient."

Two tasks remained, each of a far more personal nature. First, Simpson ensured that "Mr. McLoughlin's private property [be] packed up and forwarded to Vancouver, and his private papers separated from those that appear, on a very superficial examination, to be public." Included in this recovery effort was a highly sentimental artifact. Powkow, a Kanaka loyal to McLoughlin, had taken "a ring from the finger of the corpse," which he "gave to the woman who lived with McLoughlin." In a particularly heartless moment, Simpson made certain "this ring was afterwards taken from her and sent to Fort Vancouver with his clothes."

To complete his final duty, the little emperor again took up pen and paper. His first missive was addressed to HBC Governor Pelly. In words as cutting as they were cold, Simpson informed his superior that "Mr. McLoughlin's conduct and management, during the past year, were quite disgraceful; that he had become a slave to licentiousness and dissipation, that his treatment of the people was exceedingly violent & oppressive, and very frequently cruel in the extreme, and that, the business intrusted to his charge was entirely neglected ... in short, profligacy, waste of property and disorder characterized the management of Stikine during the past year."

FACING PAGE > Map of Fort Stikine, drawn during the initial depositions in April 1842. The effort contains a very primitive attempt at ballistic reconstruction. According to the notes, the asterisk indicates where the killer "must" have been standing, based on a trajectory that traces a straight line back from the bullet lodged in the carpentry shop door. This, in turn, suggests the map represented what Simpson wanted to believe, rather than what the eyewitnesses were telling him.

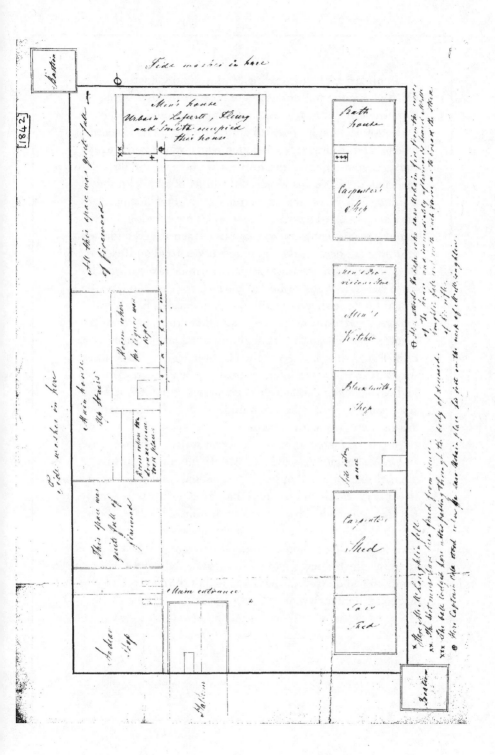

In his last act before leaving Stikine, Simpson wrote to Dr. McLoughlin to inform him of his son's demise. With complete disregard for a father's feelings, Simpson laid the blame for McLoughlin's death at his own feet: "His violence when under the influence of liquor, which was very frequently the case, amount[ed] to insanity." Salting the wound he had just inflicted, the Governor absolved the killer of all responsibility, claiming "Heroux's conduct on the fatal night still appears to have been dictated by the Instinct of self preservation more than by premeditated malice." Simpson then absolved himself, arguing that, because the shooting had occurred on Russian soil, "no legal steps against the parties can be taken by me; but my belief is, that any Tribunal by which the case could be tried, would find a verdict of 'Justifiable Homicide.'" The law had long recognized the notion of a victimless crime, but thanks to George Simpson, John McLoughlin Jr. had just become a crimeless victim. Sir George then had the temerity to conclude his letter to McLoughlin Sr. by praising the murderous crew and noting "their conduct throughout has been fully better than could have been expected under such inhuman treatment as they were frequently exposed to."

From the moment the envelope was sealed, Simpson's letter to Dr. McLoughlin claimed its place in infamy as a missive "remarkable for its callousness," a supposed condolence letter deemed so "harsh and tactless" that "even if the details which Sir George cited had been correct, the tone of his letter was uncalled for." Throughout his life, Simpson's writings had revealed him to be a museum-quality bastard, but here he sank to unimaginable new depths. Although he did not yet realize it, Simpson had destroyed what remained of the once-proud McLoughlin dynasty.

FIVE

"A Sink of Pollution"

If location is the first rule of real estate, Fort Stikine refused to play by it. The site was, at the time and in retrospect, an absolutely stupid place to build an outpost. Even George Simpson conceded it "had not been well selected...situated on a peninsula barely large enough for the necessary buildings." As a result, the fort was tiny by HBC standards, "an Establishment two hundred ft. Square."

The problem was not just space; it was also proximity to water, as John McLoughlin Jr. lamented in the fort's journal: "Tide very high last night, so much so it carried away part of the water front." The tide turned soil to mud and washed away the fort's underpinnings, leaving behind toxic sewage that triggered even the most hardened gag reflex. In his self-aggrandizing opus *Narrative of a Journey Round the World,* Simpson painted a vivid olfactory tableau of the region, thanks to "the slime that was periodically deposited by the receding sea, aided by the putridity and filth of the native villages...[filling] the atmosphere with a most nauseous perfume." One occupant summed it up best when he described the post as "a hell upon Earth with a Sink of Pollution."

Despite water on all sides, the fort's potable water was perpetually in short supply. Access to the vital resource was often threatened by hostile locals, who used it as a form of protest. Eloisa McLoughlin Rae noted, "The water was not close by the Fort there. We had a trough made with two boards for half a mile to bring in water. When the Indians got drunk or in a bad humour they would destroy the trough so that we could not get water."

When the aqueduct was out, the men were forced to drink wine or hard liquor, further hampering the rebuilding process.

Even when the trough was functional, bathing was rare, laundry was unheard of, and personal grooming was a luxury. Hair and beards grew unchecked, free from the taming influence of combs or razors. Teeth rotted in heads, unbrushed and untouched by fresh fruits and vegetables. Diseased dentition was invariably pulled or chipped out, rum being the sole form of anesthetic. Isolated from what Dr. McLoughlin deemed the "Civilized World," the men of Stikine grew feral.

It was a malodorous sinkhole fit for neither man nor beast, and it was certainly no place for a woman—at least not a white woman. The only one to ever set foot in Stikine was the aforementioned Eloisa. As the daughter of Dr. John, sister of Mr. John, and wife of the fort's first chief trader, William Glen Rae, Eloisa was HBC royalty, but she was technically not a white woman. She was every bit the "half-breed" her brother was, both being the products of a Cree mother. She was taller than a girl ought to be and had grown up in the rough and tumble of Company forts. Even so, nothing could have prepared Eloisa for Stikine. She swore, "It was a miserable place.... There were only flat rocks and no trees around close—within half a mile; just bare rocks.... It was a terrible place.... I did not like it at all; it was terrible." She was forced to endure that most terrible place for an entire year, beginning in April 1840, when she accompanied her husband as he took command of the newly acquired station. When he was later transferred to a fort in southern California, no one was happier than Eloisa.

Even filthy water seeks its own level, and the HBC quickly constructed an equally vile mate for Stikine along the fog-bound coastline, a secondary fort they dubbed Tako. Although Tako was better situated in a "landlocked harbor," it too fell prey to many of the curses plaguing Stikine. Of course, the HBC did not build Stikine—the Russians bear the ignominy for that lapse in judgement—but the Company did go to extraordinary lengths to rent it. In 1834, Governor Simpson decided the Honourable Company needed a foothold on the Stikine River, which was then under the control of the czar, Nicholas I. With flagrant disregard for international treaties, Simpson dispatched Peter Skene Ogden to establish a post at the river's mouth. Ogden was a brilliant choice to lead the charge, having successfully mounted six forays into the Snake River basin. The man was simply too belligerent for polite society, too fearless to succumb to attack, and too obstinate to fail.

Ogden met his match in the unlikely personage of Baron Ferdinand Friedrich Georg von Wrangel, an explorer and seaman who was serving as governor of Russian Alaska. Wrangel set up a blockade and fortified a village he named Redoubt St. Dionysius. Ogden, however, refused to back down. Outmanned and outgunned, he held his ground through an eleven-day standoff with the Russians. It was a noble effort, but Ogden was eventually forced to retreat. Dr. McLoughlin later mounted his own wildly unsuccessful ventures into the Stikine area, but each time his men were repelled amidst a hail of gunfire.

In 1838, the British renewed the HBC licence for another twenty-one years, extending their monopoly in a country fast running out of fur-bearing creatures. The Company's policy of environmental rape and pillage forced them ever westward in search of virgin lands, and Simpson once again decided their best hopes lay in the pristine wilds of the Stikine River basin. This time, Simpson opted for diplomacy (admittedly not his strongest suit), and the Governor booked passage to Russia, intent on brokering a deal.

After several days' wait, Simpson was finally invited to attend a state dinner. He arrived dressed in his finest frippery for his audience with Baron von Wrangel, and was, as always, underwhelmed. Physically, Wrangel was a most peculiar specimen. Eggshell bald and devoid of chin, the baron had cultivated an elaborate system of whiskers to define a face that otherwise threatened to disappear into obscurity. Simpson, a practitioner of brutal honesty, described Wrangel as "an extraordinary looking ferret eyed, Red Whiskered & moustachioed little creature." The Governor also felt the baron was "stupid to a degree," although, in fairness, Simpson thought that of everyone he met.

The two men eventually negotiated a deal, with the Russians agreeing to give the HBC a ten-year lease on their lands in return for two thousand seasoned otter skins per annum and other considerations. Simpson, immeasurably pleased with himself, headed home with a signed contract.

Wrangel was happy to be rid of that woebegone spit of land. From the start, it had proven more grief than it was worth because the region was rife with "Indian trouble." In 1802, the local tribes seized and burned Sitka, and the situation had deteriorated steadily ever since. As the Russians handed over the keys to the HBC in 1840, race relations at Stikine had reached a boiling point. Wrangel warned Simpson that the "HBC would need more men than they had in order to hold the fort," but the Governor was deaf to unsolicited advice.

On June 1, 1840, chief factor James Douglas formally took possession of the Alaska panhandle on behalf of the Company, and in a ceremony bereft of pomp or circumstance, Redoubt St. Dionysius was renamed Fort Stikine. William Rae was given full control of the outpost and its twenty-man complement, and his brother-in-law John McLoughlin Jr. was appointed as his right-hand man.

William Rae and Eloisa, his wife of two years, set up house in the fort's hastily constructed main quarters. Her role in the fort's affairs was entirely decorative, and she was trapped like a jewelled beetle in amber: lovely to behold but of little practical use. She held her nose, and her tongue, in equal measure, and soldiered on as best she could. She turned a blind eye to everything except the liquor. Her father had always preached temperance, and the men's excessive consumption shocked Mrs. Rae, who claimed to have seen "a big hogs head four feet high...emptied in one day." She was disheartened to learn her husband was emptying more than his fair share of the kegs, and so Eloisa tumbled into disenchantment, surrounded by hostile forces and repugnant conditions.

Early in 1841, Rae was recalled to Fort Vancouver and sent on to take charge of the HBC post in Yerba Buena. His departure left a void in Fort Stikine's power structure, and after much deliberation, John McLoughlin Jr. was promoted to chief trader. The final staffing decision rested with his father, who swore the arrangement bore no trace of nepotism. The good doctor later said he had appointed his son simply because he was the best man available. Although such a glowing assessment would have struck many as preposterous only three years earlier, times had changed, and so had John Jr.

To everyone's astonishment, life in the Hudson's Bay Company agreed with John McLoughlin Jr., and his earliest posting at Fort Vancouver proved to be a turning point in his maturation. Reunited with his parents and a brother he never knew, McLoughlin flourished as never before. He applied himself zealously to his duties, bragging to John Fraser, "We are in it from ½ past 6 in the morning till nine at night. I have learned more in the way of transacting business here than I should have done in Montreal in the same space of time. If you were to see our establishment you would be highly delighted with it."

His father was cautiously optimistic, seeing positive changes in both his sons now that they were within arm's reach. Dr. McLoughlin sang their praises in muted tones, saying only that John and David "are as attentive and smart at their work as most young men." Dr. McLoughlin's formidable influence stunted his offspring's growth, but John Jr.'s standing in the Company improved after his transfer to Stikine. He quickly earned a reputation as "a good disciplinarian" and did all he could to dispel Simpson's entrenched belief that "no half-breed ever amounted to much." William Rae waxed effusive of his brother-in-law, saying he could not want "a more sober, steady, or better assistant than...John McLoughlin," and adding he had little doubt McLoughlin would one day rise to full command.

Rise he did and, as McLoughlin family historian Burt Brown Barker noted, "it must have been a great satisfaction for the family to see John settling down to hard work after the wild life he had led." His younger brother noticed a discernible shift in McLoughlin following his promotion: "I believe he is well satisfied with his situation, being far away from the old Gentleman and near to the Russians, who are full of game and he being master of a post."

Not everyone held such a generous view of McLoughlin's meteoric rise through the ranks. One of his subordinates thought Mr. John "was kind and indulgent to the people" under his command, but only when sober. Others were less gracious, most notably the HBC trader George Roberts, who claimed McLoughlin was still "too young and hot headed for such a service."

McLoughlin was admittedly inexperienced and a trifle too impulsive to lead on his own—even his sister said "he had not been in long enough to be chief clerk." Fortunately, he did not have to go it alone. Dr. McLoughlin appointed Roderick Finlayson, a "congenial and competent young man," to serve as his son's right-hand. Finlayson was exactly the sort of corporate lackey prized by management. He was perpetually fearful and thus easily controlled, and his tolerance of monotony held him in good stead for Company life. He was perceived as honest to a fault; one of his supervisors described him as "Mr. Finlayson, who I am sure could not tell a lie." Finlayson was unflinchingly sober, pious, and calm, steering well clear of saloons, gambling, and women of flexible morality. He viewed pleasure and its pursuit as a character flaw to be corrected; in short, he was the perfect foil for young McLoughlin, who many feared had not yet abandoned his bacchanalian ways.

McLoughlin and Finlayson were an ideal team: a fiery and exacting disciplinarian calmed by the temperate breeze of reason. Together they had the fort so well in hand that when Governor Simpson paid a surprise visit in September 1841, even he "formed a favourable opinion of the manner in which Finlayson and McLoughlin were running the establishment."

Although Simpson normally left the day-to-day operations of the western forts to Dr. McLoughlin, he could not resist the urge to tinker. Simpson visited both Stikine and Tako during his annual tour in 1841, and "at each stop, Simpson called clerks and factors to account and transferred personnel if he thought it in the company's best interest." When the Governor returned to Fort Stikine in October of that same year, he was on the prowl for a suitable replacement for John Rowand, widely recognized as "Simpson's favourite trader." Rowand, chief factor at Fort Edmonton, was long overdue for a furlough, although many feared the corpulent trader, who weighed in at more than three hundred pounds, might not live long enough to enjoy it. Simpson wanted Rowand to accompany him on his return journey to Montreal, and so he made a seemingly simple, yet ultimately fatal, decision: George Simpson elected to transfer the capable and abstemious Roderick Finlayson in what became a protracted game of Company musical chairs.

Dr. McLoughlin did not share the Governor's enthusiasm, as Simpson's unilateral exercise in human resources "left John to govern what was reportedly one of the most difficult posts on the Pacific Coast." John Jr., however, viewed Finlayson's departure as a backhanded compliment, telling him: "I am sure that all this comes from our having had the Fort in such good order when the great Folks passed." Within a few short months, McLoughlin had morphed from profligate ne'er-do-well to the sole leader of a nascent fort. His best hope of success lay in securing another assistant equal to the indispensable Finlayson.

When the moment came to select a junior officer to help govern, decent applicants were thin on the ground. One of the primary (or perhaps only) requirements for the job was proficiency in the English language, which meant the only viable candidate was Thomas McPherson, "a poor soft half Breed Lad who out of charity had been sent to that place to be Employed in the store." Even the HBC power brokers felt "McPherson was not a fit person to act as second." Dr. McLoughlin thought the pairing of his son and the "soft and dull" McPherson would spell disaster, for he "knew McPherson to be a lazy Sleepy Drone" and a thief. John Jr. agreed, and he complained to his supervisor that McPherson "will never answer the purpose. He is a fellow that has no education." Still, Simpson had spoken, and neither McLoughlin was in any position to quibble, so McPherson — vacuous, indolent, and sticky-fingered as can be — got the job. Even in his best moments, John McLoughlin Jr. was cursed by a lack of options.

Tuesday, June 28, 1842 — Dusk

FORT VANCOUVER

John McLoughlin Sr. was a man of few vices and scant pleasures. "The Dr. never smoked—chewing was out of the question—but occasionally snuffed—but seemed afraid to trust himself." He also did not trust himself with alcohol, although he did not begrudge others the occasional nip: "Brandy was placed on the table with wine and cigars in the evening, as there was no amusement." The doctor did not care to mix food and frivolity.

After the obligatory recitation of grace, Dr. McLoughlin sat down to supper surrounded by his top lieutenants. The only tolerable sound was the scrape of knives on pewter. Conversation was to be kept to a minimum, and the sole permissible topic was work. Once the doctor had cleaned his plate and retired for the evening, the men were free to do as they pleased, within reasonable limits.

On this particular night, the room's suffocating silence was stirred by the arrival of a clerk bearing a message for the chief factor. The steamer *Cowlitz* had docked at Fort Vancouver's waterfront that afternoon, and the crew were in the midst of off-loading its cargo. The clerk produced a thick packet of paper marked confidential and addressed to the doctor's attention. The envelope bore the unmistakable scrawl and seal of Governor George Simpson.

Two months had passed since Simpson put pen to paper at Fort Stikine, and countless other HBC employees already knew what the doctor was about to learn. He threw the packet aside and finished his meal in peace. A missive from Simpson seldom brought glad tidings, and Dr. McLoughlin was in no mood for more of the Governor's self-serving edicts and unfunded mandates.

With his last bite, McLoughlin pushed back his chair, bid his officers a good night, and left them to their own devices. As an afterthought, he grabbed Simpson's envelope and headed for his room. He would soon have need of the privacy it afforded.

The doctor cracked the packet's seal and began with the top document. Simpson's words leapt from the parchment: John Jr. was dead — gunned down by his own men. The term "Justifiable Homicide" swam before McLoughlin's eyes, its meaning lost in a fog of disbelief and the anaesthetic effects of shock.

Raw grief soon gave way to an agonizing round of second-guessing and what-ifs: "Poor john, he had a great deal of trouble the short time he was in this world & if he had remained in Canada this would never have happened." The doctor was haunted by their final conversation, in which his son swore his future did not rest with the Honourable Company. John Jr. feared if he stayed in their employ, he might never escape his father's legacy or the perception he was given his job as a birthright. In his last days in Fort Vancouver, as he packed his trunk and prepared to report to Stikine, John told his father "he should Leave the country and go somewhere Else to shift for himself." He did not live long enough to make good on the promise, a thought that troubled his father.

Dr. McLoughlin returned to the ceaseless business of the Honourable Company the next morning, present in body but absent in mind and soul. Days passed as his sorrow twisted and burrowed. The true meaning behind the verdict of justifiable homicide dawned with full force, and the doctor could not accept the implications. The Governor's indifference to the shooting rattled incessantly in Dr. McLoughlin's brain, and his feelings of rage began to coalesce around a single target: George Simpson. Those in the doctor's orbit immediately noticed the shift; George Roberts felt "the chary way in which Sir Geo behaved about the death envemoned [sic] the Dr. against him." It was one thing to lose a son to murder, but it was quite another to have their mutual employer dismiss the death as both insignificant and self-inflicted.

Simpson's chary ways went far beyond that tactless letter. He had also manipulated the eyewitness statements, copies of which he included in the packet. Dr. McLoughlin knew the men of Stikine far better than the oft-absent Governor, and he soon realized "the depositions were a tissue of lies and exaggerations." The doctor was certain "many had a motive to falsify" their testimony. There was also no escaping that "some of the most important witnesses… spoke very little English," and no competent translators were present during their depositions. Dr. McLoughlin's case against Simpson was building.

McLoughlin shared his thoughts with anyone who would listen and found he was not alone in his criticism of the witness statements. The doctor's suspicions prompted chief trader John O'Brien to ask Roderick Finlayson whether Simpson's affidavits rang true, and Stikine's former second-in-command was adamant the statements were self-serving perjury. According to O'Brien, "Finlayson also showed me a letter Signed by Thomas McPherson & Countersigned by Mr. C. Dodd & Geo. Blenkinsop in which McPherson States that he did not understand the questions put to him by Sir Geo. Simpson."

The Governor's lack of investigative rigour was equally evident in his decision not to question many of the key witnesses. Simpson did not depose William Lasserte, for example, even though Lasserte was one of the few to have actually seen the shooting.

Days turned into weeks as Dr. McLoughlin obsessively picked at his wound. He read the depositions over and over, and each time he was left with more questions than answers, and with little faith in the Governor's slipshod investigation. He desperately needed to escape his grief, and so he transformed emotion into motion. He decided to launch his own inquest and began by questioning the men under his command. At that moment, Urbain Heroux was languishing in the purgatory of Sitka, but McLoughlin still had access to several other witnesses, including Pierre Kannaquassé, who was in his own strange limbo in nearby Fort Nisqually.

The doctor's initial meeting with Kannaquassé was an odd one. When McLoughlin asked who had killed his son,

Kannaquassé cryptically replied that he knew but would tell no one except Governor Simpson for fear of causing another murder. Outraged, McLoughlin stormed from the room. Determined to have his questions answered, he ordered a formal inquest be convened at Fort Nisqually. McLoughlin knew his enemy, and he feared that if he interrogated Kannaquassé himself, Simpson would dismiss the results as biased. He appointed a panel of impartial officers to head the investigation, including chief trader Donald Manson, Captain William McNeill, and the Reverend Jason Lee.

Kannaquassé was brought before the panel on July 15, 1842. His testimony was a revelation, for his recollections of the night of April 21 bore little resemblance to the story Simpson was peddling.

SIX

An Underhanded
Complement

Like the outpost that housed them, Stikine's traders were the dregs of the Honourable Company's holdings. Even the region's chief factor acknowledged that "these men had been sent to Stikine because no one else wanted them, there were no replacements and they could not desert from there." David McLoughlin said simply, "Our people here are such beasts."

Beasts they were, and of all stripes. Fort Stikine had "a somewhat volatile ethnic mix." Viewed today, the outpost's roster is an ethnographer's nightmare, for the ancestry of the fort's inhabitants defies labels or classification. How a man chose to self-identify bore little relation to how others perceived him, and it became a quagmire of cultural relativism. To full-blooded aboriginals, the fort's senior members were "white men," "Frenchmen," or "Canadians." Such epithets irked the HBC heads in Montreal and London, men to whom such labels rightfully applied. To the Company's elite, including George Simpson, John McLoughlin Jr. and his band of miscreants were "half-breeds," irrespective of what "breed" made up the non-white half. They painted McLoughlin (who was part Cree) with the same brush as his Iroquois traders, dismissing them all as *bois brûlé*, a derogatory reference to the burnt wood colour of their skin. This one-slander-fits-all approach was reflected in company documents, which slapped all indigenous peoples with the label "Indian," a word now mercifully retired to our nation's closet of politically incorrect terminology. This institutionalized cultural insensitivity led scholar Hamar Foster to argue that the fur traders "confused tribes with clans; it is therefore often difficult to reconcile their records with the writings of anthropologists."

For the sake of simplicity, and to best reflect the historical record, it is prudent to divide the men of Stikine into three groups: the "Canadians" or "white men" (including McLoughlin and McPherson); the "Sandwich Islanders" or "Kanakas" (low-level HBC employees of Hawaiian heritage); and the "Indians," "natives," or "savages" who surrounded the outpost and alternately traded with or attacked it.

Fraternization among the three groups was unthinkable, and all efforts by the Company to integrate the men were futile. The quirks of the fur trade forced them to live in close proximity, but nothing could make them interact: "They had lived apart before entering the service and separated 'by mutual consent' when encamped: 'the Iroquois had a fire; the French Canadians had a fire' and the officers had a fire." No one thought it racist at the time; it was merely the way of the world, and, as long-time HBC employee George Roberts so deftly put it, "a general comingling would not do."

In this regard, the fish stank from the head down, for George Simpson had no qualms about basing his hiring decisions solely on the ancestry of the applicant. He denied Simon McGillivray a promotion simply because he possessed "a good deal of the Indian, in disposition as well as in blood and appearance." Simpson was equally intolerant of his own kind, and he believed the Scots and the Irish were especially "inclined to form leagues and cabals which might be dangerous to the peace of the Country." Simpson was so convinced that he intentionally recruited few of his fellow countrymen and ordered they be stationed separately to keep them from organizing.

To make matters worse, this highly combustible ethnic mix was plunked down in the midst of what Dr. McLoughlin called "the most numerous and worst disposed Indians on the Coast." The fort's first commander, William Rae, understated the conflict when he informed headquarters that the locals were "by no means in good humour with us," although that may have been the liquor talking. James Douglas generously described one local band as "cheerful," even though he spent very little time at Stikine and was "probably not the best judge of how cheerful everyone was."

Baron von Wrangel's calamitous prophecy proved astute, and the fort's twenty-man complement was woefully outnumbered. The outpost's defences were "very humble indeed," a fact the locals knew all too well, as one incident in the spring of 1842 illustrates. On a quiet afternoon, five aboriginals "came to the gate and began to abuse the establishment." They had no skins to trade but demanded rum be "given to them for nothing." When no liquor was forthcoming, the visitors "threatened to kill someone," but John McLoughlin knew the game and was certain the locals were only "doing so to see if I would give them any" rum. The chief trader remained out of sight, mindful that anything he said "would have made them worse." Ignored and denied, they left, only to return a week later to wage further mischief.

The exchange casts an unflattering light on two sources of tension between the HBC and its aboriginal neighbours: language and liquor. "No one at Stikine could speak or understand 'a syllable' of the local language." Initially they relied on a female translator with little English before making a lateral move to their interpreter Hanega Joe. On the scale of poor business decisions, the Company's failure to communicate was second only to its policy of plying aboriginals with alcohol. "At Stikine the Indians got all the Rum they could purchase," and purchase they did.

When the HBC first raised its flag at Stikine, the trade currency was their iconic multi-stripe point blankets. Although the Company believed such blankets were prized because the wool retained heat even when wet, it was not long before the residents of Stikine complained of "the bad quality of our B.B. Blankets," griping "you may push your finger through them with the greatest ease." Not only were the blankets thin, they stank. Natives and employees alike described a camphoric fug emanating from the wool, the result of prolonged storage in damp cargo holds. The criticisms didn't stop with the blankets; "the natives also complain of the bad quality of our beaver traps," wrote one chief trader, who had little recourse but to offer liquor instead.

The pitfalls of frontier capitalism soon gave way to the need for security. Rae and McLoughlin had inherited a fort in name only. The perimeter was far from impenetrable, and the threatening hordes could simply walk in at their leisure. McLoughlin told his commanders, "I think it my duty to inform you that I shall have a great many alterations to make," and he decided his first order of business was to surround the fort with new pickets.

Completing the walls would have been simple, were it not for the men inside them. The HBC had drained the dregs of the employment pool to assemble the fort's roster, leaving McLoughlin very little to work with. In every letter sent up the HBC chain, McLoughlin made his needs clear: "We require men that can do their duty but the most part of the men here are not able to make themselves useful in any way." His missives are equal parts dismal augury and naked pleading: "I am here left alone with two assistants who cannot speak the language or make themselves understood. I endeavour to battle the watch as well as I can until someone is sent." As the months ticked by, McLoughlin's requests grew more and more desperate.

There is, of course, a certain irony in watching McLoughlin, a man long dismissed as indolent and useless, bemoan the sloth of his charges: "The more I see of the men, the more I have to complain of them. I am obliged to mark everything that is to be done." In fairness, the men gave him plenty to complain about. Still, McLoughlin made the best of a bad situation, and you have to admire his courage, if not his judgement. He had a weakness for lost causes, having been labelled one his entire life.

There were minor triumphs. Even without making any changes in personnel, he succeeded in adding "new pickets to one side of the Fort." The men also built a mill to process local grain and the consignment of wheat delivered by the annual trading ships, which dropped off provisions and collected the harvested skins. Under McLoughlin's leadership, the nascent fort was turning a tidy profit, and despite persistent conflict with the locals, the fur trade remained brisk.

§

According to a census in the fort's daily journal, the roster was evenly divided: there were eleven Kanakas and twelve Canadians, including Metis ("half-breeds") and Iroquois. Nearly all the Kanakas could "neither work, understand or be understood." Their names were considered too complicated for English tongues and two — Captain Cole and Joe Lamb — had adopted anglicized names to ingratiate themselves with their superiors.

On paper and in practice, the Kanakas were treated as a single entity — an easily dismissed, innocuous, eleven-headed creature. Even so, a few Kanakas earned special notice in company records. Nahua was the fort's delicate cook, prone to effusive displays of emotion. Graced with a thoughtful face that bordered on pretty, Nahua became the target for the complement's taunts and pent-up aggression. Kakepé, "who has been taught to read and write, and instructed in the Scriptures and who knoweth the nature of an oath," was one of McLoughlin's favourites, prized for his quiet strength and loyalty. Kanakanui was simply "a Sandwich Islander who has never been baptised," a meaningful distinction at the time. There were others—Okaia, Powkow, Kakulukulu, and Anahi, to name a few—who would play minor roles in the events to come, but to the Company they were simply the Sandwich Islanders: interchangeable, forgettable, and for the most part useless.

Whatever their shortcomings, the Kanakas were godsends compared to their Canadian counterparts. All the "white men" were young—in their twenties and early thirties—strongly built, and just big and dumb enough to cause real havoc. One such Canadian, Benoni Fleury, was considered by all to be "a half fool, or in other words very stupid." He was also an unrepentant drunkard, often too intoxicated or hungover to be of real use. What little obedience he may have had dissolved instantly in the booze, and he was not above taking a swing at anyone, including his boss. For all his sins, Fleury was a lovable rogue, a blistering, boisterous reprobate who won the hearts of his Stikine fellows, including McLoughlin, who forgave him every trespass and embraced the Metis as a long-lost brother.

Drunk or sober, Fleury often kept company with a fellow lout, Francois Pressé. In one of the fort's earliest journal entries, William Rae described Pressé as "a half-breed and passable." Of course, Rae had no way of knowing that "Pressé had been dismissed from Moose [Factory] for Shooting at a man."

Rae's first impressions of the other Canadians were equally tepid. Some, such as Charles Belanger and Simon Aneuharazie, were charmless but harmless, while others warranted a brief disclaimer. William Lasserte seemed to be "a smart lad," while Louis Leclaire struck the chief as "a good man." Kinder words were harder to come by for the churlish George Heron, who was dismissed as "a half fool" and a "Blackguard...who does not know his prayers." Heron got off easy compared to Oliver Martineau, who exasperated his chief trader to such a degree that official company records state Oliver "appears to be a half idiot and understands neither French or English." The mouth-breathing Martineau, in turn, paled next to the boorish Phillip Smith, widely regarded as "the most Criminal man among these men."

Although the exact nature of his crimes remains unknown, his character was immortalized by John McLoughlin Sr., who proclaimed Smith to be of "Ill Nature and Bad temper," a scoundrel who was always "getting into difficulties with the other men."

As defective as the Canadians were, a small subset garnered the harshest criticism and caused the greatest concern: the Iroquois. They were feared by their Canadian fort-mates because of "the ferocity that characterized their pagan ancestors" and a widespread belief that "they do not pay great deference to the laws of God." Physically, they were "the most uncouth, savage looking beings...mouth from ear to ear, cheek-bones remarkably high, low projecting forehead, hair like a horse's mane, and eyes red and swollen by continual intoxication." At Stikine, the Iroquois contingent numbered only three—Antoine Kawannassé, Pierre Kannaquassé, and Urbain Heroux—but what it lacked in size, it gained in terror.

Antoine Kawannassé, the least thug-like, was considered by many to be too mentally challenged to be truly troublesome. The impairment was relatively recent, as Rae noted in the fort's journal: Kawannassé was "a good man before he had the fever but has been sickly ever since." The fever had dulled his intelligence, but the HBC still handed him a gun.

Everyone knew Kawannassé was slow, but Pierre Kannaquassé prided himself on his cat-like reflexes and mental acuity. Others disagreed. Most thought Kannaquassé was more smartass than smart, and he put his lightning-fast agility to ill use. "Pierre Kanaquassi [sic] is accused of having murdered and Robbed before he came" to Stikine—a checkered past kept hidden from McLoughlin. Kannaquassé was universally described as "a blackguard" and "one of the Greatest villains in the country...whom necessity alone has obliged us to Employ." George Simpson noted that Kannaquassé "appears to have been a character so vicious that nothing but the strictest discipline could have ever hoped to govern an establishment of which such a man was a member." To this most vicious and villainous creature, the HBC handed two guns and a pistol.

Kannaquassé's pre-employment crime spree did not hold a candle to that of Urbain Heroux. The man was "addicted to liquor" and a convicted felon who had been prosecuted in Canada by his own relatives for burglary and robbery. The Honourable Company claimed they knew nothing of

Heroux's criminal history when they hired him, despite the fact "Heroux was tried and condemned for Robbery at three Rivers and subsequently taken up for Larceny when his father Bought off the Evidence." That same father eventually had his son imprisoned on account of his violent conduct, but the charges were dropped on the condition Heroux join the HBC and leave Upper Canada for good.

Heroux spoke in a patois all his own, a staccato blend of his native tongue, French, and blue-streak profanity. "He would fly into a violent rage at the slightest opposition and shower threats and curses on every one near him in the most brutal manner." William Lasserte thought Heroux's "savage looks and furious deportment made him an object of terror," and Heroux cultivated this fearsome image right down to his clothes: "Heroux's dress was remarkable, he normally wore a red worsted cap . . . and the belt of his powder horn which he also wore at the time was of red cloth more than two inches wide." Indeed, his head and hat were one, inseparable save for the rare bath. In dress and in manner, Heroux commanded attention and a certain degree of grudging respect for sheer audacity and menace. At first glance, Heroux fooled William Rae, who thought the Iroquois was a "good man."

Fort Stikine was a dumping ground for wrecked and criminal minds, and a last resort for the HBC's most problematic employees. Dr. McLoughlin told George Simpson that, "As a Body the Canadians and Iroquois were the Greatest Blackguards in the department and were sent to Stikine to prevent their giving trouble in other places." Simpson could not have cared less. In its infinite wisdom, the Hudson's Bay Company had hired criminals, issued them guns and a generous monthly allotment of liquor, and shipped them off to a cesspool. What could possibly go wrong?

§

It escaped no one's attention that Stikine's new chief trader and the region's chief factor shared the same name, and the spectre of nepotism hovered unspoken over the fort. To avoid the appearance of favouritism, John McLoughlin Jr. was ordered to report directly to an intermediary, a fellow chief trader named John Work. Irish born, Work was one of Governor Simpson's pets because he did not have a speck of aboriginal blood in him. By 1841, Work had served nearly three decades with the HBC and had earned partial credit in the Governor's book as "a very steady pains taking man... [who] bears a fair private character." Simpson thought less of Work's mien, declaring him to be "a queer looking fellow, of Clownish Manners and address, indeed there is a good deal of simplicity approaching to idiocy in his appearance." Still, Simpson reasoned, Work was superior to the mixed-race McLoughlin, and so Work became McLoughlin's boss.

McLoughlin's regular duties included sending monthly written reports to Work. He often used these dispatches to vent his dissatisfaction with the men, but he never mentioned any overt threats to his life. McLoughlin kept his fears to himself, convinced that "Work might draw negative conclusions about his capacity as a leader" if he spoke too freely. He had come too far to be branded as feckless or unstable again.

To the untrained eye, McLoughlin seemed poised and in control, but a thunderstorm raged between his ears. He was paranoid, consumed with worry, and plagued by insomnia. Between the proposed poisoning and the random bullets, there had been four serious attempts made on his life, all perpetrated by his own men. He overheard the grumbling in the barracks and knew that some of the men wanted him dead. He was terrified, but he was also proud, and his hubris would prove his undoing.

McLoughlin's pride kept him from sharing his troubles with his father, for he could not bear the thought of disappointing him yet again by losing control of his men. Discipline continued to be his stumbling block at Stikine, a threat far greater than the one posed by hostile natives. Given the criminal element under his command, McLoughlin soon learned the only way to stop violence was with violence, as it was the sole language such men understood. His efforts at governing without the liberal use of corporal punishment were not working. In an ominous letter sent to John Work in the weeks before his death, McLoughlin lamented that if things did not soon improve, "I shall be obliged to use measures which I am afraid will not be approved by the Gentleman in Charge of Columbia District."

It was a risk McLoughlin was willing to take, for he was finally basking in the glow of his father's approval. He had grown up, and grown into, the man his father had always wanted him to be. McLoughlin was a rising star in a multinational corporation and had done the impossible: regained the trust and, dare he say it, the respect of George Simpson. John McLoughlin Jr. had reached his moral apex, the denouement of his life's twisted journey. Any student of epic tragedy knows what must happen next.

Thursday, April 21, 1842 — Midnight
FORT STIKINE

From the sworn testimony of Pierre Kannaquassé.

It began with the scuffle between McLoughlin and Benoni
Fleury, although scuffle was too musical a word for it. It was a
fight, and not a fair one at that. Fleury was falling-down drunk,
barely able to form coherent sentences. McLoughlin was merely
"elevated" from a few glasses of spirits but still in command of
his faculties.

The conflict had been brewing for weeks, and the animosity
was not isolated to Fleury and his master. Many of the Canadians
were openly hostile to the chief trader; Kannaquassé "made no
secret of his dislike of McLoughlin," and Heroux "was heard
several times to threaten his life." Some men did more than make
empty threats. George Heron spent a sleepless night "at the foot
of the stairs with the intention of shooting Mr. John had he come
out of his room." Lasserte once saw Kannaquassé in the gallery
with his gun trained on McLoughlin's front door, waiting to
shoot. After countless failed attempts, all agreed "McLoughlin
would certainly be put to death that night."

Faced with a mutinous crew, McLoughlin did what he
could — he drank. Given the circumstances, it's hard to
begrudge him a little liquid courage. He could even be
forgiven for plying his would-be assassins with alcohol in
hopes of saving his own skin. Just after nine o'clock,
McPherson arrived with the first of what would be many
bottles that night. Accounts differ as to who drank and how
much, or even why. Antoine Kawannassé said that "Mr. John
had ordered him not to drink," but Kannaquassé claimed to
have seen people being forced to imbibe, and he was handed a
flagon and told to drink it by McLoughlin. Leery of
McLoughlin's motives, Kannaquassé only pretended to drink,
letting the amber liquid run down onto the front of his shirt.

Benoni Fleury found the waste of perfectly good liquor unconscionable. He drained the dregs from Kannaquassé's cup (and any others left unattended) before being carried to his room by McLoughlin. The squabble ensued as McLoughlin tried to coerce his servant into bed, although it was hard to tell who was on the losing end of the tussle. Fleury hit McLoughlin, McLoughlin slapped Fleury, Lasserte protested, and McLoughlin cuffed Lasserte for insubordination. Lasserte ran to get Urbain Heroux, setting in motion the events that would forever stain the reputation of Fort Stikine.

At Lasserte's urging, Heroux ran into the centre court shouting that Mr. John was "maltreating" Fleury, although other men recalled Heroux screaming something about McLoughlin "killing Fleury." For his impudence, McLoughlin "struck Urbain in the face." As the sound of the slap echoed off the timber walls, the entire fort's complement stilled, too frightened to draw breath. The Iroquois stood silent, his face like stone but his eyes blazing with hatred. He then hissed, "I never received a blow without revenging it." The standoff held a moment longer, the tension heavy enough to snap bones, before Heroux warned McLoughlin to take care of himself and walked away.

Heroux headed for the southwest bastion. As he passed Antoine Kawannassé, he muttered, "It would be well to put a ball through Mr. John." Heroux mounted the stairs and exited onto the gallery, looking down at McLoughlin in the square below. With the eyes of the fort upon him, McLoughlin could not let the challenge to his authority go unanswered. Glaring up at the blackened silhouette, he ordered Heroux "to come down but the latter, in a tone of defiance, dared him to come up."

Joe Lamb heard the heated exchange as he kept watch in the gallery above the back gate. Lamb made his way toward Heroux, his finger welded to the trigger of his rifle, ready for whatever came next. Suddenly the moon was obscured by cloud, and visibility dropped to nothing. As Lamb approached the southwest corner, Kawannassé "heard someone jump down," and Simon

Aneuharazie, standing near the base of the bastion, was almost flattened by the falling Heroux. Aneuharazie raised his rifle and told Heroux to give himself up but received only an "insolent refusal...in language not fit to be repeated." Heroux "appeared in a violent rage and reproached us with cowardice, saying 'you are all as much afraid of Mr. McLoughlin as a parcel of old wives but I am the man for him. I will look after him tonight.'"

What happened next suggests premeditation. Heroux turned back into the stairwell and grabbed a "gun standing against the lower door of the bastion." Heroux had loaded the gun and hidden it earlier that evening. Kawannassé ran toward the bastion and "saw Urbain taking aim at something." Heroux pulled the trigger, "but the gun appeared to be very slightly loaded and it made no report." Heroux's rifle was pointed straight at John McLoughlin.

McLoughlin ordered him to drop his weapon, but Heroux just laughed. At that moment, both men bolted toward the Kanaka barracks, where a number of Sandwich Islanders lay sleeping. The sound of McLoughlin running to his door woke Kakepé, who glanced outside to see what was happening. Through the filthy windowpane, Kakepé saw Heroux "seize Mr. McLoughlin around the body but the latter succeeded in throwing him off." As Heroux regained his footing, McLoughlin called out for the Kanakas to arm themselves and to fire on Heroux. McLoughlin then ran to McPherson's room in search of a weapon. As he passed, he ordered Kawannassé to fetch his sword, but when Kawannassé went to the chief trader's room, "his wife refused to give it up."

In McPherson's cramped quarters, a war counsel was quickly convened, made up of McLoughlin, McPherson, a sword-less Kawannassé, and McLoughlin's wife, who had followed Kawannassé in search of her husband. She was horrified to see "his shirt was torn to rags." McLoughlin, frantically clutching his arm, said, "Heroux had fired at me," brandishing his shirt sleeve as proof. The near miss shook McLoughlin, who "continued walking about the room, grasping with one hand the tick of the other arm, above the elbow, where he [said] he was wounded." There was no sign of blood.

McLoughlin told the room that "Urbain wants to kill me," but this was not news to those assembled. McPherson had often heard Heroux declare "I will shoot him," and Heroux once told Kawannassé "he would never be happy until he had put [McLoughlin] to death."

McLoughlin knew of Heroux's vile intent, thanks to his drunken valet. It was common knowledge in the fort that Fleury "was aware of everything" and told it all to his master. McLoughlin began playing "a demented sort of cat-and-mouse game with the fort's complement," throwing his knowledge of their treachery back in their faces and goading them into action. He dared the men to "kill me if you can; if you kill me, you will not kill a woman, you will kill a man."

Now, surrounded by his most trusted advisers in the relative safety of McPherson's room, his boasts rang hollow. Heroux and his confederates meant to rid Stikine of its leader, and McLoughlin's salvation lay in the unlikely form of George Simpson. The Governor had made vague promises to return with McLoughlin's new assistant, and every morning the chief trader anxiously scanned the horizon for any sign of the cavalry. As his counsellors looked on, McLoughlin took his wife by the hand and told her if Simpson "does not come soon, you will not see me again." The certainty brought McLoughlin and his wife to tears, and the onlookers shifted awkwardly at the sight of such bald emotion. Pulling himself together, McLoughlin rallied and put on a brave face, saying, "Never mind, if I die, I will take it like a man."

McLoughlin was drying his wife's tears when Phillip Smith and Simon Aneuharazie burst into the room. They, too, had heard Heroux's threats and offered to hunt down the villainous Iroquois, telling McLoughlin "that if he wished to punish Heroux, they would seize him." Their support again moved McLoughlin to tears. The crying proved contagious, and

"Smith & Simon, the latter with tears in his eyes, entreated Mr. John to remain at home and not go out," but McLoughlin was resolved, exclaiming time and again, "I must bring the matter to a point." The men continued their pleas, but McLoughlin was "losing all patience," and he prepared for war.

He told the men to arm themselves, ordering Kawannassé to load his handguns and McPherson to ready his rifle. They did as bidden, and McLoughlin snatched his long gun "as soon as it was loaded and either Antoine or Simon belted on his Pistols." McLoughlin then grabbed hold of "a stout bludgeon" as McPherson, taking up a lantern, led McLoughlin and the men out of his room.

They ran headfirst into Francois Pressé, who was hiding behind the door, waving his weapon and "looking suspicious." Gripped by fear, McLoughlin disarmed the man and hauled him off to the storage room that served as a makeshift jail cell. McLoughlin ensured Pressé's feet "were in irons" and the door was bolted before resuming the hunt for Heroux.

Just then, a bell began to peal in the centre court. It was the fort's main alarm, a signal normally reserved for aboriginal attacks. Kannaquassé rang the bell to flush McLoughlin out of hiding, but not everyone knew it was a false alarm. Chaos ensued as more than a dozen loaded men with loaded weapons scrambled to repel a non-existent enemy.

There was a long silence, then two quick pops, followed by "the reports of more than fifteen shots." Smith ran to his room in search of his gun, "but not finding it in the place where I used to keep it, I went out without it." The melee grew as Pressé, Martineau, Lasserte, and Heroux fired "each a shot, apparently without any particular object as they fired in the air and toward the outside of the fort."

As McLoughlin crept through a passageway, he stumbled and his rifle accidently discharged. Kawannassé reloaded it for him while McLoughlin ordered the Kanakas in the gallery to shoot the Canadians, "especially Lesserte [sic] and Urbain."

On his command, a dozen shots immediately erupted from the gallery. The senseless gunplay continued even after Kawannassé cried "stop, stop, stop."

With his long gun in hand, McLoughlin moved along the platform of the men's barracks, "walking cautiously" as he passed the door, hugging the wall for safety. McPherson, one floor up, scanned the fort with his lantern, letting the light fall on the chief trader. McPherson heard McLoughlin "weeping loudly" as he searched in vain for Heroux. For reasons that would die with him, McLoughlin never unholstered his pistols.

Kawannassé made his way up to the gallery, dodging the incessant gunfire. As he stood looking down from the southwest bastion, he "saw Urbain just before me, lurking by the corner of the house." Heroux's long gun was empty, its ammunition wasted in the false alarm. What happened next passed in the blink of an eye: "Urbain stepped back to where he had another gun standing and again, advancing to the corner of the house, fired." The shot was deafening, "a very loud report" that shook the fort like a hard wind. The bullet pierced its target and sailed across the courtyard before "lodging in the Carpenters shop Door." John McLoughlin "immediately fell forward upon his face," and the wooden walkway echoed with the "noise of a heavy body falling on the platform."

Captain Cole watched it all unfold from the doorway of the men's barracks. He was "quite naked, having just got out of bed" when he heard the alarm and the volley of shots that followed. He ran to the window as McLoughlin slunk past and saw "Urbain a few paces off, near the adjoining windows." After the fatal shot was fired, and the chief trader fell, Cole saw McLoughlin "lying wounded on the platform and respiring with freedom, audibly," as "the murderer walked anxiously round for a moment," then "retreated a step or two behind the corner of the house, as if to hide himself." George Heron, leaving the safety of the water closet, "saw a man laying on his hands and knees between the platform and the wood. He had a gun laying beside him. By his dress I should think it was Urbain but I am not certain."

McLoughlin was bleeding into his lungs, and the sound of his laboured breaths haunted all who heard it. As the death rattle deepened, at least one man could stand it no longer. Captain Cole watched Urbain Heroux "come on from the corner of the house," put his back to the wall, "and place his foot on the neck of Mr. McLoughlin," acting "as if to finish the tragedy."

Even with Heroux's boot on his throat, McLoughlin was "still breathing." Heroux lifted his foot and, looking down, spied McLoughlin's gun. Heroux grabbed the rifle but it was unloaded. In rage and desperation, he took hold of the barrel and "struck him a severe blow to the forehead, and in doing so, broke the rifle." As the gun splintered, Lasserte heard Heroux scream, "Get up now, see if you can strike the men with your stick." Heroux cast aside the broken long gun, and McLoughlin's agonies ceased.

Other men soon arrived at the platform. They found McLoughlin "lying on the left side with the right arm stretched forward at full height, quite dead." With a smirk on his lips, Heroux whispered, "Mr. John is asleep." Up in the gallery, Kawannassé raised his rifle, as if to claim credit for the fatal shot, shouting "hurra for my gun." Tearing the keys from the dead man's vest, Heroux ordered Lasserte to free Francois Pressé from his chains.

Heroux then turned to deal with potential witnesses. As he pushed past Captain Cole at the door of the men's house, he asked the Islander if he knew who had killed Mr. John. Fearful, Cole replied: "I do not know; bye and bye, I will tell who did it." As the Kanakas made their way down from the gallery, they too demanded to know who fired the fatal shot. This time, Heroux said, "I suppose it was the Indians [from Tako]." Up in the gallery, Kawannassé knew "it could not have been the Indians, as I had secured all their arms early in the evening and they were all lying dead drunk in my house."

Pressé arrived at the scene, relishing his freedom.
Although he had heard the commotion, Pressé was unsure
what had transpired during his captivity. At Heroux's urging,
Pressé "wrested" the gun from Kanakanui's hands. Pressé then
turned to Heroux and asked who had killed Mr. John. Heroux's
reply came in the form of a riddle: "He who killed him placed
himself near enough not to miss." Pressé could not crack the
code and pleaded for an honest answer, but Heroux offered only
a thinly veiled warning: "He who killed him will not hesitate to
take a false oath."

Captain Cole had heard enough. Thrusting an accusing
finger at Heroux, Cole declared, "You have killed the master."
Heroux wheeled and faced his accuser head-on, his eyes sharp
with menace. He put his lips to Cole's ear and whispered, "No,
it was not I."

Just then, Nahua crawled free from his hiding place and
knelt beside his master, his face bathed in tears. He had seen
it all and fixed his eyes on Heroux, asking why he had shot the
chief trader. Heroux lunged at Nahua "in a furious manner and
said it was not him who had killed Mr. McLoughlin." Heroux
cuffed the insolent cook with the back of his hand and warned
him he "had better take care how [he] spoke." Heroux then
stared down every man on the platform, forcing each to cast his
eyes to the ground lest they too incur his wrath. Having cowed
those on the platform, Heroux lifted his gaze toward the gallery
where Kawannassé stood triumphant. The two Iroquois locked
eyes as Kawannassé lowered his gun and made his way down to
where the body lay.

Pierre Kannaquassé soon joined Antoine Kawannassé, and
the three Iroquois stood over their kill, the new masters of Fort
Stikine. The Kanakas and Canadians stood back, fearful of this
strange new world order. Kannaquassé looked down at
McLoughlin's lifeless form on the ground and, without a word,
"kicked the body in the face." The sound was sickening. To
prevent further indignities, George Heron asked some of the
men to help carry McLoughlin's corpse into the house and

prepare it for burial. Heroux spit at him and sneered, saying "he would not carry a dead dog, that when he killed a dog he left the carcass there." Heron retreated, and McLoughlin remained where he fell.

According to Iroquois tradition, all kills demand a ritual, even that of a dog. Kawannassé dropped his gun, bent down, and thrust his hand into McLoughlin's gaping wound, drenching his hand in warm blood. Raising himself to full height, Kawannassé then "painted himself with the Blood of the Deceased," streaking red across his cheeks like war paint. He turned to his fellow Iroquois and with a hollow laugh said, "It was the blood of a Deer." The kill was now complete and the spirits at rest. The Iroquois retreated to the men's house to speak in private.

The blood ritual unnerved the remainder of the fort's men, who lingered around the body as though it still retained command. Many continued to question who had killed McLoughlin, and "some of the men even suspected Pierre Kannaquassé or Antoine of having committed the murder." It would take several hours for those who had seen it with their own eyes to convince the others, but by morning all agreed that "the fatal shot had been fired by one Urbain Heroux."

SEVEN

Tight Reins and
Loose Women

Peter C. Newman once quipped that the initials HBC stand for "Horny Boys' Club," a cuttingly accurate poke at a company that was often more frat house than country club. Isolating hundreds of red-blooded men in their prime and denying them all contact with women was a recipe for disaster, putting the HBC on equal footing with the military and prisons as breeding grounds of sexual misconduct. Women had no place in the Honourable Company, and by the same token an HBC outpost was no place for a lady, "for residence here among the savages was not compatible at all with the life of a highly civilized white woman."

That is not to say there were no women at Fort Stikine. They were ably represented in the form of country wives, the aboriginal paramours of the HBC clerks and traders. Although the unions were not legally recognized, some of them were long-standing, and a few might even be described as committed and loving. Most, however, were truly marriages of convenience. In exchange for the comforts they were expected to provide, the wives received trade goods, food, and shelter, but it was not necessarily a good deal for the women. They were prisoners within the outpost's walls; wives "took their meals alone, saw few visitors, and had few outings." The aboriginal consorts also had to contend with the ever-present threat of being ousted by a more suitable companion. Some local brides even resorted to infanticide while their men were away, fearing their husbands might return with a white wife. It was a difficult and precarious arrangement, fraught with far greater peril for the women than their male partners.

In this, as in all things, George Simpson set the tone. The Governor's attitudes toward women "were not enlightened, even by the standards of his age." To his way of thinking, women were merely a perfumed, pillowy means to a pleasurable end. During his footloose bachelor days, Simpson told a friend that "the White Fish diet of the district seems favourable to procreation, and had I a good pimp in my suite I might have been inclined to deposit a little of my spawn."

He was clearly so inclined, and his indiscriminate deposits resulted in a handful of illegitimate children by aboriginal women, although such dalliances caused him no end of grief. In 1822, Simpson ordered his fixer, John George McTavish, to clean up the mess he'd made with Betsey Sinclair, his current country wife who had just borne him a child. With typical indifference, Simpson declared, "She is an unnecessary and expensive appendage. I see no fun in keeping a Woman, without enjoying her charms." Although the Governor no longer had any use for her, he did not relish the idea of sharing his plaything with the lower ranks. He told McTavish to either find her another officer or else make some rather medieval arrangements: "If she is unmarketable I have no wish that she should be a general accommodation shop to all the young bucks at the Factory and in addition to her own chastity, a padlock may be helpful; Andrew is a neat handed Fellow and having been in China may perhaps know the pattern of those used in that part of the world."

Simpson often projected his own distorted issues with *les femmes* onto his colleagues. One such target was John Stuart, whom Simpson dismissed as "disgustingly indecent in regards to women." The Governor once took an interpreter to task for his "over intimacy" and "indiscreet amours" with native women. He also created a corporate culture in which it was entirely acceptable for one of his employees to cut "off the Ears of an Indian who had had an intrigue with his Woman." Simpson swore he wouldn't have minded so much had the ears been cut off "in the heat of passion or as a punishment for Horse Stealing," but to get that upset over a woman was simply a waste of energy.

Sir George was a master of the mixed message, and his words and deeds seldom matched. Blind to his own transgressions, he announced, "Almost every difficulty we have had with Indians throughout the Country may be traced to our interference with their Women." Accordingly, Simpson forbade employees from taking part in "short-term, potentially exploitive sorties in search of Indian women." Ever the hypocrite, his own sorties were exempt. Of course, the rule against fraternization was impossible to enforce, and Simpson sometimes looked the other way when it came to more formal long-term relationships, especially in remote areas.

One such exemption was Fort Stikine. Despite his recent edict, the Governor gave permission for a number of Stikine men to marry when he visited in 1841. "Fourteen or fifteen of the men of the establishment asked permission to take native wives," Simpson later wrote, "and leave to accept the worthless bargains was granted to all such as had the means of supporting a family." One of those lucky men was John McLoughlin Jr., who immediately began sharing his bed with the daughter of the local chief.

Simpson then argued both sides against the middle, drawing one breath to declare "these matrimonial connections are a heavy tax on a post, in consequence of increased demand for provisions," and then using the exhale to contend such unions formed "a useful link between the traders and the savages." Upon further reflection, he decided that link was not as mutually advantageous as he had hoped. Moving the aboriginal women into the fort "afforded the Stikine Tlingit much more information about HBC society and its foibles than the Company wanted them to know, and certainly much more than the Company knew about the Tlingit."

Simpson changed his tune yet again, denouncing country wives as meddlesome in Company affairs and branding them "petty coat politicians." Hypocritical to the bitter end, he issued a final mandate to the men of Stikine: "I must beg that good order be restored . . . and no worthless women be allowed to harbor within the stockades." Other arbitrary regulations soon followed. At one point, HBC officers were required to sign marriage contracts, and if a man abandoned his family, he was obligated to find the woman another provider. Legal scholar Hamar Foster summed up Simpson's endless flip-flopping with unwarranted diplomacy: "The Company's practice in such matters was never the model of consistency."

Sir George changed the game completely when he informed his superiors of his plan to return to London to seek a wife. It was entirely out of character for the Governor, who had always decried marriage and offspring as socially mandated fetters designed to impede a man's happiness and liberty. But it had recently been brought to his attention that he was long past that certain age when a man of status needed to tie the knot, and he had little hope of finding an appropriate match in the wilds of the New World. The board implored him to wait, and his one-time benefactor, Andrew Colvile, whispered in Simpson's ear, "A wife I fear would be an embarrassment to you until the business gets into a more complete order." The Governor, a devoted company servant, acquiesced, but he kept his eyes open. Over the next five years, he scanned the horizon for a suitable mate during his sojourns to the Continent, and just as hope soured, he found her.

Her name was Frances Ramsey. Twenty years his junior, she was his first cousin, daughter to the uncle who gave Simpson his start in the sugar trade. Simpson wrote to John McTavish with his usual blend of effusion and indiscretion: "Would you believe it? I am in love—how may I get rid of it." Lest you think the Governor had gone soft, he closed the letter: "I shall settle my Bullocks in her." Simpson married his great white hope on February 24, 1830, in a ceremony long on pomp but short on sentiment. With their union consecrated, the couple immediately set sail for Simpson's old stomping grounds at Red River. Laden with her trousseau, Frances was thrust onto the first of an endless procession of canoes bound for her new home. She was beryl-eyed and cupid-lipped, pink of cheek and boneless, pale, and uninteresting in the way of all cloistered teens. Beauty had been one of Simpson's bridal requirements, of course, as was height or, rather, a lack of it. It simply would not do to have a woman tower over the pint-sized emperor, a constant visual reminder of his limitations. There was little fear of that with Frances, who stood barely five feet. Unburdened by intellect, and bred for domesticity, Frances curled inward, cowed, contrite, and overly dutiful, a living testament to the negligible difference between "bridal" and "bridle."

Theirs was a strange and loveless union. In her private diary, Frances frequently referred to her husband as "Mr. Simpson." Despite being chronically "affection-starved," she somehow managed to produce four children who survived infancy: Webster, Augusta D'Este, Margaret MacKenzie, and, in a shameless act of brown-nosing, a son named John Henry Pelly. It did not bode well that the couple had nothing in common aside from the children.

Frances Ramsey Simpson,
Sir George's only lawfully wedded wife.

The Governor was never physically abusive, but neither was he kind. Frances existed in a gilded cage, surrounded by the trappings of great wealth, but starved for simple human touch, "a prized but almost inanimate possession."

She was not alone in her frigid pen. Simpson was unable to love anyone, and "there is no direct evidence of any kind of emotional attachment to anyone or anything beyond himself and the HBC. He could muster illusions of warmth and friendship, could give his family endearing nicknames, but beyond that it appears that at his core the Governor was not sustained by matters of the heart." He was dead inside, an empty and withered husk of a man, even with those he professed to hold dear. Heaven help those he hated.

§

Everything changed for the country wives when Simpson married Frances, as, "overnight, she created a fashion for white, church-wed wives." Class distinctions long ignored in the HBC suddenly surfaced, and James Douglas mapped the resulting evolution: "Indian wives were at one time the vogue, the half breed supplanted these, and now we have the lovely tender exotic torn from its parent bed."

Country wives became passé, and Simpson vociferously expressed "his disapproval of officers who continued in the old ways." It was yet more hypocrisy from a man who "had fathered at least five children by four different women." The Governor led by toxic example, and he demanded no less from his right-hand man, John McTavish. During their years at Red River, Simpson insulted his men when he "refused to accept mixed-bloods as suitable company for Frances." McTavish followed suit when he transferred to Moose Factory and soon had the rank and file in an uproar when he forbade his Scottish-born wife, Catherine, to "mix with their country wives."

Simpson's reactionary edict that Company men find suitable replacements for their displaced country wives came back to haunt him after his marriage. When Frances arrived to set up house in Red River, Simpson once again asked McTavish to deal with his "old concern" — his latest country wife, Margaret "Peggy" Taylor, who was pregnant with his child at the time. Simpson's contempt was on full display as he told McTavish, "Pray keep an Eye on the commodity and if she bring forth anything in proper time and of the right colour, let them be taken care of but if anything be amiss, let the whole be bundled about their business." The baby was decidedly the wrong colour, and mother and child were hastily bundled off. In accordance with his own regulation, Simpson was forced to pay Peggy £30 per year until she was "disposed of." After handing out a few annuities, McTavish finally managed to marry her off to an agreeable striver in the Company with the whimsically appropriate name of Amiable Hogue. Simpson's love life was by then an open secret, and a source of derision, within the Company. His snider colleagues mocked Taylor's demotion, chiding, "The Govr's little tit bit Peggy Taylor...what a downfall is here...from a Governess to Sow."

Simpson's vacillating beliefs and randomly enforced policies regarding country wives caused no end of headaches for John McLoughlin Jr. after he assumed command of Fort Stikine. McLoughlin heeded the rules, but the men's lust often trumped Simpson's decrees, and "the unmarried men were in the habit of secretly going out of the Fort at night, contrary to order, to visit the Indian camp." They even hung a rope for just such a purpose, gleefully "scaling the Picquets" to visit their "dusky maidens."

McLoughlin tried to curtail their midnight runs by locking down the fort and issuing curfews, actions that quickly became a source of discord. Kannaquassé swore it was his inability to bring his wife into the fort that was "the real cause of his enmity" toward the chief trader, and that "All the Ill Will the Servants of Stikine felt towards [McLoughlin] arose from his preventing them...going to the Indians as often as they wished."

McLoughlin's curfews were not the only source of discontent. The chief trader once made quite a production of beating Oliver Martineau "for giving away his clothes to women." According to one trader, "Mr. McLoughlin summoned all the men to witness the punishment, he told us that he was determined to enforce the regulations of the establishment in all cases, and punish all offenders without respect to colour or country." McLoughlin kept tight rein on his own spouse and reportedly beat Martineau and Kakepé "for allowing his wife to go outside the fort." The men resented having to keep tabs on the chief trader's woman when they were not allowed to have one, and no one took greater umbrage than McLoughlin's feeble-minded assistant, Thomas McPherson.

McPherson loved the ladies, but they didn't care for him. He wasn't much to look at and was scrawny by HBC standards. A perpetually unkissed toad, McPherson was forced to do as countless other undesirables had done before him — he paid for it. Sampling a slattern's charms did not come cheap, and McPherson was a clerk of very limited means, but he had one thing his ladies-on-loan wanted: the key to the HBC storeroom.

McPherson used that key to buy himself a little companionship to ring in the new year of 1842. While the other men drank their good health, McPherson "brought a woman of bad reputation into the house at night and paid her with goods from the store." Their rendezvous was fleeting and uninspired. For her efforts, McPherson "gave the woman 4 yards of white cotton...which [he] stole in the shop for the purpose."

McPherson coupled with other working girls over the next few weeks. Whenever the mood struck him, he "opened the Fort Gate about 3 o'clock in the morning and [took] a female into the Indian Shop, the key of which he had, and that after having kept her there about half an hour, he had put her out of the Fort," locking the gate behind him. The clerk's erotic sojourns worked to everyone's benefit. Each time McPherson entertained "a loose woman," Heroux, Kannaquassé, Heron, and others used the open gate "to spend the night in the Indian lodges."

John McLoughlin heard whispers of McPherson's nighttime escapades and called his worthless assistant to account. He had long suspected McPherson "pilfered from the Store," but after a quick check of the inventory, he finally had hard proof. Calling his subordinate into the office, "Mr. John turn[ed] McPherson out of the shop" for "running after loose women" and stealing "goods from the shop to pay them." He seized McPherson's storehouse key and suspended him for two weeks. Although the chief trader was livid, he dealt with his clerk's transgressions quietly, as "McLoughlin did not wish to bring him to open shame." McPherson was not publicly flogged, as any other man would have been.

McPherson escaped a beating, but McLoughlin imposed one last sanction, the seemingly minor penalty of "turning Thomas McPherson from his table" and forcing him to "dine with the men for a month." Demoted and humiliated, McPherson retreated to his room to ride out his involuntary celibacy.

§

McLoughlin had his difficulties with the men of Stikine, but he seemed to find solace and genuine friendship with its women. Glimpses of his warm regard for the fairer sex can be found throughout the fort's records. McLoughlin's daily journal entries were perfunctory, dull, and entirely focused on the business affairs of the outpost, except when he made reference to the women. Often such comments related to his duties as chief trader or his unofficial role as the fort's surgeon, as in this entry from Thursday, February 24, 1842: "Early this morning I was called to attend Urbain's wife [next part crossed out] who was [illegible]. As soon as I was arrive [*sic*] I began to examine her and found that she had been labouring for some time before my arrival. An hour after my arrival, she was delivered of a daughter."

But more common (and more compelling) were the curiously intimate marginalia regarding the traders' wives that popped up, apropos of nothing, amidst the corporate details. For example, the diary shows that McLoughlin kept abreast of the outpost's gossip, which he recorded for posterity along with the day's activities: "Monday April 4, 1842, cloudy all day, with frequent showers of rain. Sent the men to get wood for wedges. Today one of the men's wife went off without any excuse and says she will not return without conditions. No trade except previous." McLoughlin was a veteran of such teacup tempests, and he knew better than to interfere in a lover's quarrel, adding: "I did not listen to it nor to her husband." The journal also served as a ledger of McLoughlin's generosity toward the fort's fairer inhabitants. On May 11, 1841, he noted that among the goods received that day were "a little fish," which he gave "as a present" to his favourite of the officers' wives.

By all accounts that matter, McLoughlin treated his own country wife with care and respect. His parents had been excellent role models in that regard, and though his time with his father and mother had been limited, a few incidents clearly left a lasting impression. One indelible exchange involved a run-in between his father and an appropriately named HBC clergyman, Herbert Beaver. Despite his rampant piety, Dr. McLoughlin took an instant dislike to Reverend Beaver, and his animus was both personal and spiritual. Beaver "was of the fox-hunting type," remarkable only for being "a short stout man with a high-pitched voice and fondness for long sermons." Beaver hated everything on principle, disparaging his Company house as a "personal insult and domestic annoyance," cursed with floors "too filthy to step upon." But what the reverend detested most of all was the practice, then condoned by the HBC, of taking country wives.

One day Beaver made his displeasure known in a showpiece of passive aggression. Company policy dictated that Dr. McLoughlin review all of Beaver's outgoing reports, and in a particularly long-winded letter to Governor Simpson, the cleric berated Dr. McLoughlin's wife, Marguerite, as "a female of notoriously loose character." The doctor did not take kindly to the slight, and he confronted Beaver in the fort's compound, demanding an explanation. According to one eyewitness, Beaver replied, "If Dr. McLaughlin [sic] you require to know why a cow's tail grows downward, I can simply cite the fact." McLoughlin brandished his silver walking stick and swung it at Beaver's head. "The parson bawled to Jane his wife for his pistols, old style affairs, flint locks, half as long as my arm," but cooler heads intervened and the incident stopped just short of bloodshed. Dr. McLoughlin immediately sent the reverend packing, but he never got over the insult to his wife. From that day forward, Dr. McLoughlin insisted his "employees stand and remove their hats in her presence." The image of those doffed caps was seared into John Jr.'s brain, and when he took command of Stikine, he implemented the practice with his own country wife. The men didn't like it but obeyed. Failure to comply meant a beating, another on a growing list of reasons McLoughlin raised his hand to the men — or so it seemed.

Thursday, April 21, 1842 — Dawn
FORT STIKINE

The fort's journal entry paints a sterile, detached scene:
"Daylight, fine weather and no wind." It would have been
a lovely morning were it not for the murdered man on the
platform.

If the Iroquois had their way, Stikine would have a captain
soon enough. The first to seize the reins of command was
Antoine Kawannassé, a man with half a mind and little to
lose. He returned from his whispered plotting with Heroux
and Kannaquassé to find the scene unchanged. He rolled the
body face up, casting McLoughlin's rigored eyes toward the
heavens, although many of the onlookers felt that was as close
to the pearly gates as Mr. John would ever get. Kawannassé
began to bark orders with surprising ease. He told the
Kanakas to fetch some boards, and the corpse was "carried
on a plank to McPherson's room." Two chairs were recruited
as biers, a flimsy yet serviceable arrangement that kept
McLoughlin off the floor, the only small measure of dignity
on offer.

There were other practical matters to be attended to,
and the most distasteful of them fell to the lowest ranks.
The inescapable issue of blood demanded immediate attention,
for "the body bled profusely, there being a deep pool of blood
found around it." At Kawannassé's command, it "was washed
away afterwards by the Kanakas." Bucket upon bucket was
hauled from the well, and the pool was diluted and smeared
until the platform was stained a uniform crimson.

The blood was everywhere, on everything. At one point,
Kawannassé glanced down and saw that his "hands and front
of [his] clothing were soiled with blood." The less said about
how the blood got there, the better. The blood ritual, witnessed
by all, would soon be stricken from the official record, replaced
by Kawannassé's claim that his hands were bloodied from

carrying the body. When no one was looking, he "washed them in [his] own room," erasing the stigmata of his crime.

The mournful task of preparing McLoughlin for burial also fell to the Sandwich Islanders. Okaia, aided by two of his brethren, ensured that the body was "stripped, washed clean, decently dressed and laid out." Charles Belanger, seemingly struck by divine inspiration, ran to his room and returned with a straight razor. He did what he could to groom McLoughlin's ragged beard, steering well clear of the gaping exit wound on the dead man's neck.

The stopgap morticians had just finished their ablutions when Kannaquassé burst into the room, hawkish and crazed. He lunged at the body and, without warning or cause, "tore the shirt open on the breast" and "attempted to tear off the vest." The men watched in horror as Kannaquassé "threw the body on the floor and stamp[ed] on the face with his foot." A volley of insults soon followed, and the Kanakas "saw Pierre strike the body in the face with his fist" and "strike it on the face with a towel which he had in his hand."

For a moment, an eerie calm descended. Kakepé stepped forward, intent on returning McLoughlin to his makeshift catafalque, when Kannaquassé pushed him aside and again seized "the head by the hair and knock[ed] it against the floor several times, saying something very bad which [Kakepé] did not understand." Those who knew the tongue heard Kannaquassé scream, "While you were living you gave me many a blow but you cannot do so now." Kannaquassé then released John's hair and ended his siege. His assault left the traders shaken, and they "were all crying and told him not to use the body in that way." Kanakanui asked Kannaquassé to go downstairs and leave him to deal with the body, but the Iroquois refused to go. Reasoning with a madman rarely ends well, but the Kanakas were inherently deferential to any man possessing more "white blood" than they, and their respectful tone seemed to calm him. Kannaquassé then tried to recruit people to pray over the body, telling the Kanakas it "was customary in Canada." The request was so disingenuous, no one could bring himself to do it.

Outside, commotion drew forth the last remaining hold-outs. Oliver Martineau emerged into the breaking dawn, gormless and slack-jawed, of no tangible use to anyone. He told his colleagues he had spent the night sleeping in the southeast bastion, but the Metis trader was not just slow, he was inconsistent. When questioned further, Martineau admitted he had fired twice at the deceased. When Kannaquassé asked if Martineau had killed Mr. John, he replied, "I do not know if it was me or not." Martineau would later change his story, saying he had fired into the air, not really aiming at McLoughlin. When asked a third time, he changed again, claiming he'd slept through the entire event, only to reverse his tale for a fourth time, telling anyone still listening he'd spent the night in hiding, too terrified to move "till daylight."

The sun's rays also roused Benoni Fleury, who was nursing a hangover. He had no recollection of the night gone by, saying, "I was told by the men that they found me in the morning under my bed, where I had hid myself the previous evening." When informed of his master's untimely death, Fleury broke down and cried.

As for Mrs. McLoughlin, she had heard the shouts regarding her husband's cruel fate but was too frightened "to move out of [her] room," and she refused to "go down stairs till the next Morning." Only then did she see what remained of the man who had shared her bed. She had no rights, and her input into the funeral arrangements was neither solicited nor tolerated. There was no longer a place for her at Fort Stikine.

As the day stumbled on, the Iroquois and the Kanakas "quarrelled about who was going to obey whom." Orders were given and quickly ignored, and nothing of note was accomplished. Thomas McPherson, having remained "up all night with the body," simply assumed he was the new camp commander, and he barked orders that no one followed. During a quiet moment, he surreptitiously paced out McLoughlin's quarters with an eye to taking them over. McPherson spent the morning writing the day's entry in the fort's journal and then completed his missives to the Hudson's Bay commanders. In a letter to John Work, McPherson staked his claim as the outpost's leader by adopting McLoughlin's paranoia: "I am afraid that they will do to me the way they did to him."

Pierre Kannaquassé made his own plans. As the Canadians gathered in the dining hall, he announced, "Now Mr. John is dead, I shall go out of the fort and spend the day with my wife." Surprisingly, it was Urbain Heroux who stopped him, declaring that no one was to leave the fort. Kannaquassé told Kawannassé that Heroux was as bad as McLoughlin, treating the men as if they were prisoners. It was the first fissure in the Iroquois alliance. Kannaquassé's voice dripped with bile as he laid bare his threat: "I see we must raise the devil again with these Canadians before we can get our liberty."

As the day dragged on, whispers continued to circulate as to the killer's identity.

II

"A Skin for a Skin"

EIGHT

Casus Belli

Confronted with Kannaquassé's explosive account, John McLoughlin Sr. cushioned the blow with denial. Like Simpson before him, he embraced a narrative that suited his psyche better than it catered to the facts. He convinced himself his son's death was neither accidental nor justifiable — it was nothing short of cold-blooded mutiny. His son had been an innocent victim twice over: once to the villainous deeds of his subordinates, and now to the slanderous accusations of George Simpson.

It never occurred to Dr. McLoughlin that Kannaquassé's version of events was no more credible than Thomas McPherson's, or that both stories were stitched together from self-serving fictions. He was certain the Iroquois had told the truth, even at the risk of incriminating himself, and in the decades since, historians have agreed. W. Kaye Lamb believed Kannaquassé's account "to be much the best account extant of what actually happened at Stikine." Hamar Foster thought Kannaquassé was simply "bored by his captivity and not in the least intimidated by the Company or anyone else," and so he decided to tell the panel everything he knew.

Dr. McLoughlin bought into Kannaquassé's tale for the same reason Simpson was so enamoured of McPherson's: it reinforced the vision he already held of his son and, more importantly, it mirrored his own experiences with the Hudson's Bay Company. And, like Simpson, McLoughlin was prepared to defend his version to the death, if not for his son's sake, then for his own.

As McLoughlin reviewed the new evidence, he itemized the ways in which the two accounts conflicted. Contrary to McPherson, Kannaquassé could think of no instance in which anyone was beaten or punished without cause. Furthermore, he had seen John Jr. "elevated" on rare occasion, but he had never seen his boss drunk. Of all the disclosures Kannaquassé made, however, the ugliest was that McLoughlin's death was premeditated. According to Kannaquassé, Thomas McPherson had drawn up a contract "agreeing to murder...Mr. McLoughlin if he was not removed from the charge of Stikine," and forced all the men sign it. Killing the chief trader became the lone topic of conversation around the dining hall, and the co-conspirators kept their guns loaded and at the ready should the opportunity arise. Kannaquassé heard Phillip Smith coolly boast he did not "care for killing him more than a Dog," and Kannaquassé even admitted "that he had himself tried to shoot McLoughlin on three separate occasions." Dr. McLoughlin also learned his son knew he would die that night, and Kannaquassé felt certain that knowledge was what led to John Jr.'s "dejection of mind and his having shed tears in presence of his wife."

Dr. McLoughlin shared his list of inconsistencies in the dozens of letters he wrote to his closest allies pleading his case. He felt compelled to revisit the horrific details of his son's final moments, particularly how Heroux "put his foot on the neck of his prostrate victim, writhing in the Agonies of death."

The doctor also shared his revelations with his youngest son, who was still stationed at Fort Vancouver, and David, in turn, passed this brutal awakening on to his inner circle. He called Urbain Heroux a "Cowardly wretch," but he saved his harshest critique for Governor Simpson, who was "such a dunce as to have formed his opinion on the reports of the Murderers." Given the disparity between McPherson's and Kannaquassé's accounts, David McLoughlin was not always certain what to believe, but he could not deny "there is a mystery in this affair."

Dr. McLoughlin unleashed his wrath from the relative safety of Fort Vancouver and his coterie of servile middlemen. With little regard for the irreparable damage it would do to his own career—and indeed his sanity—he drafted a letter to Sir George challenging every one of the Governor's assumptions and conclusions, and in so doing, sealed his fate. He vented his spleen without censor, on occasion attacking Simpson personally. In a further act of self-immolation, McLoughlin copied his harangue, which ran in excess of fifty pages, and sent it to John Henry Pelly and the London Committee.

Each letter began with a counterassault on the charge most easily refuted: Simpson's accusation that Stikine's books were in disarray. Dr. McLoughlin had ordered an exhaustive review of the accounts, which revealed a discrepancy of £10 — a piddling sum he declared to be the smallest ever seen during his entire career in the fur trade. History has since borne out McLoughlin on this point. Researchers have undertaken their own audits and concur with the doctor, noting that even the post's journal was religiously maintained until one day before McLoughlin's death.

Dr. McLoughlin then broached the Governor's other allegations. He had nothing but contempt for Simpson's claim that John Jr. was a chronic drunk; it was, in his opinion, an aspersion without substance or merit. His son had his foibles, but "however badly McLoughlin may have behaved in Montreal and Paris, there was never any suggestion that he abused alcohol." McLoughlin Sr. made much of the posthumous inventory of John Jr.'s possessions, noting his son's personal liquor allowance was found to be "almost in the same state as when Mr. Finlayson left" months earlier. Dr. McLoughlin laid the blame for these spurious assertions at the feet of George Simpson, "whom the men Made Believe that my deceased Son was Given to Liquor and that when in that state he Used to Beat the Men most Unmercifully, as if one man could ill use when Intoxicated twenty two men so much as to make them murder him."

To prove the accusation was unfounded, Dr. McLoughlin pointed to the testimony of witnesses better suited to speak to his son's behaviour. He began with long-time Simpson crony John Rowand, who swore, "I did not see the deceased take a Single Glass while I was at Stikine and, as for Beating his men, I saw nothing of the kind." Roderick Finlayson also denied "having seen Mr. John McLoughlin intoxicated at any time during his residence at Stikine," adding that "he never saw Mr. McLoughlin taste raw Spirits," and that often a month or more would pass "without [Junior] tasting a drop of any kind of Spirits and [he] never exceeded one glass." Dr. McLoughlin then offered up the most compelling witness: his son's country wife. The doctor noted, "Indians do not view drunkenness as improper," and said he had never known an aboriginal woman "to screen the drunkenness of her husband."

The doctor accused Simpson of exaggerating the accounts of John Jr.'s drinking for effect, adding: "When we Examine, we see they all must refer to the same Instance." For argument's sake, Dr. McLoughlin was equally guilty of hyperbole—when all the witness accounts are reviewed, John Jr. was visibly drunk on three separate occasions—but his underestimation seems less egregious than Simpson's blatant inflation. The doctor drew this particular tirade to a close with a simple question, asking, "If it is fair, because a young man of twenty Eight years of age in a convivial moment has been known to have Been three times Intoxicated, to set him down as a man of Intemperate Habits. If such is the Standard there are many and many who will not be able to pass the Ordeal."

In a poignant historical footnote, McLoughlin's murder did effect some positive change in the Company's liquor policy, as his father noted in the postscript of a letter sent to John Fraser: "In consequence of this unfortunate affair We have been able to make an arrangement with the Russians by which no liquor is issued to Indians in that quarter and consequently no liquor is issued to Indians by the Hudson's Bay Company." Alcohol had not been the cause of his son's downfall, and as a tribute to his temperance, Dr. McLoughlin ensured it would not be the ruin of others.

Since Simpson's conclusions linked McLoughlin's drinking with his abusive nature, Dr. McLoughlin could have let the matter rest, but his grief (and his ego) would not allow it. Steaming full ahead, the chief factor then addressed the issue of abuse. He did not deny his son sometimes resorted to corporal punishment—every commander used his fists to maintain discipline—but he bristled at the notion his son was a sadistic tyrant who beat his underlings without cause. To refute allegations of excessive force, Dr. McLoughlin again turned to the observations of his son's former second-in-command: "Finlayson saw Mr. McLoughlin flog one or two Sandwich Islanders for Sleeping on their watch, he beat Fleury with his fists for Stealing rum & getting drunk, Mr. McLoughlin being perfectly sober at the time, & that to his Mr. F's knowledge, no other men were punished during his residence at Stikine." After reviewing all the witness accounts, the list of beatings grew to include the time "Capt. Cole was flogged for his sleeping on his Watch, Joe Lamb for Giving away meat out of the Kitchen, Antoine Kawanassau [sic] for fighting with Heroux, Martineau for giving away his

Blanket to an Indian Woman." Yes, Dr. McLoughlin conceded, the men were struck, but always with cause. Such accounts might never find their way into the Company's recruiting posters, but they were business as usual for the Honourable concern, even if Simpson was loath to admit it.

In Dr. McLoughlin's mind, the problem was not his son or Company policy or even the fort itself, but rather the people who inhabited it. The criminal element that made up the bulk of the HBC labour pool took "every advantage of insulting their Masters, especially when there is a favourable opportunity." Their insubordination flew in the face of one of Simpson's core beliefs: that hired hands "remote from civilization with no temptations from competitors would happily accept their lot." The men were neither happy nor accepting, but those who refused to submit were sent to outlying forts or received "summary disciplinary action," a Company euphemism for beatings. Given Stikine's desolate location, it was policy that "all the troublesome characters in the Department were sent there." In his letter to the Committee, McLoughlin posed a loaded question: "Is it surprising if such men are brought to the Country; that people are murdered in it?"

The doctor also believed many within the Hudson's Bay Company knew of the danger John Jr. faced before he was killed. For example, chief factor John Rowand had questioned Simpson's decision to remove Roderick Finlayson from Fort Stikine. After "hearing what kind of Indians [Junior] had to deal with," Rowand firmly believed "it was not safe for one Gentleman to be left alone." Dr. McLoughlin had raised similar concerns with Simpson, protesting when his son was left alone in a hostile outpost, but Sir George had turned a deaf ear. He told the doctor he "had full confidence" in John Jr., and Simpson was certain "he would do well." The Governor based this assessment on his recent trip to Stikine, where he "had found Everything in the highest order." John Jr.'s direct supervisor, John Work, also tried to warn George Simpson when he "heard from the Natives of some irregularities at Stikeen [sic] and that two of the Iroquois, Peter and Antoine, had fired at [Mr. John]," but Simpson simply coupled his deaf ear with a blind eye. He rejected Work's fears, saying his recent letter from McLoughlin made no mention of assassination attempts, nor had he heard such tales from Roderick Finlayson.

Simpson dismissed the aboriginal threat as ephemeral, as though sculpted from clouds, but denial was no hedge against a tangible threat. To show just how real the danger was, Dr. McLoughlin recounted his chance encounter with the son of a local chief named Saix. One afternoon, Saix's son came to trade skins at Dr. McLoughlin's fort; during the transaction, the doctor discovered his own son had known for some time of the men's plan to mutiny. The chief's son claimed that in the months before the murder, he had told John Jr. in confidence that four of Stikine's men had approached him and offered him liquor and trade goods to shoot McLoughlin. The man also told McLoughlin that every time he traded at Fort Stikine, the men "were in the habit of talking of murdering the deceased as a common topic of conversation." Saix's son could not say what (if anything) McLoughlin had done with this information.

Dr. McLoughlin's rage burned: even the indigenous traders of Stikine knew what the men were planning, yet Simpson had refused to act. The Governor could have saved his son, but instead chose to play ostrich. The doctor demanded to know precisely what warning sign Simpson had been waiting for, given the mutiny had been overt and well-orchestrated, conceived in broad daylight, and discussed ad nauseam. Dr. McLoughlin's hand visibly shook as he wrote that Antoine Kawannassé "had heard Heroux state some hours before that he would shoot my Son like a Dog."

Armed with this new evidence, Dr. McLoughlin had no choice but to conclude "there were three men of very Bad Characters who formed a plot to murder him." The treachery did not end there, for the doctor's conspiracy theory meant all of the "men at the fort were accomplices to one degree or another."

To determine how organized the plot had been, Dr. McLoughlin charged his trusted lieutenant Donald Manson to investigate. Manson immediately subjected Thomas McPherson to a second round of questioning, prompted by Kannaquassé's whispers of a murderous contract. McPherson vehemently denied there was a signed agreement to kill John Jr., but admitted he had prepared a petition demanding the chief trader's removal. When asked why he had not forwarded his complaint to the Governor, McPherson replied: "I destroyed the paper about a month ago because I did not want anyone to see it, as it was so badly written." Neither Manson nor McLoughlin Sr.

believed McPherson's disavowal, and Manson searched the fort thoroughly for the document, but found nothing. Dr. McLoughlin took this as evidence, informing his superiors that "we cannot find the paper, yet there are no proofs of its not being so." The doctor was forced to concede that without the damning paper it would be "impossible to convict them *en masse* of conspiracy." Still, the doctor found solace in Manson's declaration: "In my opinion, almost all the Canadians and Iroquois more or less are implicated."

Dr. McLoughlin's fervour proved contagious, and the more Manson heard, the more he was convinced John Jr.'s death had been a premeditated act of treason. At Dr. McLoughlin's behest, Manson travelled to Fort Stikine to interview the remaining witnesses. Before departing, he sent word to the fort's chief trader, Charles Dodd, to disarm the men as a precaution. Mr. Dodd went one better, placing all the Canadians in irons under Kanaka guards. Both Dodd and Manson trusted the Kanakas implicitly and were convinced the Sandwich Islanders had nothing to do with McLoughlin's death, having remained loyal to their leader to his bloody end.

After interrogating the men of Stikine and McLoughlin's wife, Manson revised his thinking and laid out a new narrative of the crime in a private letter to Dr. McLoughlin. Manson believed McLoughlin had known of the plot against him, and "in order to secure the principal ringleaders he gave them rum, thinking no doubt that when intoxicated he could more easily accomplish" their arrest. On the night in question, McLoughlin had armed the Sandwich Islanders and imprisoned Pressé, and he intended to do the same with Heroux and Kannaquassé. According to the Kanakas, Kannaquassé was as guilty as Heroux, and the conspiracy did not stop there, as Kawannassé and several others were clearly involved. In closing, Manson urged the chief factor to step up security around the Iroquois, warning that Kannaquassé would likely escape at the first opportunity, "and perhaps might be inclined to do something worse." Before he took leave of Stikine, Manson ordered that six prisoners be sent to Fort Simpson for incarceration, pending trial.

It remained an open question whether there would ever be a trial, and no one could predict the fate of Urbain Heroux. In his letter to Pelly, Dr. McLoughlin complained bitterly that Simpson "distinctly told me that all he could do in reference to Heureux [*sic*] was in the meantime to remove him to the island of Kodiak or some other distant Settlement," all the while insisting he "had no desire to screen the prisoner from justice."

The problem was one of jurisdiction, at least according to Simpson. McLoughlin's death was an international debacle involving the murder of a Canadian "at a British post in Indian Country, on land leased from the Russians." As such, the issue of jurisdictional authority was not readily resolved. The territory was controlled by Nicholas I, who could pursue the matter if he so desired. The British government could also lay claim, thanks to a historic Tudor statute that authorized the English courts to try anyone accused of murdering a British subject, even on lands outside the Crown's dominions. Even Canada had the right to prosecute. In 1803, the British Parliament passed the Canada Jurisdiction Act specifically to address lawlessness in the fur trade. The act authorized trials for offences committed on Crown lands or in "other Parts of America not within the Limits of Canada or the United States." Both Heroux and his victim were Canadians employed in the fur trade, and the crime had been committed "in other Parts of America," making it exactly "the sort of case that the Canada Jurisdiction Act had been designed to catch."

Ultimately, the sticking point was not authority, as no fewer than three countries had legitimate claims for jurisdiction over the case. The problem was apathy. Russia, England, and Canada had collectively thrown up their hands, happy to foist the prosecution onto any nation that wanted it. The only institution less interested in pursuing the case was the Hudson's Bay Company, which had the most to lose if the crime was made public. Dr. McLoughlin, consumed with impotent fury, played the only card left to him, telling his superiors he "might prosecute the case personally if the HBC did not." Although the chief factor no doubt meant what he said, everyone knew it was a toothless threat.

McLoughlin Sr.'s vow may have lacked bite, but that did not stop him from sinking his teeth firmly into Simpson's backside. The remainder of his rambling missives were dedicated to an all-out assault on the overseas governor. The doctor's opening salvo was a scathing critique of Simpson's investigative method: "Instead of conducting the examination so as to endeavour to find out what had led to the murder; you conducted it as if it had been an investigation into the moral conduct of the Deceased, and as if you were desirous to justify the conduct of the murderers."

Dr. McLoughlin was not surprised by the Governor's vitriolic attacks on his son, having watched Simpson continually disparage his colleagues in the past, but he could not let them stand. Rhetoric was all he had, and so the doctor refuted Simpson's allegations with a rhetorical question: "If the Deceased had been the Bad master these men pretend, would all those whose time was about to Expire have Re Engaged to him as they did?" McLoughlin argued Simpson himself was the strongest evidence to contradict any claims of abuse, as "the Best proof that these men were not ill treated by the Deceased is that you passed and repassed in the same Season and no complaint was made to you." Kannaquassé had tried to raise his concerns about the chief trader during the Governor's October 1841 visit to Stikine, but according to Kannaquassé, Simpson "put me off, saying by & bye." Such disregard was very much in keeping with Simpson's contempt for his inferiors, particularly those of mixed blood. Sir George had often voiced his belief that, when confronted with a troublesome "half-breed," the offender must "be allowed to make the discovery that he cannot mend his Fortune by a change of Masters."

To prove Simpson had conducted a shoddy investigation, the chief factor offered a final argument: Sir George had refused to have McLoughlin's body exhumed and autopsied. Dr. McLoughlin challenged his overlord, charging: "If you Sir had had the Corpse of the deceased taken out of the Grave and Examined...you would have found out the truth." Simpson ignored the protest, ordering that John Jr. would rest in peace at any price.

Having laid bare Simpson's inept handling of his son's murder, Dr. McLoughlin then turned his attention to the Governor's overall failings as a leader and a human being. Topping his litany of complaints was Simpson's notorious inconsistency. On this point, the doctor had ample support, for Simpson's colleagues often described his conduct as "vacillating, unsteady and arbitrary." Dr. McLoughlin believed the Governor's caprice had directly contributed to John Jr.'s demise, and his son had come to his "untimely End in consequence of Sir George's most injudicious arrangements." The case could be reduced to a simple syllogism, and the doctor "insisted, with fanatical perseverance, that the transfer of Finlayson had been the direct cause of the tragedy, and as Simpson had made the transfer he held him responsible for his son's death."

Next the good doctor called out his adversary for his blatant duplicity, marvelling at "Simpson's capacity to speak from both sides of his mouth." As illustration, McLoughlin pointed to Simpson's feigned disgust over the use of corporal punishment at Fort Stikine, even though floggings and beatings were commonplace within the HBC. McLoughlin recalled the Governor had no qualms keeping violent "blood hounds" — quick-fisted men he called "bruisers" — on the Company's payroll as "a necessary evil." And Simpson had promoted John Jr. to chief trader largely because of his demonstrated strength as a disciplinarian. Yet, in a perverse display of delusion and self-deception, the Governor once claimed, "I have, as you know, always Believed Kindness to Be the Best Disciplinarian."

Dr. McLoughlin mocked Simpson for having "become all at once very sensitive about striking the men." His point was well taken, as the Governor had always found his own lapses charming, but found similar transgressions in others unforgivable. McLoughlin claimed Simpson often resorted to corporal punishment, compensating for his diminutive stature with a big stick. McLoughlin once watched Simpson knock a man down, leading the doctor to remark, "I never saw a man get a neater blow." He also recalled that "on at least two occasions... Sir George had himself inflicted floggings and beatings, and on a third, he 'tickled' a man's shoulders 'with a canoe pole' until he had to be restrained from beating the man further." Such occurrences were legion and legendary in the fur trade.

George Simpson's incurable cognitive dissonance often left his contemporaries shaking their heads. With the brutal honesty found only in letters of resignation, one long-suffering HBC employee accused Simpson of lacking "the principles of honour and integrity which you so strongly recommend in others." Dr. McLoughlin accused Simpson of "writing for Effect on others," recounting many instances in which the Governor paid lip service to policies he had set, then refused to obey. For example, Simpson universally despised any man who was overly fond of the bottle. Simpson once complained that his house servant "washed his Throat occasionally," but he believed he could cure the man's alcoholism through sheer willpower and a clenched fist, boasting that his manservant only drank "until I gave him such a pounding as made his Bones ache for a month, which has cured him." Yet Simpson was known to hoist a glass or three in his time, partaking freely of wine and spirits wherever and whenever the opportunity arose.

Dr. McLoughlin's bile-soaked diatribe was an accurate depiction of Simpson and his personality defects, but it did more damage to its author than to its target. McLoughlin stripped his attack of all power by making it too personal, and he hurt his cause further by following up his initial letters with a handful of subsequent harangues, each longer and more vitriolic than the last.

McLoughlin's crusade bordered on obsession, and it did not escape the notice of his colleagues. J.E. Harriott observed: *The Big Doctor* is in a deplorable state, poor man, what anxiety he has experienced about that young man, and to be murdered at last with such a character as his murderers have given him." Dr. McLoughlin simply would not, could not, let the matter rest, "making each new fragment of evidence an excuse for reviewing the entire matter at what the recipients soon came to consider wearisome length." He "had lost both his self-control and sense of proportion."

More's the pity, for the Hudson's Bay Company elite had come to the realization that the shooting at Fort Stikine was anything but a "justifiable homicide." Despite Simpson's concerted efforts to plug the holes in his own investigation, "a number of new facts came to light, all of which pointed strongly to the conclusion that his assessment of what had happened was not only hastily conceived but seriously flawed."

NINE

Prior Bad Acts

The best predictor of future action is prior behavior. To understand a man's choices, you need look no further than his past, where his character is forged by the incidents and accidents of his days. Dr. McLoughlin's barbs regarding Simpson's biased investigation stuck because everyone involved—the letter's author, recipients, and subject—knew Simpson had done the exact same thing many times before. The Governor's dismissal of the Siveright matter was one example, but Simpson's tendencies were most evident during his "investigation" into the strange death of his cousin Thomas.

The cousins were born sixteen years apart and grew up in the same tiny house in the village of Dingwall, but they had never been close. Still, Simpson kept a paternalistic eye on his kin, and when Thomas came of age, the Governor convinced him to join the HBC in 1831.

In his demagogic character book, Simpson atypically heaped praise on his nepotistic hire, calling Thomas "Perfectly correct in regard to personal conduct & character." This high regard faded after the young man settled into his dual roles as Simpson's "Secty and Confidential Clerk during the busy Season...and Shopman, Accountant & Trader at Red River Settlement during the Winter."

And speaking of character, the Simpson boys offer compelling proof that narcissism is genetic. Thomas had an ego to rival Sir George's and an entrenched sense of entitlement born of being "considered one of the most finished Scholars in Aberdeen College." Despite his lowly rank, Thomas possessed something his cousin did not: a college diploma, a fact he lorded over Simpson at every opportunity. Thomas was also as indiscreet as he was arrogant, openly mocking George Simpson's management acumen in his dispatches home: "Entre nous, I have often remarked that his Excellency miscalculates when he expects to get more out of people by sheer driving; it only puts everyone in ill humour." Thomas even hinted that "when the Governorship of the country became vacant, he himself would be the person best adapted to fill it," a sentiment unlikely to endear him to the post's current occupant. Whatever his endgame, Thomas was messing with the wrong egomaniacal tyrant.

Thomas revealed his true colours at the Red River settlement. Just prior to Christmas Day, 1834, a Metis employee came to Thomas's office asking for an advance in his pay. Thomas held the same racist views as his cousin and saw the request as sheer impertinence. He proceeded to beat the man unconscious. Thomas's brother Alexander later downplayed the severity of the assault, saying only that the man "got the worst of the scuffle, coming off with a black eye and a bloody nose," but it was no mere scuffle. To prevent a full-scale Metis rebellion, "Simpson was forced to remove him from authority with breathtaking speed."

Simpson needed to find a suitable placement for his hotheaded relation, a posting sufficiently remote to shield Thomas from possible criminal charges. His solution was to send his cousin north, as far north as it was possible to go. He appointed Thomas second-in-command of an Arctic expedition captained by famed navigator Peter Warren Dease, a man Simpson once dismissed as "not calculated to make a shining figure." Their mission was to explore the uncharted northernmost coastline of Rupert's Land. The foray had the added benefit of fulfilling one of the oft-ignored covenants of the HBC's charter: to map the territory and identify trading routes.

To Simpson's befuddlement, Thomas met with great success on the expedition, mapping over 150 miles of coastline in the first three years, as well as filling in the western tail of the Northwest Passage. Indeed, Thomas was so self-satisfied he petitioned his cousin to extend both his contract and the financial support of the expedition. Simpson refused, although he took credit for the expedition's success when he met with his Russian counterpart, Baron von Wrangel. Thomas was livid when he learned Simpson had hoarded the glory, and in a full-throated tantrum he would not live to regret, he went over the Governor's head. He appealed directly to the HBC's London Committee, informing them George Simpson's "jealousy of his rising name was not but ill disguised." In a second missive sent directly to his cousin, Thomas declared: "Fame I will have, but it must be mine alone." The war of the Simpsons had begun.

Thomas's playground antics were no match for his cousin's Machiavellian games. The London Committee promptly drafted a letter to Thomas, granting his extension. The letter also contained their heartiest congratulations, as Thomas had recently been awarded the Royal Geographic Society's Gold Medal in recognition of his Arctic discoveries. Simpson intercepted the Committee's reply to Thomas and switched the missive into the wrong dispatch bag, leaving his cousin on tenterhooks in Red River for a letter that would never come.

By June 1840, Thomas could wait no longer. He left the settlement and headed for St. Paul, intent on sailing to London and making his case directly to the Committee. The route to St. Paul ran through Sioux territory, a treacherous region with standing warnings for travellers to be armed and on alert. Two weeks later, Thomas's body was discovered south of Fort Garry. The cause of death was a single gunshot wound to the head.

Governor Simpson led the investigation into Thomas's death, and his efforts were cursory at best. His official ruling was that the wound was self-inflicted, Thomas having "committed suicide while of unsound mind, after murdering two of his four Metis companions." Eyewitnesses begged to differ. One survivor swore Thomas had shot one of his Metis travelling companions, John Bird, killing him instantly before mortally wounding a second man, Antoine Legros. A third Metis—Legros's son, James Bruce—ran for the horses and rode back to the main camp. When a search party returned to the scene the next day, they came upon the remains of Legros and Bird. Lying beside them was Thomas, still very much among the living. From that moment on, accounts differ, but all agree that in the minutes that followed, Thomas died of a gunshot wound to the head.

There is no question George Simpson was instrumental in covering up the event, but writer James Raffan wonders whether the Governor's culpability ran even deeper. Raffan reasons that "if Simpson had wanted a full and impartial investigation" of his cousin's death, he could have simply ordered one. Raffan also questions why Simpson buried his cousin in a pauper's grave alongside the two men Thomas had murdered. Raffan is not alone in thinking Simpson had a hand in Thomas's death—historians Marjory Harper and Vilhjalmur Stefansson reached the same conclusion independently, although all three stop short of saying Simpson's finger was on the trigger.

Sir George certainly had the final word on Thomas's legacy, as he controlled the public dissemination of the Arctic expedition's accomplishments. He arranged to have a chronicle published that extolled the foray's successes, and he distributed the credit as he saw fit. Many took exception to Simpson's revisionist history, including John McLean, who marked his protest for posterity: "Mr. Dease's name is mentioned in the published narrative of the expedition, where he is represented as being employed merely as purveyor. It might have been said with equal propriety that Mr. [George] Simpson was employed merely as astronomer." The Governor's efforts to besmirch his cousin's memory did not stop there. Simpson also went to great lengths to repress many of Thomas's accomplishments, squelching any hope Thomas might achieve his long-desired fame posthumously. His campaign to snuff out his cousin's light ultimately failed, and in an ironic footnote, the citizens of Dingwall have since elevated Thomas to far greater heights of infamy than George Simpson.

Simpson's unchecked autocracy received a cruel validation when Queen Victoria knighted him for his limited contributions to the Arctic expedition, and the undeserved investiture caused his head to balloon. The ginger-haired whoreson was now Sir George Simpson, and those in his presence were never permitted to forget it. Once knighted, he began to rewrite his own history, crafting a biography worthy of the man he had become. To mask all traces of his ignoble birth, Simpson designed (or pilfered) a heraldic crest featuring a falcon volant resting on a garland of Scottish thistle. An unfurled banner bore his freshly coined motto, *Alis nutrior,* which translates roughly to "fed by their wings," or as one wag interpreted it, "It is sometimes pleasant to act like a madman." He even had the crest carved into his dining room chairs and stitched into some tapestries.

Simpson was made a knight bachelor, an honour bestowing the non-hereditary title of Sir to the recipient alone. He was now a paladin, but the glory was short-lived and his detractors gleefully crowed, "The bauble perishes with him." Far more galling to Simpson was the fact his superior, HBC Governor John Henry Pelly, was made a baronet, a title that would pass to his sons. It was a perverse display of aristocratic injustice, but Sir George still resented others sharing in his unwarranted accolades.

The investment ceremony was held in the throne room at Buckingham Palace on January 25, 1841. No written account survives of the event's particulars, but one historian envisioned the scene as a comedic clash of tiny titans, imagining that Simpson wore heels under his pearl grey spats, raising him to a dizzying five foot seven inches and allowing him to tower over the diminutive monarch, who stood a mere five feet tall. No doubt Sir George accepted his knighthood with his usual preening, receiving as his due that which others had achieved. His critics were more willing to call out the Governor, including John McLean, who seethed, "Sir George owes his ribbon to the successful issue of the Arctic expedition conducted by Messrs. Dease and [Thomas] Simpson. His share of the merit consisted of drawing out instructions for those gentlemen, which occupied about half-an-hour of his time at the desk."

The Governor's callous indifference to the fate of his own cousin formed the template for all future death investigations conducted under his watch, including John McLoughlin's. Simpson's corrupt handling of Thomas's demise filled Dr. McLoughlin with despair and trepidation, for if Simpson cared so little for his own blood killed in the Company's service, could Dr. McLoughlin reasonably expect more when the victim was kin to another?

TEN

An Irresistible Force, an Immovable Object

As 1842 drew to a close, the travesty of Fort Stikine no longer referred solely to the killing of its chief trader. The Company's investigation had little to do with John McLoughlin Jr. and everything to do with the escalating war of words between Simpson and the victim's increasingly irrational father. As the two men locked horns, many believed their mutual destruction was assured.

Both men refused to yield, and their relationship deteriorated. For George Simpson, such conflict was of no concern, but "McLoughlin's loyalty to the Company, which would normally guarantee discretion, was also becoming suspect." The Governor had expected Dr. McLoughlin to simply swallow "the pill without daring to complain of its bitterness," something the doctor could not bring himself to do. Consequently, Sir George no longer trusted McLoughlin to act in the Company's best interests, and so Simpson began to work in ways that were decidedly not in the doctor's best interest.

McLoughlin, in turn, accused Simpson of being deluded and heartless. The Governor's self-image was "ludicrously unrealistic," and his callousness was the stuff of legend. One oft-humiliated underling confronted Simpson, saying, "You are pleased to jest with the hardships I experienced...you ought to have considered it sufficient to have made me your dupe, and not add[ed] insult to oppression." Dr. McLoughlin believed the Governor combined "the prepossessing manners of a gentleman [with] all the craft and subtlety of an intriguing courtier," and that "his cold and callous heart was incapable of sympathising with the woes and pains of his fellow-men." Neither combatant came off well in the exchange, as the clash revealed the intractable demands of each man's ego: "Simpson expected to rule; McLoughlin was accustomed to independence."

HBC Governor Pelly took the matter seriously but refused to get serious about it. He grew weary as the squabble dragged into its second year, lost track of who said what, and did not have the patience to find his way back. As the barrage of insults rained down from both sides, the Company's stewards insulated themselves from the fray.

Their cloak of plausible deniability was torn asunder, however, when Simpson and McLoughlin stopped talking to each other and began sending their toxic missives directly to Company headquarters. The first bombshell landed early in 1843, when a thick envelope arrived in London containing Simpson's bellicose response to McLoughlin's latest letter. Like a petulant child, Simpson refused to deal with his uncompromising sibling, preferring to make his case directly to the father figure that loved him best, confident he would receive vindication.

In all things, Simpson cultivated the appearance of a man more sinned against than sinning, and his letter fashioned him the innocent victim of Dr. McLoughlin's unwarranted attacks. He did not mince words, claiming, "It is evident Mr. McLoughlin is ignorant" of how "difficult and troublesome [it is] to obtain the ends of justice." The doctor's ignorance was so egregious that Simpson had no recourse but to address all of McLoughlin's accusations. With each point the Governor masterfully blended whinging with an abdication of responsibility.

With regard to Dr. McLoughlin's critique of the first depositions, Simpson retorted: "I had no power to cross examine the witnesses...after the most rigid investigation...I still firmly believe the main features of the evidence they gave, in reference to the conduct and habits of the unfortunate young man, were substantially correct." It was a curious approach, for Simpson had never before claimed he did not have the power to do something, and in this particular case he did possess the authority to interrogate the witnesses —he simply chose not to. As to the credibility of the witnesses, the Governor grudgingly agreed there were "many worthless characters in the Service." Experience had taught Simpson that even good employees inevitably "became slothful and insolent," and this became a real concern when the hired hands started out as "the very dross and outcast of the human species." From Simpson's vantage point, the violence at Fort Stikine was simply a prophecy fulfilled. Indeed, the Governor had predicted just such an occurrence more than two decades earlier. The problem, he opined, was the loathsome necessity of hiring Canadians, who were both easily beguiled and readily treasonous: "If humoured with trifles, anything may be done with them, but if treated with uniform harshness and severity, they will Mutiny to a certainty." McLoughlin Jr. had caused his own demise through his excessive abuse of his men, or so Simpson still believed.

In a magnanimous feint, the little emperor conceded he might have been mistaken when he accused John Jr. of cooking the books, and he heaved a sigh of relief "to find it is better than I was led to suppose." Although he had never expected to be challenged on the point, the Governor knew how easily such allegations could be disproved. Simpson deftly shifted the blame to a conveniently placed straw man who "led [him] to suppose." It was a curious sleight of hand that quickly became a recurring theme throughout his screed.

Simpson then rewrote history, claiming Dr. McLoughlin had made the decision to leave his son in sole command of Stikine. In the midst of this temporal juggling act, Simpson paused long enough to disparage the son one last time: "From what Mr. McLoughlin knew of his son's previous conduct, he ought never in my opinion to have been placed in charge of Stikine; and I believe that those who knew the young man best are aware that when under the influence of liquor, he was violent to madness, and even in his sober moments he was ever more ready with his hand than was necessary or proper."

To prove John Jr. was quick with his fists, Simpson relied on the hearsay of John Rowand, chief factor of the Saskatchewan District. Rowand said Dr. McLoughlin had been "informed by their servant La Graise that the conduct of Mr. McLoughlin Jr. was exceedingly violent and irregular, and that in an act of violence, of then recent occurrence, a sword was broken." Simpson claimed to have once laid his hand on the blade, "which I afterwards found at Stikine, and if my recollection fails not, forwarded to Vancouver." He conceded that finding the broken sabre would lend some (much needed) credibility to the account, but the sword in question was never seen again.

The Governor then took umbrage at McLoughlin's allegation that his investigation had been biased and inept. Simpson stated the inquiries conducted under McLoughlin's auspices was done "at Least as much with a View of Exonerating your Son as of Eliciting the truth."

George Simpson's letter to the board was a textbook of misdirection and obfuscation, and an acid test of his power to persuade. The facts were never as important as their delivery. Simpson held tight to his conviction that the men responsible for killing McLoughlin could be trusted to give a fair and impartial account, and he alluded to evidence corroborating his theory of the killing, even if he could not produce it. But Simpson's defence of self was ultimately not based on evidence or testimony — it was a thinly veiled plea for the Committee's unwavering support. He had given his life to the Company, and he now expected the board to repay him by taking his side in this fight. For once in his fabled career, Simpson could not retreat, and so he forced Governor Pelly and Committee to stand behind him.

In the months that followed, Pelly and the board did line up behind Simpson, although their rationale had nothing to do with the arguments offered by either side, or any strong conviction as to what had happened to John McLoughlin Jr. Rather, the decision came down to a single guiding principle: "Simpson was indispensable, McLoughlin was not."

§

Dr. McLoughlin lacked Simpson's clout and charisma, but he remained a force to be reckoned with, and he could not let the matter drop. He fired off another tedious screed, then stalled for time as he waited for his latest round of evidence and newly acquired depositions to arrive in London for the Committee's consideration. The doctor's evidentiary package promised to shed "new light" on the case, proving once and for all that the "crime was clearly long pre-mediated," and that "the charges of habitual intoxication and excessive severity were trumped up after the deed was committed as a screen to the villainy of the culprits."

A new day finally dawned at corporate headquarters in 1843. After wading through Dr. McLoughlin's averments, the Company's secretary, Archibald Barclay, wrote to Simpson regarding this new evidence, and for the first time, Simpson received a gentle smack on the nose. Having reviewed each set of depositions, the Committee decided both inquiries were fatally flawed. Barclay told Simpson, "[The] evidence taken since you were at Stikine is no doubt loose, irrelevant often little to be depended upon, but it is not nearly so bad as that given before yourself at Stikine." Barclay felt the solution to halting the palace intrigue was simple: the Committee would commission a third round of witness depositions, to be conducted by an impartial third party. Actually, the process had begun earlier that year, when the board agreed such an unprecedented move was necessary to appease the two warring factions. The impartiality of the new investigator was a smokescreen, however, and Barclay privately assured Simpson that Dr. McLoughlin "has not been allowed to triumph."

Governor Pelly and the Committee also informed Dr. McLoughlin of the renewed investigation, but they were quick to reprimand him on a number of fronts. First, Pelly berated McLoughlin for not raising his objections regarding the men at Stikine before his son's death. He reminded the doctor that "the persons placed there were supposed to be fit for their several situations, and able to discharge the duties they had to perform. It unfortunately turned out otherwise; they proved incapable and worthless, but that was not the fault of Sir George Simpson." Dr. McLoughlin was again slapped on the wrist for his heated and personal attacks: "You have thus virtually refuted your own charge and acquitted Sir George Simpson of any blame that does not equally attach to yourself."

In the decades since, historians have concurred, voicing their belief that McLoughlin Sr.'s vitriol did more harm than good. W. Kaye Lamb was certain had the doctor not made his contest with Simpson so personal, the Committee might have done more. John S. Galbraith felt Simpson had "already damned himself" with his callous handling of McLoughlin's murder, forever damaging his credibility with the Committee, but that Sir George was "saved" by Dr. McLoughlin's crusade, which had "lost all sense of proportion."

But how history might view the tussle did not concern the Committee as much as the prospect of negative publicity. What all the senior officers knew—but the public did not—was that the killing at Fort Stikine was not an isolated event. Violence and murder were commonplace in the outposts, and the shareholders did everything in their power to keep it quiet. Governor Pelly and the Committee relied heavily on that code of silence, and they appealed to McLoughlin's passions as a father, as well as his rational business sense. Pelly reminded McLoughlin that his son's legacy was at stake, and that tales of barbaric corporal punishment "may be the fabrications of worthless or malicious persons, but unfortunately the effect is the same as if they were well founded: the service is injured, men of good character are deterred from entering it." The Company also needed to save face with their trading partners, for it was simply not good business practice "that such scenes as those which occurred at Stikine should be witnessed by the Natives." Surely Dr. McLoughlin, as an invested shareholder, could see that.

Dr. McLoughlin held an entirely different view, and he was in no mood to be placated or told what to think. His response to the Company's pleas for discretion cut to the quick: "Is murder not to be punished because it is Embarrassing to Both Companies?" It was now McLoughlin's turn to wield guilt as a cudgel, and he reminded the Committee his son was both a Christian and an Englishman, and therefore deserving of proper justice: "I presume there is no place under Christian Dominion where a British subject is murdered but it will be Enquired into."

Still, McLoughlin could ill afford to alienate the Committee, given that he remained in their employ and they were making positive strides to seek justice for his son. If another investigation could meet that end—particularly an inquiry devoid of Simpson's input—then so be it. He signed the truce and temporarily held his fire.

§

Enter James Douglas, the bastion of impartiality appointed to conduct the third investigation on the Company's behalf. Although chosen for his even hand, Douglas had a troubled history with Simpson and had, of late, fallen out of favour with the senior McLoughlin. Dr. McLoughlin's incessant raving had forced Simpson and the Committee to systematically strip him of his authority, and Douglas had quietly succeeded McLoughlin as the district's chief factor, a move that ruffled the feathers of the white-headed eagle.

Though not quite as tall as Dr. McLoughlin, Douglas was every bit as imposing as his predecessor. His contemporaries found him to be a "cold

An official, if awkward, portrait of Sir James Douglas, taken in 1863 by G.R. Fardon.

brave man... with a wooden hard face." Those under his command called him "Old Square-Toes," a moniker lacking in affection or discernible meaning.

Simpson also had issues with the new appointee, for Douglas was a "half-breed" of an entirely different stripe. In 1803, he was born in Demerara (now Guyana) to a Glasgow merchant, also named James, and Martha Anne Tefler, a Creole from Barbados and a black freewoman. Their coupling produced a number of offspring, but they never married. At age nine, little James was dispatched to a prep school in Scotland to secure a proper education. Scrappy and sporting a perpetually chipped shoulder, Douglas learned to "get on by dint of whip and spur." He began his career in the fur trade with the North West Company, and following the merger in 1821, he was made a clerk second class of the HBC.

His rise through the Company ranks was meteoric. On January 30, 1830, he was dispatched to Fort Vancouver to serve as Dr. McLoughlin's accountant. Douglas soon tempered Simpson's prejudice by being "imperious, penny pinching, [and] obsessed with detail and ritual." Douglas was dictatorial and a tight-fisted believer in false economy, provided, of course, the privations never touched him. By 1835, Simpson had learned to overlook the swarthy colour of his skin, and Douglas was commissioned as a "gentleman of the interior" and promoted to the rank of chief trader. In short order he was given charge of the district, supplanting his former mentor, Dr. McLoughlin.

Douglas was a study in contrasts. Peter C. Newman was clearly smitten, calling Douglas a "mulatto of elegant mien whose character was a perplexing combination of endearing romanticism and glacial tenacity." His subordinates saw only the sharper side, claiming he could be "furiously violent when aroused." Still, he possessed an effusive charm and was capable of disarming even the hardest of men.

He could be difficult, and his history was certainly spotty, but the Committee pretended Douglas was impartial, and he was their unanimous choice to lead the investigation into John McLoughlin's death. The process proved arduous as the witnesses were by then scattered over a wide geographic area. The inquest dragged on for months, and further delays ensued as the depositions were copied by hand in triplicate before making the circuitous voyage from the Pacific coast to London.

The Committee took its time reviewing Douglas's witness accounts, but their leisurely pace should not be misconstrued as thoughtful deliberation. Pelly and his backscratchers were simply hoping for a miracle. Eventually, Secretary Barclay informed Simpson and McLoughlin the new evidence would be sent to the Russian governor in preparation for trial. Dr. McLoughlin was elated, but Simpson soon snatched defeat from the jaws of victory by informing the Committee the men involved were no longer in the Company's employ.

When Dr. McLoughlin first learned of his son's tragic death in June 1842, he ordered Douglas to send those responsible to Sitka, but his command was ignored. Douglas did send Kannaquassé and Pressé to join Heroux at the prison in Sitka, but the rest of the men were quietly reassigned, by order of George Simpson. A few were sent to Fort Simpson while the rest were transferred to a new outpost, Fort Albert, where they were to be held "under watch and ward." It was a loose form of house arrest at best, and escape was as easy as walking away.

Meanwhile, the Russians had their hands full with Urbain Heroux. In custody, the Iroquois showed himself "to be a man of ferocious disposition, having attempted to murder his keeper, who prevented his escape." While still at Fort Stikine, Heroux had told Kannaquassé, "I am going to the Russian Fort and will be either banished or hung," but neither prediction came to fruition. The Russians did not want to deal with McLoughlin's killer any more than George Simpson did, and they found a legal loophole. As Heroux raged in irons (and Kannaquassé and Pressé settled in beside him), Baron Ferdinand von Wrangel informed Governor Pelly the Russian government had no jurisdiction over the case because Stikine had been leased to the HBC. Wrangel then ordered Sitka's governor, Adolph Etoline, to send the prisoners back to the Hudson's Bay Company. As fate would have it, the men were to be remanded to Dr. John McLoughlin at Fort Vancouver.

When the Russians refused to solve their problem, the HBC was forced to make a decision. Privately, Barclay told Simpson all this squabbling about jurisdiction was just "more fudge alleged to get rid of the business." The Committee secretary then stepped over the dead body of John McLoughlin Jr. and recast the Hudson's Bay Company as the true victim of this tragedy: "If these men cannot be tried by the Russians, what is to be done with them . . . they might be tried in Canada but what an expense and inconvenience to get them and the witnesses transported thither — and what an exposure too! To let them loose without trial would be a most dangerous example to others." Bribery, Barclay decided, was not out of the question. He contemplated paying Sitka to try the men, wondering aloud whether "money was the real reason the Russians were refusing to act."

It was idle speculation, as Barclay saw no need to grease Russian palms, nor was he interested in airing the Company's dirty laundry. He fixed a hard price on John McLoughlin's life, arguing that "the expense involved in bringing the case to trial was more than the Company was willing to incur. Bad publicity was virtually certain but convictions were not." And although he never admitted it publicly, Barclay felt neither McLoughlin was "worth the trouble."

§

In February 1844, Heroux, Kannaquassé, and Pressé found themselves on a steamer bound for Fort Vancouver, where they were to be delivered into the waiting clutches of their victim's vengeful father. George Simpson recognized that handing the men over to Dr. McLoughlin was tantamount to a death sentence, and to avoid further bloodshed, he sent a directive ordering McLoughlin to free the men upon their arrival. His edict met with stony defiance. In a missive which began "I am no Lawyer But," McLoughlin acknowledged the men were under "the Warrant of a Magistrate," and that "until instructions come from England, how Sir George, who is himself only a Magistrate, can take on himself to order their liberation, I know not."

Unbeknownst to Simpson or the London Committee, Dr. McLoughlin had already settled on a course of action. The moment Heroux and his confederates arrived in Vancouver, Dr. McLoughlin sent the accused (along with a dozen witnesses and an interpreter) to York Factory, with instructions they be sent on to Canada for trial. So certain was McLoughlin Sr. of their guilt, he boldly declared that if the Canadian courts were unwilling to prosecute, he would do so himself.

The doctor's unilateral action brought down the full wrath of the HBC on his snow-white head. Simpson was apoplectic, sputtering, "[If] the prisoners either escape unpunished or receive at most a trifling punishment, Mr. McLoughlin will hardly find in his own feelings any compensation for the odium which he will have heaped, and the injury which he will have inflicted, on the honourable company." McLoughlin's eastbound chain gang made it as far as Norway House before Simpson stopped them in their tracks. The shackles were removed, and Heroux and his cohort were told they were free to go.

Simpson's vengeful ire came with a price tag. The Governor informed the London office he had ordered Dr. McLoughlin "to make up a statement of all the expenses of the investigation, so that your honours may be able to decide whether the burden is to fall on the Fur trade or on Mr. McLoughlin himself." Sir George then played his communiqué time-delay advantage, refusing to wait for the Committee to decide anything. Instead, he "simply cut off McLoughlin's five-hundred-pound salary until such time as he might apologize." Simpson also knew how to mix insult and injury. Upon learning the identities of his son's murderers, Dr. McLoughlin had immediately stopped their pay. In a spiteful act of retribution, the Governor ensured the killer and his confederates received their back pay, and that McLoughlin knew it. Lest the good doctor mistake Simpson's message, Sir George gave one of the perpetrators a raise and ordered another be returned to active service.

Simpson's venom was inexhaustible, but others in the company had tired of the ordeal, and much of their frustration was directed at the victim's father. The general consensus was that Dr. McLoughlin needed to move on, for his ceaseless lamentations had grown as tedious as rain. Archibald McDonald, chief factor of Fort Colvile, marvelled that the "pile upon pile of papers the unhappy father has laboured to fill upon this harassing question to prove his son to have been what in my opinion he was not, is truly astonishing." Chief trader John Tod echoed the sentiment, writing: "I fear the Dr. has not only compromised his dignity in this affair but has also failed to excite the Sympathy of the greater part of his friends, from his very excess."

Dr. McLoughlin had become an object of pity. The matter had dragged on too long and, thanks to Simpson's petty machinations, "even McLoughlin ran out of energy, and funds." Eloisa recalled, "About that time my father was in very low spirits." McLoughlin's relationship with Simpson, never good, was now unsalvageable. The doctor had also fallen out with James Douglas, a loss he felt more keenly. Eloisa described how the men first met: "Douglas was 17 when he came to Fort Williams—he was a boy when my father was a man. My father always liked him." Whatever affection McLoughlin once had for him was trampled under Douglas's square toes during McLoughlin's demotion and the final failed round of depositions.

§

There would be no formal resolution in the murder of John McLoughlin Jr. Simpson's hope that Russia would clean up the Company's mess was an idea that withered on the vine. Equally fruitless was the notion Canada or England might step in and prosecute the case. Despite Dr. McLoughlin's repeated threats, he lacked the personal funds to bring a civil suit, a venture he estimated might cost in excess of £10,000. Even if McLoughlin could muster such resources, Simpson had already acquitted and freed the men responsible. The matter seemed closed, yet there remained one last loose end: Douglas's depositions. Having commissioned the statements, the London office felt duty-bound to do something. The Committee, in an act of unmistakable favouritism, elected to forward the latest inquest findings to their overseas governor, George Simpson, for comment. After years of legal wrangling and endless strife, the case of John McLoughlin Jr. ended precisely where it began.

The Governor's musings were recorded for posterity in the precise hand of his personal secretary Edward Martin Hopkins, who was under strict instructions to mark his every word and forward the compendium to the Committee. Simpson opened by taking strong exception to the statements, although his rancour was no doubt fuelled by past criticisms of his own flawed depositions. In a classic case of psychological projection, Simpson found fault with the exact same missteps he had committed in his earlier inquest. He challenged the credibility of witnesses with vested interests in saving their own skins, and he criticized the leading questions posed during the depositions. He struggled to find a suitable example to prove his point, finally surrendering in exasperation and stating, "We shall not quote the answer, for any answer — be it what it might — to such a question, must be worse than useless."

His contempt for the process was palpable, yet Simpson still managed to reach a verdict in the case: "From the forgained deposition we arrive at the following conclusions: 1st That John McLoughlin, with a loaded gun and accompanied by a body of armed Kanakas, hunted up Urbain Heroux, avowing at the same time his intention to destroy him; 2nd That under these circumstance, a shot was fired, proving fatal to John McLoughlin — that shot having been fired by Urbain Heroux." Gone was any mention of liquor and abuse, and he steadfastly refused to dignify the mutiny theory by giving it any serious consideration. You have to admire Simpson for sticking to his guns. His verdict had not wavered since his first proclamation, although he carefully sidestepped his previous finding of "Justifiable Homicide."

Although Simpson's verdict was slathered in bastardized legalese, such jargon was judicially meaningless or, as he was so fond of saying, "worse than useless." His conclusions, however, were good enough for John Henry Pelly and the London Committee, who declared Simpson's findings to be the final word on the subject. They used his conclusions to close the matter of John McLoughlin Jr. forever.

ELEVEN

Putting Flesh to Bone

Although the tale of John McLoughlin Jr. is "a fascinating, if somewhat pathetic, narrative," his tragic demise has not received the attention it deserves. Two-time McLoughlin biographer Dorothy Nafus Morrison dedicated only a handful of pages to his death, as did Burt Brown Barker in his chronicle of the family dynasty. James Raffan's discussion of the murder runs little more than a page, while similarly scant accounts appear in Williams's *Highlights of the First Two Hundred Years of the Hudson's Bay Company* and Galbraith's much-lauded biography of George Simpson, *The Little Emperor*. The murder warrants only a single sentence in Newman's *Empire of the Bay*: "The dispute between the two climaxed as a result of Simpson's mishandling of the investigation of the murder of McLoughlin's son in the territory." Just two chapter-length academic considerations of the crime have ever been published: Hamar Foster's "Killing Mr. John," which examined whether England, Upper Canada, or Russia had jurisdiction to prosecute the shooter; and an essay by Walter Kaye Lamb focusing entirely on the deteriorating relationship between McLoughlin's father and Governor Simpson after the murder.

Indeed, the friction between the two men seems to be the only aspect of the crime scholars care about, and much of the rhetoric hinges on a single question—whose version of events was correct: Simpson's or McLoughlin's? While the Company's ruling class threw its lot in with the Governor, historians have sided with the victim's father. Willard Ireland spoke for many when he wrote: "In all fairness, it must be added that McLoughlin was in the right."

But was he right? Was his mutiny theory any more plausible than the self-defence narrative championed by Simpson? Answering that question requires delving into the crime at a level never before attempted, and reconstructing the scene using the latest investigative methods.

Cases like McLoughlin's are the bane of modern forensic investigations. Murders masquerading as suicides, accidents, natural deaths, or even justifiable homicides are often mishandled. The scenes are not properly examined, autopsies are deemed unnecessary, and the collection of physical evidence is cursory at best. It is only after the true nature of the crime is revealed that investigators must piece together the event with whatever remains.

In this case, what remains is a series of witness statements in the Hudson's Bay Company Archives, as well as a few hand-drawn maps and some personal and business correspondence relating to the shooting. There was no police service in 1842, and no autopsy was performed on John McLoughlin. Ironically, although his medical career never amounted to much, he was the closest thing the fort had to a doctor, and as chief trader he was also its resident law enforcement. Had the bullet struck another, it would have fallen to McLoughlin to examine the body and investigate the circumstances. His untimely demise left a void no one else could fill, and, as a consequence, the specifics of his murder were recorded solely in the depositions of lay eyewitnesses.

Relying on such statements to reconstruct the crime is a perilous but necessary proposition. Eyewitness testimony is notoriously unreliable in the best of circumstances, and evidence derived from individuals with strong motives to deceive makes it all the more questionable. Such potentially biased investigations raise the spectre of a deductive ouroboros, a circular argument endlessly feeding on itself.

The lack of objective, professional scrutiny is an obstacle, but it is far from an insurmountable one. Even in the age of DNA and chemical analysis, murder investigations still rely heavily on eyewitness testimony. The former is meant to augment the latter, not replace it, as the analysis of physical evidence serves to confirm or refute the narrative of witnesses by alerting investigators to incongruities in the story being told.

Today, a number of hallmarks are used to evaluate the credibility of witness testimony. The first is consistency: does the story change with each telling? In this case, witnesses were interviewed at least three times over the course of two years by different interrogators: Governor George Simpson, chief trader Donald Manson, and chief factor James Douglas. In reconstructing the events at Fort Stikine, testimony that shifted over time was discounted, while preference was given to the narrative threads that remained constant. Second, convention holds that multiple witnesses offering identical descriptions are more credible than a single witness straying from the pack. That is not to say that the lone voice is inherently incorrect or lying, but simply that there is legal safety in numbers. Finally, testimony must match the physical evidence and obey the laws of gravity, physics, and the space-time continuum to be deemed credible. Then, as now, a person cannot be in two places at the same time, a bullet in flight behaves in predictable ways, and it is safe to assume the laws governing force and energy were not temporarily suspended in 1842.

§

The first step in any crime scene reconstruction is to understand the spatial relationships, which in this case include the fort's layout and the position of each witness when the fatal shot was fired. Not everyone present in Fort Stikine on the night of the murder is relevant to the discussion. Certain individuals—such as McLoughlin's wife, Francois Pressé, or Benoni Fleury—were excluded as suspects because they were asleep, incapacitated (drunk or in irons), indoors, or unarmed.

Maps drawn during the depositions were augmented with details from the interrogations, and the resulting diagram reveals the setting as well as the physical relationships of players central to the action.

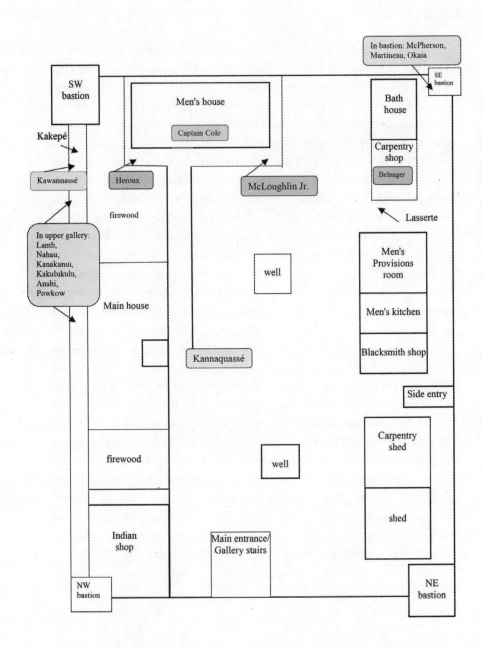

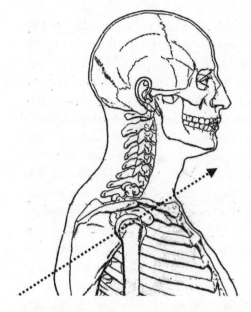

Dashed line indicates the wound track through McLoughlin's torso.

The next step is to collect the physical evidence retroactively, beginning with the body of the victim. Although no autopsy was performed, McLoughlin's injuries were well documented by his men, who described the nature of his wounds consistently, even if they disagreed as to their source.

McLoughlin's cause of death was a single gunshot wound to the chest from "a bullet which seemed to have entered his back between the shoulders and came out through the gullet above the breast bone," "having broken the spine as it passed." The slug wreaked havoc on McLoughlin's anatomy, and "the wounds made by the ball were very large, both openings being circular and three inches in diameter."

Now the comparison of physical evidence, spatial relationships, and witness statements begins. According to Kakepé, Captain Cole, and William Lasserte, McLoughlin was making his way along the front of the men's quarters when Urbain Heroux came around the southwest corner of the house. Heroux then stopped and raised his weapon—a Northwest or "Indian trade" gun, known as the Hudson's Bay fuke—firing the lethal shot as "the Deceased was about four feet from the muzzle of the Gun." Both men were on level footing, standing on the wooden platform built to protect pedestrians from tidal flooding, and both men were of similar stature.

There is only one problem: the angles are all wrong. The physical evidence and ballistics do not match the story, as is made clear by the trajectory (the bullet's flight from the gun to the target) and wound track (the path of the bullet through flesh). At a distance of four feet, a standing man firing a long gun at another standing man would inflict a level wound track, with the bullet entering and exiting the body at roughly the same horizontal plane. McLoughlin's wound track indicates the shooter was behind him and significantly below him, resulting in the gunshot wound described. Furthermore, the trajectory of a bullet travelling at the angle indicated by the wound track would not have hit the carpentry shop door, as was reported by several witnesses, but would have struck a point well above the shop's entrance.

The only armed man in a position to fire at McLoughlin from behind and below was William Lasserte, who was hiding at ground level between the bathhouse/carpentry shop and the men's kitchen. Lasserte, however, could not have been the shooter. Given Lasserte's location, the bullet needed to defy the laws of physics by completely reversing direction, hitting McLoughlin and then travelling back the way it came, in order to strike the door of the carpentry shop. Furthermore, all three witnesses repeatedly swore they saw Heroux fire the fatal shot: "The night was clear and Lasserte says when the shot went off, the flash of the powder in the pan enabled him to see Heroux most distinctly."

When such inconsistencies arise in criminal investigations, physical evidence always trumps eyewitness testimony, but in this case there is another piece of the puzzle to consider. Several witnesses stated McLoughlin was moving "in a stooping position looking very intently before him," crouching as he made his way along the platform and hugging the wall for protection. Taking McLoughlin's altered stance into account, the shooter, the bullet's trajectory, and the wound track now align.

This brings us to the crux of every homicide investigation: intent. According to George Simpson, Heroux shot McLoughlin in self-defence, yet a crouched man cowering along a wall with his back to the shooter does not represent imminent threat. Indeed, shooting a man in the back has long been thought to be an act of cowardice, not self-protection. But was McLoughlin's hunkered stance an indication of fear or of menace? Could he have been creeping along the wall, stalking his prey, Urbain Heroux? Forensic reconstruction provides proof of the victim's posture, but it cannot determine why he was in that position. McLoughlin's stance alone does not conclusively answer the question of either man's intent. It is a curious artifact, which both Dr. McLoughlin and Simpson could argue in their favour, and it remains a question best left for you, reader as hypothetical juror, to decide: was McLoughlin hiding or hunting?

§

A virtual autopsy of McLoughlin's body also helps dispel or confirm other aspects of the divergent accounts. For instance, in both historical versions of the killing, McLoughlin insisted Urbain Heroux shot him in the arm, giving the chief trader ample cause to hunt Heroux down, yet even as McLoughlin nursed his wound, doubts swirled as to the validity of his claim. He displayed his sleeve to Louis Leclaire minutes after the alleged shooting, pointing to an area near the elbow where it was torn. When Leclaire told him he heard no shots fired, McLoughlin became agitated and shouted: "Look where the balls passed through which they fired at me." A similar exchange took place moments later between McLoughlin and

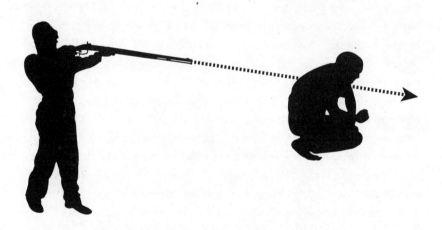

Schematic showing the relative positions of Heroux
and McLoughlin at the time of the fatal shooting.

Charles Belanger, who testified: "I examined his arm but could discover no wound nor any appearance of a ball mark on the shirt."

Leclaire and Belanger were not alone in their skepticism. Antoine Kawannassé also discounted McLoughlin's claim: "I heard no report, Which I could not have missed doing if a gun had been discharged within the fort." Thomas McPherson swore: "I saw no blood upon his shirt...I looked at his arm but saw no wound, the shirt only was torn." In fact, most witnesses believed the chief's shirt was torn as he wrestled with Fleury while trying to put the drunken man to bed, and many felt McLoughlin exaggerated the attack, either to garner sympathy or to create a reason to detain Heroux.

One witness, Simon Aneuharazie, thought McLoughlin was simply lying. Aneuharazie later testified: "I saw him tear the arm of his shirt with his teeth and exhibit the rent as produced by the passage of a ball." Aneuharazie was the lone voice accusing McLoughlin of fabricating the injury to his arm, and his allegation must be viewed with caution. What is certain is that, when the Kanakas washed and prepared the body for burial, there was no bullet wound or laceration to McLoughlin's arm.

There were, however, other injuries to the body that warrant further consideration. The first: "one of his hands were swelled from a blow he had given it some days before." The trauma may explain why McLoughlin could not load his own guns, and why he never drew his pistols. He was right-handed — his correspondence lacks the telltale ink smears of a southpaw — and though his injury would not have prohibited his use of a long gun (in which the left hand pulls the trigger), he might have lacked the grip strength or range of motion needed to fire a pistol with his wounded right hand.

The swollen hand has other implications. Both the timing and source of this injury are relevant in assessing whether McLoughlin could have brutally beaten several of the men, as George Simpson claimed. Thomas McPherson was one of two witnesses to notice the hand swelling, though all he knew of its cause was that Mr. John "had hurt it the day before." The injury likely occurred on April 19, the date of McLoughlin's last journal entry. It is unclear if the "blow he had given it" occurred during one of McLoughlin's alleged beatings or in some other manner. It can also be argued the swelling and pain related to the injury prevented the chief trader from administering such corporal punishment. Whether McLoughlin's swollen hand was the result of his excessive abuse of his troops, or evidence he was physically incapable of committing such violence, is again a question for the jury.

John McLoughlin's body sustained one final injury, "a large gash in his forehead," "a perpendicular cut...in a line with the nose." The cause of this injury was a major point of contention. Pierre Kannaquassé swore the forehead laceration occurred when McLoughlin fell on the barrel of his rifle. Urbain Heroux stated McLoughlin received the wound "from an Indian with his dog," although both Iroquois had reason to be deceitful. Less biased witnesses cite an entirely different source for the injury. Captain Cole was in his room when he heard the gunshot just outside his door. As he ran out, he saw McLoughlin "lying on his side, but still breathing audibly and Urbain...seized [McLoughlin's] rifle and struck him a severe blow to the forehead, and in doing so broke the rifle, after which he replaced it by the body."

Cole's insistence that John was alive and breathing is at odds with Kannaquassé's recollection, in which Kannaquassé approached the body "and with one hand under the neck raised the head and trunk when a deep aspiration followed which was the last sign of animation. He had previously perceived no signs of life." All other eyewitnesses side with Captain Cole. According to many of the Sandwich Islanders, the gunshot wound was not instantly fatal, and McLoughlin "did not appear to be quite dead, as there was a slight motion of the chest." Several Kanakas also reported hearing McLoughlin draw a few laboured breaths, "writhing in the Agonies of death."

Captain Cole offered a more detailed account, testifying that McLoughlin "made an attempt to rise after he fell." This statement may seem implausible, given McLoughlin's traumatic chest injury, but medical evidence supports Cole's claim. The wound path destroyed his upper thoracic vertebrae but bypassed the cervical column and the nerves of the brachial plexus. Therefore, the injury was low enough on the spinal column to allow at least the potential for movement in the neck and arms. Cole's testimony is also corroborated by others. From his vantage point on the upper gallery, Kakepé saw Heroux put his foot on McLoughlin's neck "to prevent his rising." Heroux kept his foot on the dying man's neck, "as if determined to accomplish his villainous purpose," and he pressed "upon it with his whole force, until Mr. McLoughlin ceased to breathe and life was extinct."

Curiously, none of the men who prepared McLoughlin's body for burial noted the presence of bruising or lacerations on his neck. That is not unusual with this particular type of injury, and the absence of evidence must not be misconstrued as evidence of absence. The sloe, or characteristic discolorations associated with bruising, takes time to develop fully. In modern autopsies, histological sections (tissue samples examined microscopically) are needed to accurately assess contusions, especially in the immediate aftermath of an assault. Today it is customary to put victims of suspected blunt force trauma on a twenty-four-hour "bruise hold" to give sufficient time for the contusions to manifest after death. McLoughlin also had a full beard, which may have hidden any damage associated with this specific injury. Even after his face was scraped clean by Belanger's razor, it is possible the sloe would not yet be evident.

§

The final physical evidence to consider is the guns, specifically McLoughlin's firearms. The question is whether McLoughlin had a working gun when he was shot, as it is crucial to the issue of self-defence. In his narrative, Kannaquassé was adamant that, as the killer stood over McLoughlin's body, "Urbain had no gun." Charles Belanger was equally certain Heroux had "seized the deceased's rifle and struck him in the forehead, after which he pushed the rifle under the body." Captain Cole's account concurred, adding that Heroux struck with such force, he "broke the rifle." Had Heroux grabbed a loaded long gun by the barrel and struck it down with sufficient force to break it, the gun would have discharged, potentially harming or even killing the man holding it. That the weapon did not fire indicates it was not loaded.

Others tell different tales regarding the damaged rifle. Kakepé swore that when McLoughlin was shot, he fell so hard against "the door of the men's house … as to break the stock of his rifle." George Heron believed the gun fractured when McLoughlin dropped it after being struck by the bullet. Heron did not see the actual event, but from his hiding place he heard "a noise as if a musket had fallen on the platform." All he could say for certain was he later "saw Mr. John's rifle standing against the house with the stock broken." Although the men could not agree how the rifle was broken that night, virtually all agreed it was irreparably damaged, a fact that becomes relevant in light of what followed. To garner support for Simpson's ruling of justifiable homicide, the depositions taken by Donald Manson and James Douglas specifically addressed whether McLoughlin was armed when he died. Each witness was asked "Was his rifle loaded when he was killed?" Most deponents replied they did not know or offered hearsay, swearing only that they "heard it was."

Two men gave more specific answers. Thomas McPherson and Antoine Kawannassé claimed to have loaded McLoughlin's weapons in the moments before he died. When asked if McLoughlin's rifle was functional, Kawannassé replied, "When he first came out with his Rifle, he fired a shot at random. I reloaded it and he did not again discharge it. It was loaded when he fell." McPherson corroborated Kawannassé's account in his deposition before Donald Manson. McPherson also swore that, on the day after the murder, he fired McLoughlin's rifle and pistols, proving his guns were still loaded.

Perjury can be difficult to recognize in the moment, and nothing in McPherson's claim struck Manson as questionable. Even the victim's father missed the inconsistency when he reviewed the statement sometime later. But in hindsight, McPherson's sworn statement reads false on one crucial point: how was he able to fire a broken rifle? In his testimony, McPherson made no mention of the weapon being damaged in any way, and he had no idea it had been rendered inoperable during the murder. Claiming to have fired it the next day suggests intentional deception, and, as will soon be evident, it was not the only lie Thomas McPherson told regarding the death of John McLoughlin Jr.

TWELVE

The Judas Goat

Sometimes it is what is not captured in the historical record that speaks loudest.

Simpson's machinations in the John McLoughlin investigation had turned it into a sordid potboiler that appealed to the baser instincts of his HBC colleagues. Company men of long tenure inevitably drew parallels between the faulty investigations of McLoughlin's killing and the unnatural demise of Simpson's cousin Thomas. Sir George had learned how to rewrite history when he whitewashed his cousin's death, and the same telltale signs of manipulation are evident in the documentation relating to John McLoughlin.

Take, for example, the testimony of Benoni Fleury, who hinted in his depositions that McLoughlin was very controlling of his country wife, and who claimed to have witnessed domestic violence on at least one occasion. Fleury testified that McLoughlin "attempted to use a dirk Against a woman who lived with him," an assault which his valet "prevented by snatching it away."

On closer inspection, this account becomes suspect. No other trader witnessed such aggression, and McLoughlin's wife never mentioned any violence during her interview. Indeed, she expressed nothing but love for her husband, although such denials do occur with battered women. Furthermore, those who knew him best felt McLoughlin actually had very little tolerance for the abuse of women; indeed, the mere suggestion that McLoughlin beat his wife once angered him to the point of violence. Joe Lamb said McLoughlin tried to stab him with a knife on Christmas Day "because I told the other Kanakas he had been thrashing his wife."

Digging still deeper, it appears Fleury's tale of abuse was lost in translation. On the night McLoughlin died, all in attendance agreed the fatal sequence of events began with the quarrel between McLoughlin and Fleury, but what Simpson's initial depositions failed to record was the true catalyst of that fight. According to eyewitnesses, the squabble was not the result of Benoni's intoxication but, rather, his actions as he retired for the evening: "Fleury began soon afterwards to beat his wife, and Mr. McLoughlin went into his house to endeavour to quiet him." The testimony of other traders revealed that it was McLoughlin who wrenched the bludgeon from Fleury's hand on the night of the murder. The narrative in the Governor's deposition was easily altered because Benoni testified in French, but his statement was recorded in English by Simpson. It now falls to the jury to determine whether the mistranslation represents legitimate human error or intentional manipulation.

The same holds true with Simpson's persistent insinuations that McLoughlin had played fast and loose with the books. Early in the investigation, Sir George told the dead man's father there had "been a very wasteful expenditure of property, given by the deceased to women, which has not been charged to his account." Had Simpson bothered to examine the inventories, he would have known McLoughlin kept meticulous records. When Donald Manson searched McLoughlin's desk after his death, the following note was discovered: "Deliver the following goods to Fleury's wife, and keep this note to show me this evening...8 yds Regatta cotton, blue; ½ lb white En. Beads; 1 Yd corn blue strands;...1 Rice, Cotton Handfs; 1 sm Blkt...4 Leaf Tobacco; 6 Yds White cotton; 1 Fine Ivory Comb,1 Doz Needles...Saturday October 30th, signed J. McLoughlin Jun. B.O."

Why McLoughlin bestowed these trinkets on another man's wife was not committed to paper. If the goods were intended as a love offering to a secret paramour, as Simpson implied, McLoughlin was a poor Romeo indeed, for the gift and its mode of delivery would have failed to warm any woman's heart. The note was addressed to Thomas McPherson, who procured the materials for the lady in question under the following loveless instructions: "If their [sic] is no Blue Regatta in the shop, I can suit you a little — but endeavour to make her take what there is. (Signed) McL." The entire exchange was well documented, right down to a cover letter reading "goods given to Fleury's wife on my acc. Signed JML," rendering Simpson's accusations of theft and underhanded dealings moot.

Simpson's poor opinion of McLoughlin extended beyond the fort's storeroom and into the dead man's bedroom. On this point, the Governor found an unlikely ally in Roderick Finlayson, McLoughlin's former assistant and supposed friend. McLoughlin's body was not yet in the ground when rumors began circulating that Finlayson had joined McLoughlin in his excesses of drink, theft, and debauchery. Finlayson caught wind of the malicious gossip, and he feared Simpson might believe such idle chinwags. When he was later questioned as to his boss's predilections, Finlayson felt compelled to explain why he had not told his superiors of McLoughlin's more sordid "habits," and he spoke out to protect his own reputation.

Finlayson was "an extremely proper young man, virtuous, religious, perhaps even a little self-righteous, and very worried about his job." He was eager to please and had heard tales of McLoughlin's indiscretions through the Company grapevine, yet when pressed for his recollections, Finlayson swore, "The only thing I had to bring forth was his criminal connexion with Indian women." Although he was McLoughlin's right-hand, Finlayson never saw him drunk or needlessly violent, and he had never known McLoughlin to steal from the Company store. The only thing troubling young Finlayson was "the deceased's attachment to women, which was well known to Sir George & others."

Finlayson did not have the stomach to detail McLoughlin's transgressions. Given his priggish nature, the offense was likely as inconsequential as McLoughlin taking a local bride or perhaps some saucy talk around the office, although Simpson tinkered with the statement until it alluded to something more. Regardless, Finlayson wanted the brass to know he had never joined McLoughlin "in having sexual relations with the Indian women," adding that once he made his lack of interest clear to his superior, McLoughlin never again "troubled me with such a proposal."

In hindsight, Finlayson's statement to the Company reads more as self-promotion than as an indictment of McLoughlin. Finlayson was adamant that "Mr. McLoughlin, tho' he was my master, could not divest me of my self-control." Indeed, he used his deposition to blow his own horn, claiming "the deceased's good Conduct while I remained with him may be mainly attributed to the influence of my example in resisting many temptations which, if I had indulged in, would now have given me much reason to blush with shame." He went on to credit himself with any good behaviour evident at the outpost: "All hands in the Fort, as soon as they were rid of my presence, began to pic & steal every description of property on which they could lay their hands & deal it out...to their Indian paramours." According to Finlayson, he alone stood between order and chaos at Stikine.

Finlayson closed by saying he shared "the general opinion" of many in the Company that McLoughlin's "appetite for women had provoked a number of the 'ruffians' in the fort's complement to rid themselves of him." In truth, his observation was far from the consensus. Both Simpson and, McLoughlin Sr. had support for their respective theories, but at no point did they believe that John Jr. had fornicated his way into an early grave.

Although Finlayson failed to take the Company's temperature regarding the motive for the killing, he was not far off when he pinpointed women as the catalyst of McLoughlin's demise. McLoughlin's appetite for the "dusky maidens"—whether real or imagined—had been troublesome, but it was his reported taste for one particular woman that ultimately led to his downfall.

§

For now, set aside all talk of liquor and beatings, conspiracies and contracts, for they are secondary to the cause. John McLoughlin was not killed in self-defence or as part of a mutinous rebellion. His death had much more biblical roots, for he was murdered in a jealous rage after "allegations surfaced that McLoughlin had taken 'liberties' with Heroux's wife on the very night he was killed."

Only one witness testified as to the "liberties" taken: Phillip Smith. Just after ten o'clock on the evening of April 20, 1842, Smith "met Mr. John near the door in company with Heroux's wife." Phillip's testimony reads: "On seeing me, he said 'is that you, Smith?' I answered it was and he told me to keep a good look out." This tepid dialogue represents the only evidence of indiscretion on the part of McLoughlin. The chief trader was never alone or unaccounted for in the hours before his death, and he had no time or opportunity to engage in sexual relations with Heroux's wife, nor did Smith claim to have seen any inappropriate touching or intimacy between the two when he encountered them in the doorway. It appears the entire exchange was taken out of context. Thomas McPherson claimed that, just moments before, McLoughlin had asked each man if he had seen Simon's "wife or Antoine's wife or Joe the interpreter's wife." Why he was searching so fervently for the women was not clear, but it indicates McLoughlin's interest in Heroux's wife was neither sexual nor specific.

McLoughlin's tête-à-tête with Heroux's wife was innocent, but no one could convince Heroux of that. By this point, Heroux was certain there was something illicit between the two. When questioned, Antoine Kawannassé said, "I think Urbain's hatred of Mr. John arose chiefly from jealousy, as he suspected an intrigue between Mr. John and his Wife." Curiously, the statement prompted no follow-up questions during Kawannassé's interrogation. Other men revisited the topic in later depositions. On July 24, 1842, Donald Manson asked Charles Belanger if he believed "Urbain was jealous of Mr. John McLoughlin with respect to his wife?" Belanger replied: "Yes but I do not believe he had any cause. I never saw nor heard from any other man in the fort that he had any cause for being so." Once again the matter was dropped without further questioning, dismissed as inconsequential gossip.

Although there was no legitimate evidence to support the insinuation, the question of whether McLoughlin was actually carrying on with Heroux's wife was irrelevant. Urbain Heroux believed he was, and that was motive enough to kill. The rumours were baseless but they were well planted, and if we trace the perfume back to its flower, the whiff of scandal emitted from a single fetid source: Thomas McPherson, the final crucial piece of the Fort Stikine puzzle.

§

Recall, if you will, the moment John McLoughlin caught Thomas McPherson stealing from the storeroom and turned him from the captain's table. That insult wounded McPherson's fragile ego, and he came undone after McLoughlin "put him with the men and made him work as a common man." In that moment, McPherson began to plot revenge. His scheme would require all of his nefarious talents, but luckily he could lie effortlessly and without conscience, and his ability to manipulate was second only to that of George Simpson.

Banished to his quarters and stripped of the storeroom key, McPherson became an object of pity. He carried his wounds for all to see, and in so doing, he managed to rally the other men to his cause, which was to rid Fort Stikine of its tyrannical leader. He found strong allies among the camp's Canadians, particularly the Iroquois; McPherson played to their independent spirit and their refusal to submit to any form of servitude. His message particularly resonated with Urbain Heroux, who strained the hardest against the Company's shackles. McPherson truly believed he would assume command once McLoughlin was out of the picture, and he dangled a tantalizing carrot: the promise of liberal access to local women once he was in charge. McPherson bore his suspension as if it was a death sentence, and although the reprimand had been relatively light, Heroux was angered by the punishment because it restricted his own ability to leave the fort at night and visit his country wife.

Heroux was never interrogated by any Company official, but a record of his thought process survives nonetheless. Mere minutes after McLoughlin was shot, Antoine Kawannassé asked Heroux why he had pulled the trigger. His answer surprised everyone: "The reason he gave was Mr. McLoughlin's ill usage of McPherson, who had been punished for a theft he had committed." Heroux's trivial motivation sickened Dr. McLoughlin, driving him to ask: "Can any man Blame my son for punishing this villain who steals the provisions of the Fort to give to Indian whores?" In the final analysis, McPherson's suspension may have been the first tipped domino, but it would not be the last.

The first step in McPherson's plan was to wage a misinformation campaign. He began by warning his fellow traders that McLoughlin had a wandering eye and to keep close watch on their wives. He also harped on the lawless nature of the northern wild; he used the Iroquois to spread his propaganda, yet every malicious word can be traced back to McPherson. Pierre Kannaquassé told Joe Lamb and several Kanakas that "men were not hung in Canada for murder," a feeble effort to convince the Sandwich Islanders "that we had nothing to fear if we killed" Mr. John. Lamb and his cohort refused to take the bait, so Kannaquassé tried his luck with

Okaia, urging the Kanaka to kill the chief trader, "as the life of the people at the fort would be much improved with him gone." Okaia was fine with the status quo, and he too declined to serve as assassin.

Urbain Heroux tried to convince another trader that McLoughlin Sr. would personally thank any man who killed his son. Phillip Smith said he had heard Heroux say sometime before the murder "that Mr. John's Father would be happy if he was put out of the way." The blatant lie failed as a recruitment tool, and McPherson urged Heroux to try a different target: George Simpson. Heroux told some locals he had heard of a case in Montreal involving a trader who "was never punished" for killing his superior, as Governor Simpson had turned a blind eye to the whole affair. Heroux went on to say "that he thought if Sir George Simpson knew of Mr. John's misconduct, he would not prosecute anyone that would murder him." It proved to be a prophetic statement; Heroux was not wrong—the HBC archives are littered with such cover-ups—but the aboriginals were not convinced.

There can be no privacy in a fort the size of Stikine, and it was not long before John McLoughlin overheard the assassination plot. He grew paranoid and added an additional two weeks to McPherson's suspension. McPherson was incensed and launched the next phase of his scheme in February 1842. He began to "prepare the paper," a document Dr. McLoughlin later described as the contract on his son's life.

The paper was also another sign of the growing allegiance between McPherson and Heroux. In their depositions, all the men stated the petition was kept in Heroux's house, but they signed it at Thomas's insistence. Once again the confederates targeted the Kanakas and coerced them into signing the paper. McPherson convinced Nahua to add his name by telling him "it was a good paper to be sent to Vancouver." Joe Lamb acquiesced after he was told "the paper contained nothing bad." Anahi affixed his signature at McPherson's urging, "merely to please him." McPherson and his co-conspirators were only a skosh more honest with the Canadians. William Lasserte signed the pledge, saying, "[I] cannot read myself but I was told that it mainly contained charges against Mr. McLoughlin." McPherson later claimed the document was simply a petition, intended for George Simpson, demanding that McLoughlin be stripped of command. McPherson swore he was only trying to get McLoughlin fired, not killed, but at the time Pierre Kannaquassé openly referred to it as the "kill McL" paper. As McPherson secured the last few signatures, he suddenly found himself back in McLoughlin's good graces, although how he came to be there was a matter of opinion. According to Pierre Kannaquassé, McPherson's suspension simply ended, and "Mr. McLoughlin then took him back." McPherson, on the other hand, claimed he was reinstated only after McLoughlin fell ill and was forced to stay in bed for several days. Either way, "McPherson destroyed the petition immediately after he was restored to his place."

With McLoughlin temporarily sidelined, McPherson expected to return to business as usual, but McLoughlin kept a tight hold on the storeroom key, handing it over to McPherson only as needed and then demanding its immediate return. The chief trader also took to sleeping with the keys in his room. Lust is a powerful motivator, and McPherson soon found a way to circumvent McLoughlin's punitive measures. He entered the "room in the night while [McLoughlin] was asleep, and took the keys of the Fort from the table to bring a strumpet into the Fort." McPherson did this on several occasions, and the master knew nothing of it.

McPherson's luck did not hold, and McLoughlin caught him red-handed. Once again, McLoughlin chose not to berate McPherson in front of the men; instead, he simply cut McPherson off at the source. Less than one week before he was murdered, McLoughlin had his craftsmen fabricate a barricade to bar his bedroom door from the inside. That bar, and all it represented, was the final domino.

§

On April 20, 1842, McPherson no longer restricted his pilfering to fabric and trinkets for whores. Sometime between 9:00 and 9:30 p.m., McLoughlin handed McPherson the keys to the stores, along with an order to extract some rum and give it to the five Indians from Tako. McPherson opened the warehouse and proceeded to give rum to "Every Canadian and Iroquois in the place, one Bottle of pure Spirits Each." Although McPherson "told Sir George that on the night of the Murder, the deceased gave them liquor," he later confessed he "did it of my own accord, contrary to Mr. McLoughlin's orders."

His compatriots found McPherson's sudden generosity to be "highly unusual," for, as one of them said, "[He had] never gave us rum at any former time without his masters orders." Many of the windfall's recipients knew nothing of McPherson's deception, or so they claimed. William Lasserte recalled, "There was a light in the passage into which the store door opened and there was no appearance of dishonesty in the transaction. If I had known that he took action without orders, I would not have taken it." Charles Belanger was more forthcoming: "The porch was dark so that it was easy to carry anything out of the stores without being discovered." When questioned, McPherson said he hoped "the men would drink it quietly, in their houses, and that the theft would never be known," but even his co-conspirators did not believe him. Although the liquor flowed freely to all, it was intended only for one. The true motivation behind McPherson's largesse was revealed in an offhand comment made by Charles Belanger, who said McPherson never "gave Heroux any rum, except on the night of the murder."

Once the men were pliably drunk, McPherson set his plan in motion, although how much of the plot was orchestrated and how much was providence is unknown. At some point in the evening, Heroux loaded at least three rifles and hid them in strategic points throughout the fort. The conspirators —McPherson, Heroux, and Kannaquassé, at a minimum—agreed that, at a given signal, Kannaquassé would sound the attack alarm, rousing the men to arms.

The squabble between McLoughlin and Fleury set the stage, and as Heroux joined the melee, his confederates took up their positions, and McPherson took up a lamp. Many testified that as McLoughlin made his last desperate run through the fort, the lone source of light (aside from the moon) was McPherson, "who carried a lantern." The lamp served triple duty. First, it was the signal for Kannaquassé to sound the fort's alarm. Second, McPherson planned to stay in close proximity to McLoughlin, so he held tight to the lantern to ensure he would not be mistaken for McLoughlin and shot accidentally. Finally, he kept the lamp trained on his master, painting McLoughlin with a target of light to aid his would-be assassin.

There was only one small glitch in the plan. Kannaquassé's false alarm drew the men to the fort's perimeter, but they did not immediately open fire. As McLoughlin crouched along the front of the men's house, McPherson ran to the gallery level via the southeast bastion. The men still did not fire their weapons, so McPherson turned to the nearest man—the dolt, Oliver Martineau—and ordered him "to fire two blank shots into the air." Martineau did as instructed, and his shots unleashed a hail of gunfire, providing the necessary cover for Urbain Heroux to step out of the darkness and fire the fatal shot at McLoughlin.

Thomas McPherson learned quickly that what a rogue does with you, he will do to you, for Heroux turned on McPherson as surely as he had been turned against McLoughlin. Kawannassé recalled that, in the moments after McLoughlin died, "I saw Heroux in a violent rage at McPherson, and heard him say that he would certainly shoot him if he said a harsh word to him." There would have been a certain poetic justice in McPherson being destroyed by his own creation, but Simpson's timely arrival at Stikine saved McPherson and ultimately rewrote the narrative.

McPherson's assumption that he would gain command after McLoughlin's death proved unfounded. His reign over Fort Stikine was mercifully short-lived, ending the moment Simpson set foot on the dock. The Governor bypassed McPherson completely, choosing instead to install Charles Dodd as the outpost's chief trader and George Blenkinsop as second-in-command. Thomas was unceremoniously demoted to the status of clerk, but he once again extracted revenge in his own inimitable fashion. Dodd foolishly removed McLoughlin's bedroom barricade, and McPherson resumed his magpie ways, creeping into Dodd's room in the dead of night to pilfer the storeroom keys and buy the temporary affections of the local harlots.

McPherson may also have used his brief stint in the chief's office to conceal his life of crime. In his quest for love, he stole a large quantity of goods, including the very trade wares Simpson first noticed missing. It is possible that, in the hours after the murder, McPherson forged the note and inventory of materials given to Fleury's wife, placing it in McLoughlin's desk to account for the items he had taken. It bears noting that many of the articles included on the list are those McPherson admitted to stealing, and that the spelling and grammatical errors in the inventory and cover letter are more consistent with McPherson's writing than that of McLoughlin.

§

In the end, the killing of John McLoughlin Jr. accomplished nothing for those who conspired to do it, but it also cost them nothing. Thomas McPherson escaped all earthly reckoning for the crime, as did his confederates Urbain Heroux and Pierre Kannaquassé. McPherson even remained on the HBC payroll for years following the murder. In 1844, McPherson and a dozen others were sent by John McLoughlin Sr. to Upper Canada to stand trial, but McPherson went as a witness, not a defendant. When Governor Simpson ordered them to stop, McPherson and his cohort disappeared into the mists of time — unreprimanded, unrepentant, and unremembered.

Neither Simpson nor Dr. McLoughlin understood McPherson's role in the crime, but there was one man in the Honourable Company who recognized his culpability. In a letter to Governor Simpson, Committee secretary Archibald Barclay wrote: "If ever men deserved hanging, Urbain Herous, [*sic*] Pierre Kanaquasse [*sic*] and the scoundrel McPherson ought to be *strung up*." But Simpson would hear none of it. He had based his knee-jerk verdict on McPherson's self-serving account, and his elephantine ego would not allow him to reverse his decision. The Governor fired back at the Committee, defending himself against allegations that McPherson was too addled to be trusted and too mendacious to be credible: "Thomas McPherson...I firmly believe perfectly understood every question I put to him; and I further believe that his statements are true." What other choice did Simpson have? To condemn McPherson after the fact would be to concede he had made a mistake. In the end, Simpson's pride saved McPherson, just as his apathy had spared Heroux.

Thursday, April 21, 1842 — Midday
FORT STIKINE

The last of the morning fog burned away as Louis Leclaire made a coffin, finishing the solemn task around eleven o'clock. The body of John McLoughlin was laid inside and the lid securely nailed. For want of a better location, the box was then taken from the carpentry shop to the bathhouse. As the pallbearers laid the casket down, Urbain Heroux surprised everyone by pleading, "My friends, pray do not suspect me. I have a wife and child to provide for and I am not wicked enough to commit such a deed." His defence rang hollow, for no one within earshot questioned Heroux's capacity for evil. To soothe the simmering tensions, "McPherson gave the men a dram" of spirits. It was a curious choice, given how poorly the last round of drinks had gone down, but it was the only way he knew to buy the men's loyalty. As dusk approached, the fort's complement settled in for a fitful night.

The morning of April 23, 1842, dawned clear, with a light westerly wind. The time had come to commit John McLoughlin's remains to the *Sandy Hills*. The fort's journal records the event without sentiment: "The men were employed digging the grave for the body and about 12:00 at noon it was deposited in the ground." Ceremony was hard to come by. They lowered the fort's flag to half-mast, and "the corpse was carried to the grave by Lasserte, Pressé, Leclaire, and some Kanakas, but Urbain did not touch it." As the coffin hit bedrock, "the salute of a gun" rang out across the barren tidal plain. The grave was dug some distance from the fort, just beyond the high-water line, and marked with a rugged wooden cross. In a final hollow gesture, "the men drank another dram," a cynical toast to their fallen leader's good health.

Unwanted, unwelcome, and unprotected, McLoughlin's wife left the fort immediately after the burial, running back to the shelter of her father, the tribal chief. As "McLoughlin's wife" once again became "Quatkie's daughter," life at Fort Stikine returned to normal, or what passes for normal in hell. Time, tide, and fur wait for no man, and the day's journal records the officers of Stikine traded "five black bear skins for various articles" that afternoon. They also welcomed visitors when "Several canoes arrived from up the river." John McLoughlin was not yet two hours in the ground, and already every last trace of him had been erased.

THIRTEEN

Endgames

The Hudson's Bay Company closed the book on the death of John McLoughlin, but the fallout reverberated for years. Dr. McLoughlin never relented, even when all hope of victory (as he defined it) was lost. He ignored Simpson's edict and ordered his son's body exhumed, but the remains were too decomposed to autopsy. John Jr. was reinterred at Fort Vancouver on October 25, 1843, in a "divine Service which was chanted for him." His bones were buried "on the rising ground near to the woods" in a simple ceremony attended by his parents, Paul Fraser, and James Douglas. The removal of McLoughlin's mortal remains from Stikine began as an impotent protest, but the gesture soon transformed into a powerful symbol of paternal love and guilt. His grave was marked and faithfully tended by his father in a display of care rarely evident during McLoughlin's tumultuous life.

As for the fort that had witnessed such misery, it continued to be dogged by intrigue and scandal: "Stikine remained open long enough to fill a few more despatches with news about another plot against officers' lives." Simpson's plan to phase out the west coast trading posts soon came to pass. Fort Tako was closed as scheduled, and Stikine was abandoned in 1849, although Simpson insisted McLoughlin's murder did not figure in his decision. The fort closures were entirely a matter of economics, as over-trapping had "beavered out" the region, and "the posts were not remunerative."

John McLoughlin Jr. was not the only casualty of Fort Stikine. The outpost's first commander, William Rae, also met his end with a single bullet. In Simpson's 1832 assessment of the troops, Rae earned praise as "a very fine high spirited well conducted Young man...Stout, Strong and active," who also happened to be "quite a Mechanical Genius." Blindness in one eye disqualified Rae "from constant Desk Work," but the Governor marked him as "a rising Man in the country." Simpson later hand-picked Rae to establish a new California outpost, but that fort struggled from its inception. When Simpson visited Yerba Buena in 1841, he dismissed the location (now downtown San Francisco) as "a wretched place." The Governor saved some disdain for Rae, berating him for granting easy credit to settlers. Sir George, thoroughly disgusted with the fort's limp bottom line, ordered the post closed. Dr. McLoughlin wanted to give Rae more time to turn things around and delayed the closure, but Simpson was adamant. On the morning of January 19, 1845, William Rae took his company-issue revolver and "shot himself in his wife's bedroom."

Rae had always been a troubled man. He was a heavy drinker and had "indulged in a torrid affair with a Spanish woman." Yet Dr. McLoughlin blamed Simpson for the man's death, just as he blamed the Governor for all of life's misfortunes. In another rambling, bitter letter to Pelly and the London Committee, McLoughlin placed Rae's suicide on Simpson's shoulders, citing the closure of the outpost in Yerba Buena as the catalyst for his son-in-law's downward spiral. Sir George counterpunched, saying Rae had simply "collapsed under the strain of work and alcoholism." Whatever culpability Simpson or the Company had in the man's death, the net result was the same: less than four years later, the HBC closed its operations in California and retreated northward.

Rae's body and soul lingered in the abandoned outpost, producing a curious footnote. In 1858, workmen digging new sewer lines near the old Yerba Buena trading post found a "glass-covered coffin containing the headless remains of Rae." These remains were buried later in a less fraught location, forever freeing him from the clutches of the Honourable Company.

The fort at the mouth of the Stikine River — that hell upon earth with a sink of pollution — had been operational for less than five years, but it had extracted a heavy price from Dr. John McLoughlin. The fur trade had made him a very wealthy man, but it had stolen everything of value, and the doctor tallied his losses with a simple equation: "Sir George Simpson's Visit here in 1841 has cost me Dear."

The unnatural deaths in his family were not the only price Dr. McLoughlin paid. His erratic behaviour had unnerved Governor Pelly, and in the spring of 1844 the London Committee decided to terminate McLoughlin's superintendency of the Columbia District. In a terse letter from the board, the doctor was told "he would no longer be in charge west of the mountains, and he was on furlough and leave of absence from mid-1846." Broken in heart and spirit, he vacated Fort Vancouver as soon as the notice arrived in 1845, although technically he would remain in the Company's employ until 1849.McLoughlin's unquenchable rage at the mishandling of his son's death forever tainted his view of the corporation to which he had given his life's blood, but it was not the only reason he and the Company parted ways. A few of the doctor's contemporaries thought the falling-out had more to do with his rabid commitment to the territory of Oregon. In his 1878 oral history of the region, J. Quinn Thornton claimed the rift developed over the HBC's treatment of immigrants. The popular media of the age was filled with favourable depictions of the west coast's limitless bounties, and those images enticed scores of desperate families to the Pacific Northwest. Many of the pioneers were poorly equipped, and few had any experience in growing crops so far north; as a result, hundreds soon teetered on the brink of starvation. Dr. McLoughlin could not allow American settlers to starve, even if those homesteaders threatened the HBC's monopoly, and his compassion put him at odds with Company policies. McLoughlin told his superiors: "I found women & children there in a suffering condition; they were in want of food & clothing & while, as a Trader, I could have wished they had not come, yet as a man and as a Christian, I could not turn away from them." Thornton recalled how battle lines were drawn after "Dr. McLaughlin [sic] furnished them with seed & Cattle & some tea. His fellow officers found fault with this and accused him of assisting the Americans to occupy the country; that without such assistance they could not sustain themselves here and must leave. He said he did not wish them to come but they were here and he could not see them suffer."

Tales of the doctor's largesse reached George Simpson, who called McLoughlin on his reckless charity and "generous treatment of potential American settlers." The two adversaries also differed over how to harvest the Pacific coast. Simpson's policy was "to destroy [the fur-bearing animals] along the whole frontier," ensuring "every effort be made to lay waste the country, so as to offer no inducements to petty traders to encroach on the Company's limits." Dr. McLoughlin had always known their fur trading days were numbered, and so he established mills and farms to help sustain the employees. Simpson thought it was all a colossal waste of time, preferring to trap a region clean and move on, sustainability be damned. Their fiercest disagreement, however, pivoted on whether the HBC should use ships, as Simpson advocated, or fixed trading posts (McLoughlin's method of choice) to service the west coast. The two men almost came to blows over a single vessel, the SS *Beaver*, a hulking steamship Simpson had commissioned in hopes of "overawing the natives," but which Dr. McLoughlin dismissed as "a travelling circus." If you look closely, you can see the ghost of John McLoughlin Jr. hovering over every conflict.

Whatever professional alliance Simpson and McLoughlin once had, the two men no longer saw eye to eye on anything, least of all how best to deal with people. Both were dangerously pig-headed, willing to fight to the death to be proven right. They held wildly divergent business philosophies: Simpson was myopic and favoured minimal investment, while McLoughlin was in it for the long, expensive haul. They were also oceans apart when it came to their goals, for Simpson was running a company while McLoughlin was building a new world.

Something had to give. The Committee summoned Dr. McLoughlin to London and "rebuked him sharply" for his actions with the settlers, as well as for his disregard of Simpson's orders. The doctor could take no more. McLoughlin squared his shoulders, steeled himself with all the dignity he could muster, and in a cool calm voice declared: "Gentlemen, I have served you some many years.... I have served you faithfully and the Hudson's Bay Company service under my administration has achieved a wonderful success.... And I will serve you no longer." With that, the doctor "threw up his commission" and resigned.

McLoughlin's exit was graceful, but in his letter of resignation to Governor Pelly, he wrote: "I have Drunk and am Drinking the cup of Bitterness to the very Dregs...So Distressed am I at being disgraced and Degraded." His ignominy did not stop at the water's edge, for there remained the issue of an outstanding debt he had incurred for the materials given to the

American immigrants. Out of sheer spite, Simpson wanted McLoughlin to pay back the balance owing on the credit he had extended to the settlers, but it was a bill the doctor never paid.

Simpson could be ruthless, but he was not entirely without heart. After McLoughlin formally resigned, Sir George — who had once cut off the doctor's pay to teach him a lesson — did not fight the Committee when they voted to award McLoughlin "a very generous pension." It was the closest Simpson ever came to benevolence.

In his heyday, Dr. McLoughlin had been feared, but in his senescence he was to be pitied. His son's death, and his subsequent abdication from the Honourable Company, left him a shadow of his former mountainous self; "his word was no longer law...he had, at the age of sixty-one, like Samson, been shorn of his power." The resignation had stripped him of all authority and wounded his pride, leaving him "fairly crushed in a business like but kingly way."

He retired to Oregon City and applied for US citizenship, hoping to find solace among those he had once helped, but the settlers now viewed him with suspicion. Certain "American demagogues" accused McLoughlin of having "caused American citizens to be massacred by hundreds of savages." It was a stinging rejection of their guardian angel, who once claimed to have "saved all I could."

The man who would one day be heralded as the "Father of Oregon" received no such recognition in his lifetime, and he spent the remainder of his days in "a continuous protest against this dethronement." Riddled with guilt, cast aside by the fur trade, and set adrift in a hostile land not his own, McLoughlin filled his final days and letters with acrimonious regret: "I might better have been shot forty years ago than to have lived here and tried to build up a family and an estate."

His bitterness was briefly tempered by a single piece of paper, a document the doctor "prized most" in this world. His salvation came in the form of an Apostolic Brief, dated February 27, 1846, and signed by His Excellency Pope Gregory XVI. The brief declared John McLoughlin Sr. to be a Knight of St. Gregory the Great. The honour, bestowed on civilian and military Roman Catholics for outstanding service to the Holy See, came as a great comfort to McLoughlin in his darkest hour. It was printed on the finest vellum, the sort of stock normally reserved for diplomas or currency. The proclamation bore enough embossed seals to assure its authenticity and was accompanied by a red and yellow ribbon affixed to a medal, an octagonal cross to be worn "at the breast on the left side after the ordinary fashion of Knights." For a man terrified of introspection, this last token of external validation sustained him in his final days. Dr. John McLoughlin died in stiff-lipped discontent on September 3, 1857. He was seventy-three.

His wife, Marguerite Wadin McKay McLoughlin, outlived the first of her sons and the latter of her husbands. She died on February 25, 1860, at the family home in Oregon City. Marguerite had never shared the piety that earned her husband his papal knighthood, and as she lay on her deathbed, she initially refused the sacraments. For the sake of appearances, the local archbishop dispatched some nuns from St. Mary's Academy in Portland to attend Marguerite in her final hours. She tolerated this eleventh-hour scrimmage to save her soul, lingering for five days "in a sort of agony which is at length terminated by a most peaceful death."

§

A disillusionment of sorts also plagued the saga's last surviving headliner, Sir George Simpson. After his knighthood, Simpson bullied his way into the gentrified class, leaving behind his carefully crafted persona as the rugged "wilderness administrator" to become "a diplomat and international financier." For a man devoid of a moral core, the shift was disquietingly simple, but the transition was not without difficulties. Splitting his focus robbed him of his power base within the HBC, which he had taken to calling the "harassing service." As he felt his dominance slipping, the Governor overcompensated with frivolous ceremony and empty ritual. His annual inspection tours devolved "into theatrical productions," and it became difficult to take the little man seriously. By the 1850s, Simpson's "swath of absolute power could no longer hold," and he was progressively marginalized by the company he once ruled.

His few remaining cronies stepped in to salvage his wounded ego. They arranged for the Governor to be presented with "a very valuable piece of plate...as a mark of respect and esteem; and as proof of his popularity," a ridiculous bit of burlesque conjured up by those seeking the favour of a dying king. To commission the meaningless trophy, Simpson's covey of minions took up a petition, forcing others to sign, "well knowing that none dare refuse." Simpson had earned such odium, for he had crafted the Company in his own image, infecting every last crevice with his "pontifical sternness" and incurable need to belittle others for his own amusement.

Simpson appeared indestructible, but the lone chink in his armour had always been his health. He was convinced he suffered from "determination of blood to the head," a condition which holds no modern equivalent. He often groused of chronic headaches, what he called "my old complaint in the head," brought on by his frequent bouts of insomnia. Cold weather inevitably triggered "affections of the Lungs and Bowels," and his delicate constitution was further taxed by overwork. Simpson both complained and boasted that he "fagged Night & Day and became so unwell in consequence." He obsessed over his own well-being, convinced he would be struck down at any moment by an attack of apoplexy. Others suffered for his fear, including William Todd, the chief trader and surgeon of the Red River outpost, as Simpson kept Todd on call around the clock. Simpson demanded to be bled almost to the point of exsanguination, a request Todd often refused at the risk of being fired. Simpson was so accustomed to having his orders followed and was so anxious to receive Todd's ministrations that when the surgeon was summoned to bleed him, he always found the Governor with his "arm bared up and ready for the operation." A diagnosis of hypochondria would not be out of the question.

Given his druthers, Simpson would have lived and ruled forever, but his mortality won out in the end. Failing health and a lifetime of excess took their toll on the once immutable Caesar, and in 1844, Simpson ordered long-time HBC employee Duncan Finlayson and his wife, Isobel (Frances Simpson's sister), to move into his palatial estate in Lachine to serve as his personal assistant and nurse. At this stage in his life, there were few people Simpson could trust. The Finlaysons reluctantly agreed and were soon ensconced in the servant's quarters, replete with a soul-crushing view of the HBC warehouse across the way. Finlayson complained privately to a friend that he hated his "enforced intimacy with the governor, who was accustomed to having his own way," and confessed he intended to resign from the service simply to be rid of Simpson.

Sir George had only been thinking of his own welfare when he ordered the Finlaysons to move in, but it was soon Frances who was in need of constant care. Always fragile, she had never adapted to the ceaseless travel that was a major part of her life as Sir George's better half. In her final days she sat, pale and consumptive, racked with a persistent cough that threatened to tear her twig-boned frame asunder. Frances was no match for the ravages of tuberculosis and died peacefully at home on March 21, 1853. She was just forty years old.

§

By the mid-nineteenth century, the HBC's monopoly was under siege on all fronts. A new wave of settlers encroached on Company-held territory after the railroad opened the American west, and many pioneers crept northward in search of arable land. Those years also saw the deaths of many of the key players in the fur trade, including Pelly, Peter Skene Ogden, and John Rowand. The changes threatened to sink Simpson, and his detractors delighted in his lost potency. Edward Ermatinger gleefully chronicled his decline: "Our old Chief, Sir George, as you describe him, tottering under the infirmities of age, has seen his best days. His light canoe, with choice of men, and of women too! can no longer administer to his gratification." Yet despite their prognostications as to his limited future, Simpson soldiered on, so much so that "some suspected he must be in league with the powers of darkness."

Simpson's pact with Satan was leading him into dangerous territory with the HBC. By his own reckoning, the Company's charter was now of little value, and Simpson argued it was best sold while others still saw some worth in its holdings. The charter was offered first to the obvious choice: the English. The British government, however, knew all too well what troubles lurked in Rupert's Land and decided to pass, leaving Canada as the lone potential buyer. Unfortunately, in 1850, the colony could not afford to purchase the territory. It wanted the land for free, as a large and vocal segment of the Canadian populace felt the region was rightfully theirs. Those in favour of annexation waged a ruthless campaign, attacking the Company's monopoly and its flagrant exploitation of the aboriginal people. A groundswell of support grew louder as the anti-HBC rhetoric (which included calls for the expansion of western settlement and the promise of prime farming land) found a receptive audience.

Simpson tried to stem the tide by declaring the country to be useless for agriculture or settlement by Europeans. The Governor was called before the Canadian Parliament to represent the interests of the Honourable Company, where he emphatically announced, "I do not think that any part of the Hudson's Bay territory are well adapted for settlement." He was even less discreet in private, telling John McTavish he was "quite disgusted with the country."

Simpson's clumsy defence of the Company angered its senior members and converted Dunbar Douglas, the sixth Earl of Selkirk, once an ardent Simpson supporter, into an outspoken advocate for the Governor's retirement. Selkirk called Simpson's lacklustre performance at Parliament a "wretched expedition," and the lord's displeasure was soon shared by the Committee as a whole, which came to see Simpson as "deficient in sound judgement," and felt "his nerves had quite given way." Conveniently forgetting his prior calls to sell off the charter, Simpson reversed his stance and began campaigning to retain the HBC's monopoly. The sale of Rupert's Land was temporarily shelved.

With his wife dead and the Committee no longer in his thrall, Simpson made do as best he could. He sloughed off the care of his four legitimate children to lesser mortals and resumed a punishing work schedule, but his health continued to decline. Simpson shrank in frame and persona, and his once inexhaustible dynamism was reduced to a simpering mewl. Seizures and intermittent bouts of idiopathic blindness kept him bedridden until even he was forced to concede he could no longer fulfill his professional obligations. As he had so often said of others, "'Tis high time he should make room for a better man," even as he steadfastly maintained there were no better men than he.

Faced with the inevitable, Simpson tendered his resignation in a confidential yet surprisingly emotional letter to the Committee. He reflected on his four decades of service: "I have never been off duty for a week at a time, nor have I ever allowed Family ties and personal convenience to come in competition with the claims I considered the Company to have on me." He also developed a strangely nostalgic view of life in Canada, fondly recalling his days in the bush. He often sighed "for the Indian Country, the squaws, and skins, and savages," the same aboriginals he had so ruthlessly disparaged while in their domain. Following his resignation, he stepped back from the Company's day-to-day operations, but he retained a ceremonial role that left one foot firmly planted in Rupert's Land.

The first test of Simpson as decorous figurehead came in the summer of 1860 when he was asked to play host to the Prince of Wales during his tour of the colony. Simpson wanted the future monarch's inspection of Île Dorval to eclipse his prior stops in the Maritimes and Montreal, visits much lauded by the press. To that end, Sir George crafted an excessive bit of pageantry grounded in his fond remembrances of a once-vibrant fur trade. He arranged for a flotilla of canoes, but as the vast majority of traditional Canadian voyageurs were now dead or retired, Simpson was forced to marshal the services of some local Iroquois. The Governor thought the aboriginals were second rate, claiming they could not hold a candle to the "dash, vivacity and song" of the Metis.

On August 29, 1860, His Royal Highness made his way toward Dorval in the imperial carriage. Three miles out, the party boarded a barge to cross to the island and Simpson's waiting extravaganza. Rain had plagued their voyage, but as the ferry approached the dock, sunlight burst from the heavens. Taking their cue from the weather, the flotilla of canoes (each bearing twenty men) descended on the royal retinue. Frustrated by the lack of proper voyageurs, Simpson had overcompensated by dressing the men in war paint, feathers, and red serge, transforming his actual Iroquois into stereotypical "Indians" suitable for the European palate. All who witnessed the theatrics declared Simpson's effusive display to be "a social triumph."

For one brief moment, Sir George Simpson had reclaimed the admiration of the London Committee, and he intended to make the most of it. On September 1 he took a final victory lap through the HBC offices in Montreal, giving his former colleagues ample opportunity to congratulate him. Drenched in felicitations, Simpson then mounted his carriage and was headed to his home in Lachine when he fell violently ill. He took to his bed, where he languished for six days, drifting in and out of lucidity. One moment he thought his nurses were trying to murder him, while the next, struck by a wave of guilt-induced generosity, Simpson wrote sizable bonus cheques to his long-time employees. After his death, the executors of his estate refused to honour the drafts, claiming the very existence of such gifts proved Sir George was not of sound mind when he issued them.

John Henry Lefroy, a scientist who travelled throughout Rupert's Land, once joked that Simpson was "a fellow whom nothing will kill," a hyperbole that begged to be refuted. In the end, George Simpson died at half past ten on September 7, 1860, the victim of his own faulty circulatory system. His official cause of death was haemorrhagic apoplexy, with convulsion — Victorian medical speak for a massive stroke — although historian Frits Pannekoek is convinced Simpson actually succumbed to tertiary syphilis. Given the damn-the-torpedoes manner in which he lived, Governor Simpson died with far less fuss than one might expect.

This being Simpson, however, fuss was inevitable. He was laid to rest at Mount Royal Cemetery in Montreal beneath a monument fit for an emperor, a job description to which he aspired and arguably ascended. He no doubt would have loved the pomp and circumstance accompanying his funeral, although his ego would not have allowed him to see that many in attendance were more jubilant than mournful. Even in death, his enemies were legion. Far more curious was the seemingly authentic display of grief from representatives of the First Nations community. As the funeral procession wended its way to the cemetery, "the Caughnawaga Indians escorted the melancholy cortege…the red men and their squaws sung a wild, and doleful but solemn dirge," a tender and somewhat remarkable show of respect for a man who had shown them nothing but contempt. The few who still harboured warm feelings for Sir George took some measure of comfort from the timing of his death. Dugald Mactavish observed: "The Little Emperor's light has gone out, just after he basked in a final blaze of glory."

Simpson was gone but his legacy was secure. Even his detractors conceded his reign had been a success, just as surely as "his own friends will admit that much of that success must be ascribed to his good fortune rather than to his talents."

Over Simpson's dead body, Canada finally purchased the rights to the Company lands, assuming ownership on December 1, 1869. Sir George Simpson and Dr. John McLoughlin helped build the Hudson's Bay Company into one of the most profitable corporations in the world, and their creation outlasted them both. The monopoly once denounced for doing business "as if drawn by a dead horse" lives on in the venerable department stores that bear its name and still sell the iconic striped point blankets that were the currency of its trading days. Three of its largest forts became provincial capitals—Fort Garry (now Winnipeg), Fort Edmonton, and Fort Victoria—while others, such as Fort Vancouver and Fort William, have been preserved as national heritage sites.

Not surprisingly, nothing remains of Fort Stikine. The fort lay abandoned until 1868, when the US military built Fort Wrangell near Stikine's crumbling, waterlogged footprint. Those who ignore the lessons of the past are condemned to repeat them, and the American soldiers experienced the same horrific conditions as their HBC predecessors. The US army gave up the site as a lost cause in 1877. The city of Wrangell rose slowly around the fort's listing walls, although a fire in the early 1950s razed all traces of the town's historic past. Those visiting Wrangell today would be hard pressed to find any sign of the fort, John McLoughlin Jr., or this sad chapter in the Hudson's Bay Company's history.

§

Justice does not always look the way we want it to. John McLoughlin Jr. did not deserve to die as he did, nor did he earn the character assassination that followed. We cannot retroactively punish McPherson or Heroux, but we can amend our image of the victim. Let history record that John McLoughlin Jr., the so-called bastard of Fort Stikine, was neither a bastard by birth nor in bearing; he was simply a fatherless son. The indifferent response to his death spoke more to the damaged character of George Simpson than it did of McLoughlin's failings. There was nothing about his death that was "justifiable."

It bears noting this case was always solvable, for this was not a murder that lay dormant for decades, patiently awaiting the advent of new technologies in order to be resolved. No genetic testing or cutting-edge computer simulations were needed to ferret out the identity of those responsible. Ultimately, all that was required was an impartial eye and a systematic assessment of the evidence. This crime could have been solved the day it was committed, were it not for Governor Simpson, Dr. McLoughlin, and their respective agendas and personality disorders.

The mechanics of the crime are now credibly established. Urbain Heroux fired the fatal shot, at the urging of Thomas McPherson, and with the help of Pierre Kannaquassé and Antoine Kawannassé. More than 170 years on, even the question of why can be addressed with some certainty. An exhaustive search of the historical archive has yielded all the relevant information touching on the murder of John McLoughlin. What gaps remain will likely never be filled, given the capricious whims of time, but the motivation of those involved was clear.

Although Dr. John McLoughlin was quick to label what happened at Fort Stikine a mutinous conspiracy, the truth is far more mundane. It was a conspiracy, in that there were multiple perpetrators acting in concert, but it was not mutiny. In the end, Thomas McPherson did not stage a coup so much as throw a lethal temper tantrum. And so it falls to us as jurors to decide whether the killing of John McLoughlin was an act of treason or self-preservation, or the premeditated endgame of a petulant clerk and his malleable henchmen.

Perhaps the solution lies in the answer to another question: who was the real bastard of Fort Stikine? Although the epithet was first affixed to John McLoughlin, it no longer sticks. With so many reprehensible candidates on offer — Thomas McPherson, Urbain Heroux, Pierre Kannaquassé, George Simpson — it may be impossible to choose just one.

Murder is a loud word, and it easily distracts us from the second tragedy of Fort Stikine: the self-inflicted destruction of Dr. John McLoughlin. Embalmed alive by guilt and enshrouded by impotent rage, the doctor died alongside his son at Fort Stikine; it simply took him longer to lie down.

Some of us never learn to mourn, particularly great hulking "lords of the lands and the forests." Dr. McLoughlin was a product of a time when men lived by their wits and the strength of their spines. Emotions were a luxury they could not afford, a trifle best suited to women. Dismissing McLoughlin's inability to grieve as an artifact of his era or his sex is tempting but facile, for unprocessed sorrow can mire anyone, anytime, anywhere.

McLoughlin's quicksand was his unacknowledged guilt. He needed the Company to assign the blame for his son's death to Simpson so that he would not have to deal with his own culpability. He could have saved his son but he failed to act, to pay attention. This was a lifelong dynamic between the distant, demanding father and his untethered son who sought love and acceptance through his achievements.

Dr. McLoughlin demanded that the HBC, as the de facto legal system, deliver justice as he defined it, then railed when they refused to do so, a pattern that continues to manifest in courthouses to this day. Like McLoughlin, those who leave the courtroom disillusioned or bitter have entered with unrealistic expectations, narrow parameters for success, and the misguided belief that extracting their pound of flesh will alleviate their own suffering. We cannot expect the courts to do for us that which we cannot do for ourselves: make peace with our circumstances.

The pain we seek to avoid cannot be foisted onto others. Protection from harm, accountability, and punishment has its place in our collective search for justice, but it is not what brings peace. In the wake of tragedy and loss, the resolution must come from within.

Acknowledgements

My sincere thanks to Jennifer Keyser and Scott Rook of the Oregon Historical Society and Heidi Pierson of the National Park Service for their assistance in tracking down the only known images of John McLoughlin Jr. and his mother, among others. Thanks also to Theresa Langford, curator for the National Parks Service, for helping me search for McLoughlin's current gravesite. My undying gratitude to the archivists at Library and Archives Canada, who worked small miracles to get me materials in whatever ridiculous timeframes I gave them—I am truly thankful. Praise and gratitude also flow to the good folks at the provincial Archives of Manitoba, home to the Hudson's Bay Company Archives. I would like to single out Sjoeke Hunter and Mandy Malazdrewich in particular for thanks. A tip of the hat is also due Kelly-Ann Turkington, permissions/licensing officer for the Royal BC Museum.

There are some lovely people up in Wrangell, Alaska, who helped track down the ghosts of Fort Stikine, including local historian Bonnie Demerjian and Carol Rushmore, economic development director of the City and Borough of Wrangell. Kay Jabusch, librarian at Irene Ingle Public Library in Wrangell, hunted down some sources. A heartfelt thanks to you all.

Words cannot express my gratitude to the wonderful people who work the reference desks at the Killam Library at Dalhousie University and the Spring Garden branch of the Halifax Public Library for all their help. As always, I am indebted to Dorothy, Ken, and Sandy at the Annapolis Royal branch of the Annapolis Valley Regional Library for their willingness to push the interlibrary loan system of the Nova Scotia library system to its limits.

Thanks also to the Eastend Arts Council, the Arts Council of Saskatchewan, and the generous citizens of Eastend, SK, for bestowing on me the Wallace Stegner Award for the Arts 2014. I loved every minute I spent in Wallace's historic home, and it was the perfect place to revise this manuscript.

Photographer Dan Froese has the patience of a saint and is deserving of some sort of award for what he has to put up with when working with me, but my sincere thanks will have to suffice. I am also indebted to my literary agent, Carolyn Swayze, for helping this book series see the light of day. Thanks also to an unsung group of heroes, friends, and early readers who have offered support, a kind word, or a kick in the pants as needed: Dr. Sarah Lathrop, Paula Sarson, Dr. Stephanie Davy-Jow, Karen Fowler, Dorothy McDonald, "Richard the Fabulous," and so many more.

I have been incredibly lucky to have found a home for this series at Goose Lane Editions. My heartfelt thanks to Susanne Alexander, Julie Scriver, Martin Ainsley, Angela Williams, Kathleen Peacock, Colleen Kitts-Goguen, Chris Tompkins, Viola Spencer, and everyone who had a hand in bringing these books to life. Special thanks are due to my editor, Sarah Brohman, and copy editor, Audrey McClellan — you both made me a better writer, and for that I am eternally grateful.

Finally, a shout-out to Dr. Kent Fowler, a master of technologies modern and ancient, for working magic with his computer and rescuing more than a week's worth of archival research. You saved the day, Kent.

Illustration credits

Notes

Whenever possible, quotations were drawn from the original source material, and the spelling and punctuation were faithfully replicated. In some cases, quotations derived from secondary sources have modernized the language and sentence structure to make the text palatable to today's audiences.

There was tremendous variation in the spelling of surnames throughout the historical documentation, as well as in subsequent popular accounts. The spelling used in each individual's first deposition or witness statement was taken as the standard.

Preface

9 **Condition of the body and burial**: Details were taken from BBC News reports on September 12, 2012 ("Richard III dig: 'Strong evidence' bones are lost king," http://www.bbc.co.uk/news/uk-england-leicestershire-19561018) and February 4, 2013 ("Richard III dig: DNA confirms bones are king's," http://www.bbc.co.uk/news/uk-england-leicestershire-21063882).

DNA confirmation of identity: Nick Britten and Andrew Hough, "Richard III: Skeleton is the king," *The Telegraph*, February 4, 2013, http://www.telegraph.co.uk/science/science-news/9846693/Richard-III-skeleton-is-the-king.html.

Identification as biohistory's sole focus: A few investigators have pushed the boundaries of biohistory, casting new light on the health and lifestyle of past notables, such as questioning the origins of insanity in artist Vincent van Gogh (J.R. Hughes, "A reappraisal of the possible seizures of Vincent van Gogh," *Epilepsy and Behavior* 6, no. 4 [2005]: 504-10) and serial killer Jeffrey Dahmer (J. Jentzen et al., "Destructive hostility: The Jeffrey Dahmer case. A psychiatric and forensic study of a serial killer," *American Journal of Forensic Medicine and Pathology* 15, no. 4 [1994]: 283-94), or determining whether lead poisoning was the cause of Ludwig van Beethoven's deafness— Russell Martin, *Beethoven's Hair* (New York: Broadway Books, 2000).

Identification of Mengele: See, for example, M.E. Rogev, "The medicolegal identification of Josef Mengele," *Legal Medicine* (1993): 115-50.

Tentative identification of the apostle Luke: C. Vernesi et al., "Genetic characterization of the body attributed to the evangelist Luke," *Proceedings of the National Academy of Sciences USA* 98, no. 23 (2001): 13460-63.

10 **Investigators misuse DNA testing**: In 2004, a team of medical ethicists looked at the unbridled growth of biohistory and were disturbed by what they saw (see L.B. Andrews et al., "Constructing ethical guidelines for biohistory," *Science* 304 [2004]: 215-16). Chief among their concerns was the common practice of testing for testing's sake, and the study concluded that "historical analysis is undertaken for commercial considerations or mere sensationalism."

Wednesday, April 20, 1842—Midday

15 **"Indian Wife"**: This expression appears frequently throughout the documentation; see, for example, Dr. John McLoughlin's letter to George Simpson, February 1, 1844, D 5/10, Hudson's Bay Company Collection in the Provincial Archive of Manitoba (hereafter HBCA).

"Quatkie's daughter" and **"McLoughlin's wife"**: Narrative of Quatkie's daughter (McLoughlin Jr.'s wife) before Donald Manson, August 29, 1842, E13/1, folio 1-63, HBCA (hereafter "Narrative of Quatkie's daughter").

"I have had all the troubles": McLoughlin Jr. to John Work, February 14, 1842, E 13/1, folio 110-111, HBCA.

"I have had scarcely any rest": McLoughlin Jr. to John Work, December 2, 1841, E 13/1, folio 108-109, HBCA.

"situated...among a horde": The comment was attributed to George Simpson and was taken from "Remarks on the depositions taken by John McLoughlin Esq, by James Douglas Esq & by Donald Manson, Esq, respectively and on various letter declarations and regarding the death of John McLoughlin Junr at Fort Stikine on April 21, 1842. In the handwriting of Edward Hopkins, 1844," E13/1, folio 368-377, HBCA (hereafter "Remarks on the depositions").

"attempted to scale": From the entry for June 21, 1840, in the Fort Stikine Journal, 1842, B209/a/1, HBCA. Although the journal is marked 1842, it includes entries from the fort's creation dating back to 1840.

16 **Destruction of the bridge and capture of the chief:** Recounted in Hamar Foster, "Killing Mr. John: Law and jurisdiction at Fort Stikine, 1842-1846," in *Law for the Elephant, Law for the Beaver*, ed. John McLaren, Hamar Foster, and Chett Orloff (Pasadena, CA: Ninth Judicial Circuit Historical Society, 1992), 152 (hereafter "Killing Mr. John").

"Mr. John has bad white men": From an "Indian report" received by Chief Factor John Work, cited in Foster, "Killing Mr. John," 149.

Kannaquassé's repeated assassination attempts: Described in a statement given by one of Fort Stikine's clerks: Kakepé's deposition before Donald Manson, July 24, 1842, E13/1, folio 197, HBCA.

"to poison McLoughlin": Nahua's deposition before James Douglas, May 18, 1843, E13/1, folio 246-248, HBCA.

"would do no such thing": Ibid. In his deposition, Pierre Kannaquassé freely admits asking Nahua and other Kanakas to poison McLoughlin. All refused. See Kannaquassé's deposition taken at Nisqually, July 15, 1842, with two separate addenda from July 16, 1842, E13/1, folio 89-103, HBCA (hereafter "Kannaquassé's deposition").

Needed to await McLoughlin Sr.'s decision regarding punishment: Nahua's deposition before James Douglas, May 18, 1843. Nahua claimed he told John Jr. of the threat and that McLoughlin "beat Pierre" and said "he would tell his father, who would punish him properly."

"I am still amongst the living": McLoughlin Jr. to John Work, December 2, 1841, original emphasis.

"all that does not trouble me": Ibid.

17 **"the Blue devils":** Ibid.

"I do not know what to do": McLoughlin Jr. to Roderick Finlayson, February 26, 1842, cited in W. Kaye Lamb's "Introduction" in E.E. Rich, ed., *The Letters of John McLoughlin from Fort Vancouver to the Governor and Committee, First Series, 1825-38*, vol. IV (London: Hudson's Bay Records Society, 1941), xxxvii.

"was always trying to catch": Charles Dodd's deposition regarding the murder of John McLoughlin Jr., August 1842, with an addendum from November 9, 1842, E13/1, folio 124-126, HBCA.

Beat the guard for sleeping: Kannaquassé's narrative regarding the murder of John McLoughlin Jr., July 1842, E13/1, folio 82-89, HBCA (hereafter "Kannaquassé's narrative").

Nahua does not bring breakfast: Nahua's deposition before James Douglas, May 18, 1843. Nahua would later testify he had left the fort without permission to fetch water.

Details of the day's weather: From two sources. The first is the fort's journal entry for April 20, 1842, which reads: "Weather cloudy with several showers of rain. Wind moderate from south east." The second source is the narrative of Quatkie's daughter, which noted that the day was "very rainy and cold."

18   **"a little English":** Cited in Foster, "Killing Mr. John," 189.

      "every night before he went": Narrative of Quatkie's daughter.

I: "Lamentable Deficiency"
Chapter One: L'Enfant Terrible

21   **"l'enfant terrible":** Burt Brown Barker, *The McLoughlin Empire and Its Rulers* (Glendale, CA: Arthur H. Clark Company, 1959), 107 (hereafter *The McLoughlin Empire*).

      McLoughlin Jr.'s birthplace: Ibid., 38. The only means of narrowing down the location is his father's correspondence. McLoughlin Sr. was stationed at Vermilion Lake in 1811-12. On March 22, 1812, he sent a letter from Vermilion Lake; however, on August 12, 1812, he wrote from Fort William. (Barker also considers Lac La Pluie a remote possibility as John Jr.'s birthplace.)

      "proud giant" and **"such a figure as I should not":** From the entry for McLoughlin Sr. in "The Character Book of Governor George Simpson, 1832" (hereafter "Simpson's Character Book"), reprinted in Glyndwr Williams, ed., *Hudson's Bay Miscellany 1670-1870*, Publications of the Hudson's Bay Record Society 30 (Winnipeg: Hudson's Bay Record Society, 1975), 176.

      "Stature tall. Hair white": Eloisa Harvey, "The Life of John McLoughlin, Governor of the Hudson's Bay Company possessions of the Pacific Slope at Fort Vancouver," volume 1, B-12, (1887): 25, MG 29 C15, Bancroft Collection, Library and Archives Canada (LAC) (hereafter "The Life of John McLoughlin").

22   **"he had a rapid way of speaking":** J. Quinn Thornton, "Oregon History," volume 1: 10, MG 29, C15, Bancroft Collection, LAC.

      "tolerably well" and **"a good deal of influence":** Williams, *Hudson's Bay Miscellany*, 176.

      "My father was very quick tempered": Harvey, "The Life of John McLoughlin," 11.

      "ungovernable Violent temper": Simpson's Character Book, 176.

      "stubborn, irascible": John S. Galbraith *The Little Emperor: Governor Simpson of the Hudson's Bay Company* (Toronto: Macmillan, 1976), 100 (hereafter *The Little Emperor*).

      "was well known for his use": Ibid., 45.

      "what he said must be so": Harvey, "The Life of John McLoughlin," 23.

"I think he required those about him": Ibid.

"Right off he cooled down": Ibid.

"the lords of the lakes and the forests": Cited in Galbraith, *The Little Emperor*, 18.

23   **McLoughlin Sr.'s birth details:** Barker, *The McLoughlin Empire*, 23.

McLoughlin Sr.'s petition to practise medicine: Reproduced in Barker, *The McLoughlin Empire*, plate #10.

"behaved honestly, he possesses talents": Ibid., plate #11.

McLoughlin Sr. pushes soldier into the mud: Peter C. Newman, *Caesars of the Wilderness* vol. 2 of *Company of Adventurers* (Markham, ON: Penguin, 1987), 206; and Dorothy Nafus Morrison, *The Eagle and the Fort: The Story of John McLoughlin* (Portland, OR: Western Imprints, The Press of the Oregon Historical Society, 1984), 4 (hereafter *The Eagle & the Fort*), among other sources. All Dr. McLoughlin ever said on the matter was: "It was entirely my own want of conduct that I came up to this Country. It was not a matter of Choice but of Necessity on my part" (from an unidentified letter, cited in Morrison, *The Eagle & the Fort*, 3).

McLoughlin Sr. dispatched to Kaministikwia: Dr. McLoughlin to Simon Fraser, July 1, 1808, reprinted in Barker, *The McLoughlin Empire*, 147-48.

"his sad Experiment": Cited in Morrison, *The Eagle & the Fort*, 15.

"giving full legal status": Barker, *The McLoughlin Empire*, 38-39. It bears noting that Dr. McLoughlin had taken a prior "country wife" before Marguerite, with whom he had a son named Joseph (Morrison, *The Eagle & the Fort*, 18). Although details are scant, it is assumed the first wife died while Joseph was very young.

24   **Dr. Simon Fraser's biography:** From his last will and testament, probated June 28, 1844, and reprinted in Barker, *The McLoughlin Empire*, 294-95.

"on account of the habit": Simon Fraser to John McLoughlin Jr., January 12, 1836, in Barker, *The McLoughlin Empire*, 218-20.

"I blamed your mother for this": Ibid.

"corrupted the morals": Ibid.

"a *very poor* letter writer": George Roberts, "Recollections of George B. Roberts," volume 1, A-83, (1878): 66, MG 29, C 15, Bancroft Collection, LAC, with original emphasis.

25   **"I am so situated":** Dr. McLoughlin to Simon Fraser, March 15, 1825, reprinted in Barker, *The McLoughlin Empire*, 175-77.

"I feel very much obliged": Dr. McLoughlin to Simon Fraser, January 2, 1823, in Barker, *The McLoughlin Empire*, 173-74.

Three years without a letter: Barker, *The McLoughlin Empire*, 108.

"You are perfectly at liberty": Dr. McLoughlin to Simon Fraser, September 14 1823, in Barker, *The McLoughlin Empire*, 174-75.

26   **"a frail child":** Barker, *The McLoughlin Empire*, 44.

"my object is not to give her": Dr. McLoughlin to Simon Fraser, March 15, 1825, in Barker, *The McLoughlin Empire*, 175-77.

"the Girl cannot be a nun": Simon Fraser to Dr. McLoughlin, April 20, 1827, in Barker, *The McLoughlin Empire*, 182-84.

Invoice of £80 for tuition: Barker, *The McLoughlin Empire*, 45.

"never at ease with a problem": Williams, *Hudson's Bay Miscellany*, 153.

"a filthy irregular place": Attributed to George Simpson, cited in Galbraith, *The Little Emperor*, 32.

27   **"meet any drafts necessary":** Barker, *The McLoughlin Empire*, 45.

Simpson's daughters in Scotland: James Raffan, *Emperor of the North: Sir George Simpson and the Remarkable Story of the Hudson's Bay Company* (Toronto: Harper Collins, 2007), 118 and 148 (hereafter *Emperor of the North*).

No relationship with daughters or mothers: Ibid., 50.

"been taught to be afraid": Cited in Galbraith, *The Little Emperor*, 128.

"was never fully a parent": Ibid., 202.

"the offense of absenting himself": George Simpson to Simon Fraser, March 14, 1828, reprinted in Galbraith, *The Little Emperor*, 186-87.

"flew into a violent passion": Ibid.

"instead of showing the least contrition": Ibid.

"to collect his Books": Ibid.

"the poor Schoolmaster was quite horror": Ibid.

"keep him another Week for £500": Ibid.

28   **"Up to the time the first complaint":** Ibid.

"him a Seat in our Counting House": Ibid.

"I have never been so grossly deceived": Ibid.

"full of wise and kind counsel": Barker, *The McLoughlin Empire*, 110.

Their entire relationship reduced to letters: In his letters, Dr. McLoughlin often belittled his son over petty offenses. For instance, he took the boy to task for his penmanship, noting: "Your hand writing is not such as it ought to be considering your age and the time you have been at school (it is very inferior to your sisters writing) which is certainly owing to yourself and shews you did not apply as much as you ought." Dr. McLoughlin to John Jr., February 1, 1830, quoted in Barker, *The McLoughlin Empire*, 190-91.

"could not go further with him": Barker, *The McLoughlin Empire*, 109.

"I cannot complain of your son": Simon Fraser to Dr. McLoughlin, April 20, 1827, quoted in Barker, *The McLoughlin Empire*, 182-84.

Wednesday, April 20, 1842 — Dusk

29 **The details of the day's work schedule:** come from Kannaquassé's narrative as well as Kannaquassé's deposition.

The evening's weather: described in William Lasserte's deposition before James Douglas, April 22, 1843, E13/1, folio 216-219, HBCA.

McLoughlin Jr. orders the squaring of logs: Louis Leclaire's deposition before Donald Manson, August 19, 1842, with an addendum August 25, 1842, E13/1, folio 1-63, HBCA.

Measurements and work schedule: William Lasserte's deposition before Donald Manson, August 11, 1842, with an addendum August 25, 1842, E13/1, folio 1-63, HBCA.

"five Indians from Tako": Narrative of Quatkie's daughter, along with every other deposition taken. The lone point of consensus among the men was that there were "five Indians from Tako" in the fort that night — every deposition taken agreed on this point, right down to the language used.

Simpson plans to close Tako: Foster, "Killing Mr. John," 158.

"considered improper": Narrative of Quatkie's daughter.

30 **"went out of the fort":** Nahua, deposition before James Douglas, May 18, 1843.

Nahua burst into tears: Francois Pressé, deposition before Donald Manson, August 20, 1842, with addendum from August 25, 1842, E13/1, folio 1-63, HBCA. Pressé recalled the cook was "crying while Mr. John was beating him."

31 **The diet at Stikine:** Stikine relied on the aboriginal groups for provisions, and numerous references can be found in the fort's journals and correspondence of the men's complaints regarding their repetitious and limited diet. See also Foster, "Killing Mr. John," 151.

"brackish water": Cited in Foster, "Killing Mr. John," 152.

Fleury carried to his room: Benoni Fleury's deposition before Donald Manson, August 19, 1842, with addenda dated August 23 and 25, 1842, E13/1, folio 1-63, HBCA.

"became very noisy and": Antoine Kawannassé, deposition before James Douglas, April 22, 1843, E13/1, folio 200-204, HBCA.

"my lad [mon enfans]": William Lasserte's deposition before James Douglas, April 22, 1843.

McLoughlin Jr. ties Fleury to the bed: Benoni Fleury's deposition before Donald Manson, August 19, 1842.

"Mr. John did this without anger": Phillip Smith, deposition before James Douglas, May 22, 1843, E13/1, folio 248-251, HBCA.

32 **McLoughlin Jr. slaps Fleury:** William Lasserte's deposition before James Douglas, April 22, 1843.

"got intoxicated": Fort Stikine Journal, 1842, entry for September 4, 1841, recorded by Roderick Finlayson.

McLoughlin Jr. slaps Lasserte: William Lasserte's deposition before James Douglas, April 22, 1843, and before Donald Manson, August 11, 1842.

"staring him in the face": Cited in Foster, "Killing Mr. John," 188.

"Do you wish to kill me": Kannaquassé's deposition, corroborated in William Lasserte's deposition before Donald Manson, August 11, 1842.

"fore entering his room": Antoine Kawannassé, deposition before James Douglas, April 22, 1843.

"We spent the evening in": Simon Aneuharazie, deposition before James Douglas, April 22, 1843, E13/1, folio 220-221, HBCA.

Chapter Two: Reckless Deeds on Distant Shores

33 **"I have written my friends":** Dr. McLoughlin's letter to John Jr., February 1, 1830 in Barker, *The McLoughlin Empire*, 190-91.

"I do not know what to do": Dr. McLoughlin, letter to Simon Fraser, March 19, 1826, in Barker, *The McLoughlin Empire*, 177-79.

"purchasing an Ensigncy for him": Simon Fraser's letter to Dr. McLoughlin, April 20, 1827, in Barker, *The McLoughlin Empire*, 182-84.

34 **"too infirm to control":** Barker, *The McLoughlin Empire*, 97.

"I do not expect to see": Sister St. Henry, letter to Simon Fraser, June 17, 1835 (translated from the original French), reprinted in Barker, *The McLoughlin Empire*, 213.

"he would fall from excesses": Sister St. Henry, letter to Simon Fraser, May 11, 1835, (translated from the original French), reprinted in Barker, *The McLoughlin Empire*, 210-11.

"The best thing that can be": Simon Fraser's letter to Dr. McLoughlin, April 20, 1827, in Barker, *The McLoughlin Empire*, 182-84.

"boys of mixed blood": Barker, *The McLoughlin Empire*, 109.

McLoughlin Jr. sent to Paris: Ibid., 111.

"young as you were": Simon Fraser's letter to McLoughlin Jr., January 12, 1836, in Barker, *The McLoughlin Empire*, 218-20.

Dr. McLoughlin learns of McLoughlin Jr.'s departure: From the postscript of John McLoughlin Jr.'s letter to Simon Fraser, October 26, 1831, reprinted in Barker, *The McLoughlin Empire*, 191-92.

"did not know John's age": Cited in Barker, *The McLoughlin Empire*, 108, paraphrasing Simon Fraser's letter to Dr. McLoughlin, April 20, 1827.

"I spent the winter very gay": McLoughlin Jr.'s letter to John Fraser, May 18, 1832, reprinted in Barker, *The McLoughlin Empire*, 192-93.

"I have been to the Kings": McLoughlin Jr.'s letter to John Fraser, February 24, 1833, reprinted in Barker, *The McLoughlin Empire*, 196-98.

36 **"I am received in the first":** McLoughlin Jr.'s letter to John Fraser, February 18, 1833, reprinted in Barker, *The McLoughlin Empire*, 196.

"I have learned to fence": Ibid.

"I have been attacked and called": Ibid.

"I shall always endeavour": McLoughlin Jr.'s letter to John Fraser, August 8, 1833, reprinted in Barker, *The McLoughlin Empire*, 199.

"Ah what can be the cause": McLoughlin Jr.'s letter to Simon Fraser, February 24, 1833, reprinted in Barker, *The McLoughlin Empire*, 196-98.

"Alas can I ever cease": Ibid.

"I have passed the examination": Ibid.

"I do not like to say much": Ibid.

37 **"the gesture angered John"**: Barker, *The McLoughlin Empire*, 115.

"very considerable" and **"very very rich"**: John Fraser, letter to McLoughlin Jr., August 1833, reprinted in Barker, *The McLoughlin Empire*, 201-2, with original emphasis.

Back rent owed by McLoughlin Jr.: I.H. Trudeau, letter to Simon Fraser, April 29, 1835, reprinted in Barker, *The McLoughlin Empire*, 207.

"having been deceived": Connet Confectioners, letter to Simon Fraser, June 1, 1835, reprinted in Barker, *The McLoughlin Empire*, 211-12.

"all expenses made by your nephew": Ibid.

38 **"I was much affected on Learning"**: Dr. McLoughlin's letter to John Fraser, February 14, 1836, reprinted in Barker, *The McLoughlin Empire*, 220-22.

"Is Junior so destitute of feeling": Ibid.

"I respect myself too much": Ibid.

"incorrigible": Simon Fraser's letter to McLoughlin Jr., January 12, 1836, in Barker, *The McLoughlin Empire*, 218-20.

"I am convinced you are depraved": Ibid.

"You must know that you are illiterate": Ibid.

39 **"spending freely for a man"**: Dr. McLoughlin's letter to Simon Fraser, February 4, 1837, reprinted in Barker, *The McLoughlin Empire*, 232-35.

"go to Montreal to resume": Ibid., original emphasis; Dr. McLoughlin refers to the postscript of a letter McLoughlin Jr. had written to Mr. Epps, administrator at the medical school, on November 21, 1835.

"when he made this most impudent": Dr. McLoughlin's letter to Simon Fraser, February 4, 1837.

"Conducts himself as a Gentleman": Ibid.

"any sum...under": Ibid.

"for my Uncle's negligence": McLoughlin Jr., letter to John Fraser, March 25, 1835, reprinted in Barker, *The McLoughlin Empire*, 205.

"squandered": McLoughlin Jr., letter to John Fraser, June 23, 1835, reprinted in Barker, *The McLoughlin Empire*, 213-14.

"It is certainly very strange": McLoughlin Jr., letter to Simon Fraser, June 15, 1835, reprinted in Barker, *The McLoughlin Empire*, 212.

40 **"Do not disappoint me"**: McLoughlin Jr., letter to John Fraser, February 14, 1835, reprinted in Barker, *The McLoughlin Empire*, 204.

"Who is then to pay my": McLoughlin Jr., letter to John Fraser, June 23, 1835, reprinted in Barker, *The McLoughlin Empire*, 213-14.

"I think my father himself would": Ibid.

"Will you be so kind": McLoughlin Jr.'s letter to John Fraser, August 28, 1835, reprinted in Barker, *The McLoughlin Empire*, 217.

"make a little money": Ibid.

"such heavy debts": Foster, "Killing Mr. John," 155. Although this is a highly credible source, Foster offers no citation to support the claim, and I could find no independent source to verify it.

"John has written me": Dr. McLoughlin, letter to Dr. Simon Fraser, February 16, 1836, reprinted in Barker, *The McLoughlin Empire*, 224.

McLoughlin Jr.'s physical resemblance to father: Dr. McLoughlin's letter to the Governor and Committee of the Hudson's Bay Company, November 20, 1844, reprinted in E.E. Rich, ed., *The Letters of John McLoughlin from Fort Vancouver to the Governor and Committee, Third Series, 1844–46*, vol. VII (London: Hudson's Bay Record Society, 1944), 48-93.

"concerned about the increasingly limited": Foster, "Killing Mr. John," 155.

41 **"made it my study"**: George Simpson, letter to Andrew Colvile, May 20, 1822, cited in Galbraith, *The Little Emperor*, 63.

"I am convinced": Ibid.

"racist attitude toward non-whites": Raffan, *Emperor of the North*, 191.

"an enlightened Indian": George Simpson, letter to Andrew Colville, May 20, 1822, in Galbraith, *The Little Emperor*, 63.

"a little too much addicted": Cited in John S. Galbraith, "The little emperor," *The Beaver* 40, no. 3 (1960): 22.

"prone to act on them": Barker, *The McLoughlin Empire*, 124.

"thoughtless, dissipated and depraved": Cited in Williams, *Hudson's Bay Miscellany*, 154.

"They look upon me": Cited in Newman, *Caesars of the Wilderness*, 199.

"qualified to cheat an Indian": Entry for Donald McIntosh, Simpson's Character Book, 188.

"bits of brown": Cited in Raffan, *Emperor of the North*, 229.

"his bit of circulating copper": Cited in Williams, *Hudson's Bay Miscellany*, 158.

"Japan helpmate": Cited in Galbraith, *The Little Emperor*, 69.

"washerwoman": Raffan, *Emperor of the North*, 202.

42 **"Father of the Fur Trade":** Newman, *Caesars of the Wilderness*, 259.

"rather imposing mien": Malcolm McLeod, ed., *Peace River: A Canoe Voyage from Hudson's Bay to Pacific by Sir George Simpson in 1828—Journal of the Late Chief Factor Archibald McDonald (Hon. Hudson's Bay Company), Who Accompanied Him* (Edmonton: M.G. Hurtig, 1971), 27.

"red-headed magpie": Newman, *Caesars of the Wilderness*, 221.

Simpson's salary: Raffan, *Emperor of the North*, 289.

"a gorgeous cloak of red Scottish": Morrison, *The Eagle & the Fort*, 60.

"unsung, unlettered and uncouth": Peter C. Newman, *Empire of the Bay: An Illustrated History of the Hudson's Bay Company* (Markham, ON: Penguin, 1989), 112 (hereafter *Empire of the Bay*).

"penchant for speed": Galbraith, *The Little Emperor*, 31.

43 **Simpson's speed records:** Raffan, *Emperor of the North*, establishes this fact beyond any shadow of doubt.

"moccasin telegraph": Ibid, 94.

"little to commend": Cited in Raffan, *Emperor of the North*, 186.

"had the exact same complaints": Ibid., 191.

"his caprice, his favouritism": John McLean, *Notes of a Twenty-Five Years' Service in the Hudson's Bay Territory, Volumes I and II, 1849*, ed. William Stewart Wallace (Toronto: Champlain Society, 1932), 389 (hereafter *Notes of a Twenty-Five Years' Service*).

Simpson's edicts were final: Those signed to the HBC realized the walls had ears, and one misstep could prove fatal: "the clerk knows that if he is heard to utter a word of disapprobation, it is carried to the ears of his sovereign lord and his prospects of advancement are marred for ever" (McLean, *Notes of a Twenty-Five Years' Service*, 386).

"know better" and **"their assent":** Ibid., 334.

Monday, April 25, 1842—Nightfall

45 **Simpson's personal bagpiper:** Raffan, *Emperor of the North*, 237.

"don his beaver topper": Newman, *Empire of the Bay*, 140.

"The stillness that prevailed": George Simpson, letter to McLoughlin Sr., April 27, 1842, E 13/1, folio 79-80, HBCA.

"filled with apprehension": Ibid.

"a scene which no pen": Ibid.

46 **"hurried into eternity"**: Ibid.

"to make me believe": Thomas McPherson's letter to John Work, Esquire, April 21, 1842, B.223/b/29, folio 21d, HBCA; also in E13/1, folio 82-83, HBCA.

"superficial investigation": Barker, *The McLoughlin Empire*, 48.

Chapter Three: The Honourable Company

47 **"left behind a legacy of alcoholism"**: Newman, *Caesars of the Wilderness*, 5.

"a man of intense loyalties": The quotation is attributed to historian Hugh Trevor-Roper, cited in Newman, *Empire of the Bay*, 33.

48 **The use of liquor and trade goods to curry favour:** noted in Raffan, *Emperor of the North*, 74. The rumour of mixing poison in tobacco is reported in Rosanna Seaborn, "Old-time company tactics," *The Beaver*, Outfit 292 (Spring 1962): 52-53.

"proud of having so many": Roberts, "Recollections of George B. Roberts," 21.

"scourged the poor Indians dreadfully": Ibid., 13.

Outbreaks coincide with ship arrivals: Ibid.

"all the Indians": Ibid., 21.

"Between you and me I have": McLoughlin Sr., letter to Simon Fraser, October 5, 1818, reprinted in Barker, *The McLoughlin Empire*, 169-71.

HBC and NWC almost bankrupt: Raffan, *Emperor of the North*, 61.

"sheer manpower" and **"ability to make"**: Newman, *Empire of the Bay*, 16.

Wintering partner: A wintering partner (or "winterer") was a shareholder in the NWC who participated in a pelt-sharing program that equally divided profits among all participants. The partners were required to spend two out of every three winters in-country, actively trapping, in order to remain eligible for profit sharing.

49 **"one of real affection"**: Barker, *The McLoughlin Empire*, 46.

McLoughlin's transformation from employee to shareholder: is described in Williams, *Hudson's Bay Miscellany*, 153. The employee participatory scheme awarded chief factors two shares each, while chief traders held a single share. Company regulations stipulated that only chief traders were eligible for promotion to factors, while any salaried clerk could be made a trader. The Company had no compulsory retirement, and a "dead man's shoes" offered the only real prospect for promotion to chief factor (ibid., 164).

Fort George not to Dr. McLoughlin's liking: McLoughlin Sr.'s letter to Simon Fraser, March 15, 1825, in Barker, *The McLoughlin Empire*, 175-77.

"the country was not worth a war": Roberts, "Recollections of George B. Roberts," 49.

"with unorthodox methods": Newman, *Empire of the Bay*, 141.

"too firmly in his own incorruptibility": Newman, *Caesars of the Wilderness*, 285.

"very Zealous in the discharge": Simpson's Character Book, 176.

"I always heard that my Father": Harvey, "The Life of John McLoughlin," 20.

"were afraid of him": Ibid.

"a very bustling active man": Simpson's Character Book, 176.

50 **"a disagreeable man":** Ibid.

"an island of luxury": Morrison, *The Eagle & the Fort*, 61.

"the New York of the Pacific": Attributed to Whitman, cited in Morrison, *The Eagle & the Fort*, 85.

"There was no society": Harvey, "The Life of John McLoughlin," 5.

"One thing occurs to me": Roberts, "Recollections of George B. Roberts," 40.

"that this country should not be inhabited": Thornton, "Oregon History," 5.

Beaver skins a finite resource: Even with its monopoly, the fortunes of the Hudson's Bay Company in Rupert's Land were on the wane. Over-trapping had depleted the stock near Montreal, and the Company had no choice but to move west into uncharted territory. Worse still, the market for *Castor canadensis* had bottomed out. "Once considered the world's most valuable fur" (Newman, *Empire of the Bay*, 14), the beaver had fallen out of favour. A beaver hat was *de rigueur*, the only means a rakish man had to combat the elements. But fashion is fickle, and the Company needed to change with the times. They ordered their trappers to expand operations to include bear, deer, mink, and marten. This in turn changed the trading culture, which had operated for decades with the beaver skin as its de facto currency. The HBC had built their trade empire on trade, and a beaver pelt could be exchanged for a blanket or gun or a predetermined allotment of tobacco, sugar, or liquor. Diversification meant the skins of other animals, such as the highly prized ermine, had to be converted into units known as "made beaver" (Raffan, *Emperor of the North*, 214).

McLoughlin Sr. never drank spirits: Roberts, "Recollections of George B. Roberts," 45-46.

51 **"a convert to Catholicism":** Galbraith, *The Little Emperor*, 77.

"they kept Sundays": Harvey, "The Life of John McLoughlin," 7.

"a British subject": Thornton, "Oregon History," 5.

"a gentleman of large heart": Ibid.

"neither more enlightened": McLean, *Notes of a Twenty-Five Years' Service*, 315.

"as ignorant of Christianity": Ibid. Not everyone agreed. While George Roberts recognized the Company did a "disservice" to their aboriginal charges by "Baptising indiscriminately," he stopped short of saying the HBC leaders "were all the vilest of the ill" ("Recollections of George B. Roberts," 17).

"The Indians came and asked": Harvey, "The Life of John McLoughlin," 4.

52 **"the HBC settled such incidents":** Foster, "Killing Mr. John," 147.

"as matters of corporate discipline": Ibid.

McLoughlin Sr.'s rule was absolute: Harvey, "The Life of John McLoughlin," 7.

"It is strange": Roberts, "Recollections of George B. Roberts," 9-10.

"You see the Co.'s chiefs": Ibid., 14, original emphasis.

"My father's method": See Harvey, "The Life of John McLoughlin," 12, for both the quotation and the accompanying story.

"the punishment was always": Ibid., 14-15.

53 **Selkirk's land grant:** Newman, *Empire of the Bay*, 117.

Selkirk's only visit to Red River: Newman, *Caesars of the Wilderness*, 138.

54   **"overburden of self-importance"**: Newman, *Empire of the Bay*, 122.

"a stern proclamation": Ibid., 123.

Walked into an ambush: One of the more colourful second-hand accounts of the Seven Oaks attack can be found in McLean, *Notes of a Twenty-Five Years' Service*, 369-72.

"damned rascal": Cited in Newman, *Empire of the Bay*, 123.

Grant shot Semple: George Simpson, in his Character Book (210), absolved Grant—whom the HBC later hired and employed for years—of all wrongdoing in the massacre, writing that Grant was "a generous Warm hearted Man who would not have been guilty of the Crimes laid to his charge had he not been drawn into them by designing Men."

"the dead were stripped": Newman, *Empire of the Bay*, 124.

55   **"like a kilted messiah"**: Cited in ibid., 125.

"piddling lord": Cited in Newman, *Caesars of the Wilderness*, 178.

"receiving, relieving, comforting": Cited in Morrison, *The Eagle & the Fort*, 27.

Burning documents in the stove: Newman, *Caesars of the Wilderness*, 179.

Sent to Canada for trial: There is some disagreement as to where the trial was held. Newman (*Caesars of the Wilderness*, 170-80) contends it took place in Montreal while Morrison (*The Eagle & the Fort*, 29) reports the trial was held in York, the capital of Upper Canada (now Toronto).

"was taken lifeless": Cited in Barker, *The McLoughlin Empire*, 41, although the original source is unclear.

"a haunting fear of death": Ibid., 43.

McLoughlin Sr. never at Seven Oaks: Morrison claims the doctor was in a canoe, en route to Red River, when the massacre occurred (*The Eagle & the Fort*, 26).

56   **Jury deliberated forty-five minutes:** Ibid., 29.

"not guilty": Barker, *The McLoughlin Empire*, 39.

Traders kill twenty-three men: Newman, *Caesars of the Wilderness*, 287. However, Dorothy Nafus Morrison, whose two biographies paint McLoughlin Sr. in a near mythic light, takes exception to the claim. In *The Eagle & the Fort* (59), she writes: "But when one of his expeditions killed a large number of innocent natives, he was so angry that he blocked the promotion of its leader."

"placate the Company's death squads": Newman, *Caesars of the Wilderness*, 287.

"a skin for a skin": Raffan, *Emperor of the North*, 5.

57 **"a tour de force":** Williams, *Hudson's Bay Miscellany*, 166, with original emphasis. Williams was quick to point out, in Simpson's defence, that the book was written during a period of great emotional turmoil surrounding the death of Simpson's son (ibid., 156) and should be viewed accordingly.

Victims identified by number: Ibid., 156. The book was not even officially listed in the HBC archives until 1923, and Simpson's exercise in character assassination remained a historical curiosity until 1935, when archivist Leveson Gower discovered the key to the coding system among George's private papers. The cracking of the number code and a discussion of its significance can be found in the introduction to Simpson's Character Book in Williams, *Hudson's Bay Miscellany*.

"a readiness, almost an eagerness": Williams, *Hudson's Bay Miscellany*, 154.

"has such tact": The quotation is cited in Raffan, *Emperor of the North*, 162, and is loosely attributed to Lord Selkirk, although in his footnote on page 443, Raffan raises concerns the attribution is in error.

"Damning & Bitching": Quotation attributed to Simpson, cited in Williams, *Hudson's Bay Miscellany*, 161.

58 **"an outstanding example":** Alan Cooke, "Review of John S. Galbraith's *The Little Emperor: Governor Simpson of the Hudson's Bay Company*," *Archivaria* 30, no. 2 (June 1977): 124-25, although Glyndwr Williams cautioned that Simpson's pathologies were "a matter for the psychologist rather than for the historian" (Williams, "Introduction" to Simpson's Character Book, in *Hudson's Bay Miscellany*, 162).

"a perfect Hypocrite": Williams, "Introduction" to Simpson's Character Book, in *Hudson's Bay Miscellany*, 195.

"firmness and decision of mind" and **"a weathercock":** Alexander Simpson, *The Life and Travels of Thomas Simpson, the Arctic Discoverer* (London: Richard Bentley, 1845), 80.

"it is his foible": Cited in Galbraith, "The little emperor," *The Beaver* 40, no. 3 (1960): 22.

"had unrivalled opportunities": Cooke, "Review of John S. Galbraith's *The Little Emperor*," 125.

"one of the best-hated": Ibid., 124.

"despised": Galbraith, *The Little Emperor*, 23.

"plausible and full": A. Simpson, *The Life and Travels of Thomas Simpson*, 40.

"severe and most repulsive master" and **"guilty of many little meannesses":** Ibid., 80.

"a bastard by birth": Newman, *Empire of the Bay*, 140.

"non-conjugal relationship": Raffan, *Emperor of the North*, 28.

Simpson's birth and early years: The date has caused discord among prior biographers. No birth records survive, and what documentation remains is contradictory. In the Canadian census of 1851, Simpson's age was listed as fifty-five, suggesting a birth year of 1796. His obituary in the London *Times* noted he was sixty-nine when he died, but his tombstone puts him at seventy-three. Historian John S. Galbraith suggests 1787 was most likely his year of birth and it seems as good a date as any (Galbraith, *The Little Emperor*, 11-12). As for the place of the blessed event, the possibilities include Dingwall — Dale Terrence Lahey, *Fed by Their Wings: The Descendants of Sir George Simpson* (Guelph, ON: Datel Publishing, 2003), x — and the parish of Loch Broom — Arthur S. Morton, *Sir George Simpson: Overseas Governor of the Hudson's Bay Company* (Toronto: J.M. Dent, 1944) — both in the Scottish Highlands, north of Inverness. All agree Simpson spent his formative years under the care of his aunt Mary in Dingwall, where he received an adequate if uninspired education. Also in attendance in the same two-room schoolhouse was Duncan Finlayson, a boy four years Simpson's junior, whose "private conduct & character" Simpson considered "models worthy of imitation." Duncan, "a highly upright honourable correct" lad, would become a childhood friend and lifelong colleague (all quotations from Simpson's Character Book, 186-87).

59   **"where his talents soon advanced":** McLean, *Notes of a Twenty-Five Years' Service*, 383.

Simpson traded in sugar: Raffan, *Emperor of the North*, 44-45.

"sufficient promptness and determination": Cited in Galbraith, *The Little Emperor*, 22.

"chosen for his courage": Cited in ibid., 24, although the original source was not credited.

"did not allow consideration": Ibid., 17.

"no background or demonstrable skills": Newman, *Empire of the Bay*, 139.

"an authority combining the despotism": McLean, *Notes of a Twenty-Five Years' Service*, 333.

"the North-West Company had previously": Ibid., 388.

"heir apparent": Newman, *Empire of the Bay*, 139.

Simpson ignores the conditions of his post: George Simpson's letter to Mr. Pooler, February 23, 1820, cited in Raffan, *Emperor of the North*, 62-63.

"the ultimate absentee landlords": Newman, *Empire of the Bay*, 205.

"with the lordly hauteur": Ibid., 140.

60 **"despotic":** McLean, *Notes of a Twenty-Five Years' Service*, 238.

"as if we had been": Ibid., 33.

"clothed with a power": Ibid., 333-34.

"acting as uncrowned king": Newman, *Caesars of the Wilderness*, xx.

"more absolute": McLean, *Notes of a Twenty-Five Years' Service*, 386.

"his role in Hudson's Bay": Raffan, *Emperor of the North*, 185.

"the slowness of the communications": Newman, *Caesars of the Wilderness*, 247.

"old and useless men": Attributed to George Simpson, cited in Galbraith, *The Little Emperor*, 60.

"parsimony of a very": McLean, *Notes of a Twenty-Five Years' Service*, 360.

"economy so ill-timed": Ibid., 243.

61 **"mangeur du lard" — a "pork-eater":** Cited in Galbraith, *The Little Emperor*, 211.

Simpson wins over all but Dr. McLoughlin: John S. Galbraith believed Simpson should not have claimed all the credit. The NWC factors were, after all, men of business, and their economic interests were better served by conglomeration, even under Simpson (*The Little Emperor*, 54-56).

"in the art of getting his way": Galbraith, *The Little Emperor*, 56.

"sham": McLean, *Notes of a Twenty-Five Years' Service*, 334.

"could outvote me": Attributed to George Simpson, cited in Williams, *Hudson's Bay Miscellany*, 154.

"The Committee received": McLean, *Notes of a Twenty-Five Years' Service*, 385.

62 **"tidbits and wine":** Newman, *Caesars of the Wilderness*, 230.

"Hudson's Bay sauce": Raffan, *Emperor of the North*, 166.

"Clothes that had once": George Simpson, *Fur Trade and Empire: George Simpson's Journal Entitled Remarks Connected with the Fur Trade in Course of a Voyage from York Factory to Fort George and Back to York Factory, 1824-25, with Related Documents*, rev. ed., ed. Frederick Merk (Cambridge, MA: Belknap, 1968), 23, original emphasis (hereafter *Fur Trade and Empire*).

Simpson dressed like a voyageur: Raffan, *Emperor of the North*, 168.

"a Radical" and **"would be a troublesome man":** Simpson's Character Book, 176.

Thursday, April 21, 1842 — Midnight

65 **As recounted by Thomas McPherson:** McPherson's account is an amalgamation of statements, including his deposition before Sir George Simpson on April 26, 1842 (E13/1, folio 69-81, HBCA) and his letter to John Work on April 21, 1842, as well as statements made by other witnesses that mirror McPherson's version of events.

"half-seas over": McLean, *Notes of a Twenty-Five Years' Service*, 53. Claims of McLoughlin's intoxication come from McPherson's deposition before Sir George Simpson, April 26, 1842: "on the 20th it was perceived about One Clock P.M. that Mr. McLoughlin was the worse of liquor, as the Day advanced he became more so; toward evening he became very drunk."

"I fell to bed": Benoni Fleury's deposition before Donald Manson, August 19, 1842, with addenda dated August 23 and 25, 1842.

"became outraged and thrashed": Benoni Fleury's deposition before Donald Manson, August 19, 1842.

"flew at Lasserte": Ibid.

McLoughlin Jr. strikes Lasserte a second time: Ibid., and corroborated by the testimony of Phillip Smith, who swore McLoughlin began beating Lasserte "repeatedly." Phillip Smith, deposition before George Simpson, April 26, 1842, E13/z, folio 189-190, HBCA.

McLoughlin Jr. grabs Aneuharazie by the throat: Simon Aneuharazie, deposition before Donald Manson, August 22, 1842, with an addendum from August 24, 1842, E13/1, folio 1-63, HBCA.

66 **"became outrageous":** William Lasserte, deposition before Donald Manson, August 11, 1842, with an addendum August 25, 1842.

"there is a danger near me": Pierre Kannaquassé's narrative.

"appeared particularly irritated": Simon Aneuharazie, deposition before James Douglas, April 22, 1843.

"take care of yourselves": Benoni Fleury's deposition before Donald Manson, August 19, 1842, corroborated by William Lasserte's deposition before Donald Manson, August 11, 1842, with an addendum August 25, 1842.

Fleury passed out cold: Benoni Fleury's deposition before Donald Manson, August 19, 1842.

"They have wounded me": Francois Pressé, deposition before Donald Manson, August 20, 1842, with addendum from August 25, 1842.

Kanakas: Kanakas were low-level HBC employees of Hawaiian heritage.

"Aux arms, aux arms": Antoine Kawannassé, deposition before James Douglas, April 22, 1843.

"You also want to kill me": Francois Pressé, deposition before Donald Manson, August 20, 1842.

67 **"any bad intention":** Antoine Kawannassé, deposition before James Douglas, April 22, 1843.

"his rifle fell": Francois Pressé, deposition before Donald Manson, August 20, 1842. Thomas McPherson, in his deposition before George Simpson, reversed the order of events, saying: "Mr. McLoughlin fell when his Rifle went off."

"succeeded in extricating": Francois Pressé, deposition before Donald Manson, August 20, 1842.

"in dread for my life": Ibid.

"The first Canadian": Ibid.

Seven or eight shots in quick succession: Ibid.

"seriously alarmed": Ibid.

Canadians: National, cultural, and tribal affiliations are difficult to categorize retrospectively. "Canadians" (as it is used throughout the text) referred to those of European or mixed European/aboriginal descent. Identities such as "Canadian" and "Kanaka" are defined in greater detail on pages 99 to 100.

Leclaire hides in the smithy: Louis Leclaire's deposition before Donald Manson, August 19, 1842, with an addendum August 25, 1842.

Heron hides in the toilet: George Heron's deposition before Donald Manson, August 19, 1842, with an addendum August 25, 1842, E13/1, folio 1-63, HBCA.

Martineau hides and sleeps: Oliver Martineau's deposition before Donald Manson, August 23, 1842, E13/1, folio 1-63, HBCA.

68 **"was walking about the floor":** Thomas McPherson, deposition before James Douglas, April 22, 1843, E 13/1, folio 210-215, HBCA.

McPherson the only sober man: In a letter written to John Work on April 21, 1842, McPherson claimed: "All hands and himself [McLoughlin] were drunk except me."

"About 9 P.M., [McLoughlin] called": Thomas McPherson, deposition before George Simpson, April 26, 1842.

"thought he saw a person": Thomas McPherson, deposition before James Douglas, April 22, 1843.

"to see who it was": Ibid.

"apprehensive of Mr. McLoughlin's violence": Thomas McPherson, deposition before George Simpson, April 26, 1842.

"1½ Gallons" and **"began to fight":** Thomas McPherson's letter to John Work, April 21, 1842.

"ran out of the House": Ibid.

"Mr. McLoughlin, who": Thomas McPherson, deposition before George Simpson, April 26, 1842.

"search of Urbain and Lasserte": Ibid.

"for what object": Thomas McPherson, deposition before James Douglas, April 22, 1843.

"went around in the Gallery": Thomas McPherson, deposition before George Simpson, April 26, 1842.

69 **"ran down into the area":** Ibid.

"3 shots were fired": Ibid. In a later deposition before Donald Manson on August 20, 1842, McPherson revised his statement, saying he heard three shots: "the first was fired about half a minute before the second." The third shot was fired "a few seconds" after the second. "The first shot was fired from the NE Breastwork." The other two were fired from the SW corner of the main house (E13/1, folio 1-63, HBCA).

"the ball passing through": Charles Belanger, deposition before Donald Manson, August 13, 1842, with an addendum from August 25, 1842, E13/1, folio 1-63, HBCA.

"one of those Shots": Thomas McPherson, deposition before George Simpson, April 26, 1842.

Location of McLoughlin's body: Simon Aneuharazie, deposition before Donald Manson, August 22, 1842.

"lying on his face": Charles Belanger, deposition before Donald Manson, August 13, 1842.

Shot through the chest: Thomas McPherson's letter to John Work, April 21, 1842.

"he did not even say": Ibid.

"We do not know": Charles Belanger, deposition before Donald Manson, August 13, 1842.

"some said it was": Ibid.

"I do not know the very man": Thomas McPherson's letter to John Work, April 21, 1842.

"the fatal shot": Lamb, "Introduction," in Rich, *McLoughlin's Fort Vancouver Letters, First Series,* xxxi.

Chapter Four: Dickson's Folly

71   **"air of command":** Elizabeth Arthur, "Dickson, James," in *Dictionary of Canadian Biography,* vol. 7 (Toronto/Quebec City: University of Toronto Press/Université Laval, 2003), http://www.biographi.ca/en/bio/dickson_james_7E.html.

"covered with huge whiskers": Ibid.

Dickson's prior association with the US military: Ibid.; see also Grace Lee Nute, "John McLoughlin, Jr., and the Dickson filibuster," *Minnesota History,* 17 (1936): 444-47; "James Dickson: A filibuster in Minnesota in 1836," *Mississippi Valley Historical Review* 10 (1923): 127-40; and "Documents relating to James Dickson's expedition," *Mississippi Valley Historical Review* 10 (1923): 173-81.

Dickson's grandiose plan: Grace Lee Nute, in her introduction to "The Diary of Martin McLeod," *Minnesota Historical Bulletin* 4 (1921): 351-439. The article includes a full transcription of the diary (hereafter "The Diary of Martin McLeod").

72   **"to aid the cause":** Barker, *The McLoughlin Empire,* 229.

"half-breeds": Ibid., 228.

"Quixotic career": "The Diary of Martin McLeod," 354, original emphasis.

"quite sanguine of success": Ibid., 359.

"movements at Buffalo": Ibid., 360.

"Remained one day at Toronto": Ibid., 356.

McLoughlin Jr. enlists: Sister St. Henry, in a letter to John Fraser, July 11, 1836 (translated from the original French, reprinted in Barker, *The McLoughlin Empire*, 227-28), wrote that four days prior, John Jr. had "left for Montreal in order to meet a Gentleman who one thinks is called *McKenzie* who has been in the N. West service, this person is now in the Texan Army, he promised a commission to John."

73   **"Secretary of State"** and **"Brigadier General":** From the footnote in Barker, *The McLoughlin Empire*, 227.

McKenzie's death: Ibid.

"encountered many interesting anecdotes": McLoughlin Jr. to John Fraser, September 1, 1836, reprinted in Barker, *The McLoughlin Empire*, 228-29.

"Crossing the lakes Erie and Huron": Ibid.

"courage and resourcefulness": Ibid.

"For the devotion": Ibid.

"McLoughlin and his men": "The Diary of Martin McLeod," 360.

"Rambled through Detroit": Ibid., 362.

74   **"saw some of its curiosities":** Ibid., 363, original emphasis.

"his unwashed followers": Ibid., 365.

Killed oxen worth $150: McLoughlin Jr. recounted the details of the sheriff's pursuit in a letter to John Fraser, who in turn repeated the account in his letter to McLoughlin Sr., April 13, 1837, reproduced in Barker, *The McLoughlin Empire*, 235-38.

"an ignorant brute": "The Diary of Martin McLeod," 364.

"the person who talk[s]": Ibid.

"his squaw" and **"some excellent Salmon":** Ibid., 367.

"Some savages": Ibid., 379.

"Such is the manner": Ibid., 390.

75   **"The coat must be red worked":** McLoughlin Jr., letter to John Fraser, October 11, 1836, reprinted in Barker, *The McLoughlin Empire*, 230-31.

"already prepared": "The Diary of Martin McLeod," 359, original emphasis.

"endeavoured to persuade": Ibid., 393.

"casting lots to eat each other": Ibid, original emphasis.

"Out of Provisions": Ibid., 414.

"Dog's meat excellent eating": Ibid.

"Since I last wrote you": McLoughlin Jr., letter to John Fraser, August 8, 1837, reprinted in Barker, *The McLoughlin Empire*, 239-41.

"long living on corn and pork": McLoughlin Jr.'s letter to John Fraser, October 11, 1836, reprinted in Barker, *The McLoughlin Empire*, 230-31.

76   **"The more I think on"**: McLoughlin Jr.'s letter to John Fraser, July 29, 1838, reprinted in Barker, *The McLoughlin Empire*, 241-42.

"a man such as your Dixon": John Fraser's letter to McLoughlin Jr., April 16, 1837, reprinted in Barker, *The McLoughlin Empire*, 238-39.

"join your Honorable Father": Ibid.

77   **"Trail of Tears"** and **"civilized tribes"**: Foster, "Killing Mr. John," 156.

Simpson offers jobs to Dickson's men: Barker, *The McLoughlin Empire*, 229.

"By detaching them you will": Cited in Lamb, "Introduction," in Rich, *McLoughlin's Fort Vancouver Letters, First Series*, xxvii.

"got a letter from Gov. Simpson": McLoughlin Jr., letter to John Fraser, August 8, 1837, reprinted in Barker, *The McLoughlin Empire*, 239-41.

McLoughlin Jr.'s job title and salary: Foster, "Killing Mr. John," 157; Barker, *The McLoughlin Empire*, 47.

McLoughlin Jr. had not been paid by Dickson: John Jr. told John Fraser, who in turn told McLoughlin Sr. John Fraser, letter to McLoughlin Sr., April 13, 1837, reproduced in Barker, *The McLoughlin Empire*, 235-38.

"chose to keep him": Foster, "Killing Mr. John," 157.

"Dickson's disordered mind": "The Diary of Martin McLeod," 352.

"the invasion ended in": Barker, *The McLoughlin Empire*, 229.

78   **"made a laudatory speech"**: Barker, *The McLoughlin Empire*, 229. Grant was one of Dickson's last remaining officers.

Monday April 25, 1842 — Full Dark

79   **"Mr. McLoughlin was in the habit"**: Thomas McPherson, deposition before George Simpson, April 26, 1842.

"addicted to the Bottle": George Simpson's letter to Robert McVicar, September 26, 1820, cited in Raffan, *Emperor of the North*, 111.

"was exceedingly violent": Thomas McPherson, deposition before George Simpson, April 26, 1842.

"the worst of all those": McLoughlin Jr.'s letter to John Fraser, October 11, 1836, reprinted in Barker, *The McLoughlin Empire*, 230-31.

80 **"could not get them to work":** Ibid.

"before I get to red river": Ibid.

"McLoughlin in other respects": Thomas McPherson, deposition before George Simpson, April 26, 1842.

"Simpson's penchant for early starts": Raffan, *Emperor of the North*, 334.

"The business of the post": George Simpson, letter to McLoughlin Sr., April 27, 1842.

"Ledger books and post journals": Raffan, *Emperor of the North*, 145.

81 **"because it confirmed his views":** Barker, *The McLoughlin Empire*, 124.

"had simply reverted to type": Lamb, "Introduction," in Rich, *McLoughlin's Fort Vancouver Letters, First Series,* .

"this dreadful act": George Simpson's letter to McLoughlin Sr., April 27, 1842.

"I have no Doubt": The words are attributed to George Simpson, repeated in Dr. McLoughlin's letter to Governor Pelly and the Committee, June 24, 1842, reproduced in E.E. Rich, ed., *The Letters of John McLoughlin from Fort Vancouver to the Governor and Committee, Second Series, 1839-44*, vol. VI (London: Hudson's Bay Record Society, 1943), 74-76.

"shot a man in cold blood": Simpson's Character Book, 195.

Siveright's career in the HBC: From a footnote in Williams, *Hudson's Bay Miscellany*, 195.

"he was more influenced": Simpson's Character Book, 195.

"in self defence": Lamb, "Introduction," in Rich, *McLoughlin's Fort Vancouver Letters, First Series*, xxxi.

82 **"attract much unfavourable attention":** Ibid.

Simpson's suspect hiring practices: Foster, "Killing Mr. John," 175.

"he had access to": Ibid.

"perception was everything": Raffan, *Emperor of the North*, 312.

HBC's perspective: Hamar Foster ("Killing Mr. John," 159) later summarized Simpson's conundrum: "Neither the company nor its monopoly were popular.... rumors of how harshly it treated both the Indians and its *engages* were common. If one of its clerks had so abused his men that they had killed him in self-defense, a trial in Canada would be (what today is termed) a public-relations disaster."

"In the whole case": George Simpson's letter to Governor Pelly and the Committee, June 21, 1844, reprinted in Rich, ed., *McLoughlin's Fort Vancouver Letters, Second Series*, xvi-xvii.

"Neither by this course": Ibid.

"conveniently antiseptic solution": Foster, "Killing Mr. John," 160.

"Mr. [Charles] Dodd, chief Mate": George Simpson's letter to McLoughlin Sr., April 27, 1842.

83   **"a respectable young man":** Ibid.

"Notwithstanding the melancholy": George Simpson's letter to Charles Dodd, April 27, 1842, E 13/1, folio 77-78, HBCA.

"McPherson and Smith, who": Ibid.

One final threat at Stikine: In his April 21, 1842, letter to John Work, McPherson claimed "now we are in danger from the Indians of this place as they want to attack the Fort when they heard [McLoughlin] was killed."

"the Indians, who are collected": George Simpson's letter to McLoughlin Sr., April 27, 1842.

"The indian interpreter Hanaga Joe": George Simpson's letter to Charles Dodd, April 27, 1842.

"he had been guilty": Lamb, "Introduction," in Rich, *McLoughlin's Fort Vancouver Letters, First Series,* iii.

"to be forwarded to Canada": George Simpson's letter to Governor and Committee, July 6, 1842, reprinted in Glyndwr Williams, ed., *London Correspondence Inward from Sir George Simpson, 1841-1842*, vol. XXIX (London: Hudson's Bay Record Society, 1973), 162.

84   **"had done all that":** Lamb, "Introduction," in Rich, *McLoughlin's Fort Vancouver Letters, First Series,* xxxi.

"Mr. McLoughlin's private": George Simpson's letter to McLoughlin Sr., April 27, 1842.

"a ring from the" and **"gave to the woman":** Powkow, deposition before James Douglas, May 18, 1843, HBCA E13/1, folio 242-243.

"this ring was afterwards": Ibid.

"Mr. McLoughlin's conduct": Cited in Lamb, "Introduction," in Rich, *McLoughlin's Fort Vancouver Letters, First Series,* xxxi.

86 **"His violence":** George Simpson's letter to McLoughlin Sr., April 27, 1842.

"Heroux's conduct": Taken from McLoughlin Sr.'s letter to George Simpson, February 1, 1844, in which he cited Simpson back to himself.

"no legal steps against": George Simpson's letter to McLoughlin Sr., April 27, 1842.

"their conduct throughout": Ibid.

"remarkable for its callousness": Foster, "Killing Mr. John," 160.

"harsh and tactless": Glyndwr Williams, *Highlights of the First Two Hundred Years of the Hudson's Bay Company* (Winnipeg: Peguis Publishers, 1976), 64.

"even if the details": Barker, *The McLoughlin Empire,* 48. Lamb also described the letter's tone as "definitely unsympathetic and, considering the circumstances, the wording is frequently harsh in the extreme" (Lamb, "Introduction," in Rich, *McLoughlin's Fort Vancouver Letters, First Series,* xxxi).

Chapter Five: "A Sink of Pollution"

87 **Stikine's location:** Ernest Voorhis, *Historic Forts and Trading Posts of the French Regime and of the English Fur Trading Companies* (Ottawa: Department of the Interior, 1930). Voorhis noted that Stikine was located on a flood plain four miles from the mouth of the Stikine River.

"had not been": George Simpson, *Narrative of a Journey Round the World, 1841-1842* (London: Hudson's Bay Record Society, 1847).

"an Establishment two hundred ft. square": McLoughlin Sr., letter to George Simpson, February 1, 1844.

"Tide very high": From the entry dated March 28, 1842, in Fort Stikine Journal, 1842.

"The slime that was": Simpson, *Narrative of a Journey.*

"a hell upon Earth": John Rowand's letter to McLoughlin Sr., March 11, 1843, printed in Appendix A in Rich, *McLoughlin's Fort Vancouver Letters, Second Series,* 355-56.

"The water was not": Harvey, "The Life of John McLoughlin," 13.

88 **"Civilized World":** In a letter to Simon Fraser, February 24, 1840, Dr. McLoughlin refers to life outside the HBC outposts as "the Civilized World." Letter reprinted in Barker, *The McLoughlin Empire*, 244.

"It was a miserable": Harvey, "The Life of John McLoughlin," 13.

Fort Tako: also appears in documents as "Taco" and "Taku." Fort Tako was built near Stephen's Passage (Voorhis, *Historic Forts and Trading Posts*). According to Roberts ("Recollections of George B. Roberts," 7), "The Russians permitted the building of Tako still further north — the rent was paid in wheat — butter & East side Otter."

"landlocked harbor": Voorhis, *Historic Forts and Trading Posts*.

89 **The eleven-day standoff:** Peter Skene Ogden's adventures are recounted in Newman, *Empire of the Bay*, 141-42.

McLoughlin Sr. tries to infiltrate Stikine: Raffan, *Emperor of the North*, 299.

Simpson goes to Russia: Ibid., 300. According to Galbraith (*The Little Emperor*), HBC Governor Pelly accompanied Simpson to Russia, a fact overlooked by some biographers and historians, because Simpson's account of the trip rarely mentioned the presence of his boss.

"an extraordinary looking": Cited in Alice M. Johnson, "Simpson in Russia," *The Beaver* 291 (1960): 4-12. The quotation appears on page 11.

"stupid to a degree": Ibid.

Two thousand otter skins: Raffan, *Emperor of the North*, 304; Foster, "Killing Mr. John," 149.

90 **"Indian trouble":** Foster, "Killing Mr. John," 151.

"HBC would need": Ibid.

"a big hogs head": Harvey, "The Life of John McLoughlin," 13.

91 **"We are in it":** McLoughlin Jr. describing his experiences in Fort Vancouver, in a letter to John Fraser, March 15, 1840, reprinted in Barker, *The McLoughlin Empire*, 244-45.

"are as attentive and": McLoughlin Sr., letter to John Fraser, October 24, 1840, reprinted in Barker, *The McLoughlin Empire*, 246.

"a good disciplinarian": Lamb, "Introduction," in Rich, *McLoughlin's Fort Vancouver Letters, First Series*, xxx.

"no half-breed ever": Ibid.

"a more sober": William Rae's letter to McLoughlin Sr., April 20, 1843, E13/1, folio 189-190, HBCA.

"it must have been": Barker, *The McLoughlin Empire*, 48.

"I believe he is": David McLoughlin, letter to John Fraser, April 7, 1842, reprinted in Barker, *The McLoughlin Empire*, 247-49.

"was kind and indulgent": Phillip Smith, deposition before George Simpson, April 26, 1842.

"too young and hot headed": Roberts, "Recollections of George B. Roberts," 22.

"he had not been": Harvey, "The Life of John McLoughlin," 14.

"congenial and competent": Lamb, "Introduction," in Rich, *McLoughlin's Fort Vancouver Letters, First Series*, xxx.

92   **"Mr. Finlayson, who I am sure could not tell a lie":** John Work, letter to George Simpson, May 1, 1842, D 4/7, HBCA.

"formed a favourable opinion": Foster, "Killing Mr. John," 153.

"at each stop, Simpson": Raffan, *Emperor of the North*, 342.

"Simpson's favourite trader": Newman, *Empire of the Bay*, 144.

"left John to govern": Barker, *The McLoughlin Empire*, 48.

"I am sure that all this comes": McLoughlin Jr., letter to Roderick Finlayson on December 2, 1841, cited in Lamb, "Introduction," in Rich, *McLoughlin's Fort Vancouver Letters, First Series*, xxxviii.

93   **"a poor soft half":** McLoughlin Sr. to the Governor and London Committee, June 24, 1842, reproduced in Rich, *McLoughlin's Fort Vancouver Letters, Second Series*, 74-76.

"McPherson was not a fit person to act as second": John Rowand's letter to McLoughlin Sr., March 11, 1843.

"soft and dull": McLoughlin Sr., letter to George Simpson, February 1, 1844.

"knew McPherson to be a lazy Sleepy Drone": Ibid.

"will never answer the purpose": McLoughlin Jr., letter to John Work, October 2, 1841, E 13/1, folio 295, HBCA.

Tuesday, June 28, 1842 — Dusk

95   **"The Dr. never smoked":** Roberts, "Recollections of George B. Roberts," 32.

"Brandy was placed": Ibid.

Other HBC employees knew before McLoughlin Sr.: Lamb, "Introduction," in Rich, *McLoughlin's Fort Vancouver Letters, First Series,* xxxviii.

96 **"Poor john":** David McLoughlin, letter to John Fraser, March 19, 1843, reprinted in Barker, *The McLoughlin Empire,* 246-47.

"he should Leave": McLoughlin Sr., letter to George Simpson, February 1, 1844.

"the chary way": Roberts, "Recollections of George B. Roberts," 7.

97 **"the depositions were a tissue of lies":** Lamb, "Introduction," in Rich, *McLoughlin's Fort Vancouver Letters, First Series,* ii.

"many had a motive": Foster, "Killing Mr. John," 174.

"some of the most": Ibid.

"Finlayson also showed": John O'Brien, statement regarding the death of John McLoughlin Jr., June 4, 1842, E13/1, folio 84, HBCA.

Lasserte not deposed, saw shooting: William Lasserte, deposition before James Douglas, April 22, 1843. He stated: "It was a clear moon light night and I could see both Mr. McLoughlin and Heroux distinctly." When later asked why he had not "informed against Heroux," Lasserte replied: "I had no opportunity of information against him before Sir George Simpson, during his short stay at Stikine, as I was not examined by him but I have given Mr. Manson all the particulars of the murder" (William Lasserte, deposition before James Douglas, May 8, 1843, E13/1, folio 252-253, HBCA). Lasserte added two additional comments: first, that he did not say what he had witnessed "before Urbain Heroux was removed from Stikine as I feared the man." Second, "I also think that Pierre Kannaquassé was an abettor of the murder" (ibid.).

98 **Kannaquassé would only identify the killer to Simpson:** Kannaquassé's narrative.

Manson, McNeill, Lee: Foster, "Killing Mr. John," 162.

Chapter Six: An Underhanded Complement

99 **"these men had been sent":** McLoughlin Sr. to Governor Pelly and the Committee, February 1, 1844, reprinted in Rich, *McLoughlin's Fort Vancouver Letters, Third Series,* 39-42.

"Our people here are": David McLoughlin, letter to John Fraser, March 19, 1843.

"a somewhat volatile": Foster, "Killing Mr. John," 149.

bois brûlé: Raffan, *Emperor of the North*, 370.

"confused tribes with clans": Foster, "Killing Mr. John," 150-51.

100 **Dividing the complement into three groups:** As an anthropologist, it pains me to do this, but to apply labels retroactively would be to artificially introduce a concept that was meaningless at the time, and is misleading now.

"They had lived apart": Foster, "Killing Mr. John," 175. The source of the internal quotations was not specified.

"a general comingling": Roberts, "Recollections of George B. Roberts," 9.

"a good deal of the Indian": Simpson's Character Book, 190.

"inclined to form leagues": Cited in Foster, "Killing Mr. John," 175.

"the most numerous": McLoughlin Sr., letter to George Simpson, February 1, 1844.

"by no means in good humour": Cited in Foster, "Killing Mr. John," 152.

"cheerful" and **"probably not the best judge":** Ibid., 151.

101 **"very humble indeed":** Fort Stikine Journal, 1842, from the entry dated Friday, June 19, 1840.

"came to the gate": Ibid, entry for Tuesday, March 29, 1842.

"given to them": Ibid.

"threatened to kill someone": Ibid.

"doing so to see": Ibid.

"would have made": Ibid.

"No one at Stikine": Foster, "Killing Mr. John," 152.

"At Stikine the Indians": McLoughlin Sr. to George Simpson, February 1, 1844.

"the bad quality" and **"you may push your finger":** Donald Manson, letter to Dr. John McLoughlin, September 3, 1842, E13/1, folio 292-294, HBCA.

"the natives also complain": Ibid.

"I think it my duty": McLoughlin Jr., letter to John Work, March 3, 1841, Judge Howay Collection, Library of the University of British Columbia.

Surrounded the fort with pickets: Ibid.

102 **"We require men"**: Ibid.

"I am here left": Fort Stikine Journal, 1842, from the entry dated Sunday, October 3, 1841.

McLoughlin Jr.'s letters grow desperate: In a letter McLoughlin wrote to John Work (March 3, 1841), he lamented, "If no exchange of men takes place, I shall not be able to do more than half of the work. . . . if it is in your power to remove some of the useless hands, I should be very thankful."

"the more I see": McLoughlin Jr., letter to John Work, June 3, 1841, Judge Howay Collection, Library of the University of British Columbia.

"new pickets": Ibid.

Trade was brisk: Fort Stikine Journal, 1842, from the entry for Monday, June 15, 1840.

Metis: Metis is "an elusive term" used to describe people of mixed European/aboriginal heritage (Newman, *Empire of the Bay*, 120).

"neither work, understand": McLoughlin Sr., letter to John Fraser, April 12, 1843, reprinted in Barker, *The McLoughlin Empire*, 249-51.

103 **"who has been taught"**: Kakepé, deposition before James Douglas, May 1, 1843, E13/1, folio 232-233, HBCA.

"a Sandwich Islander": Kanakanui, deposition before Donald Manson, August 24, 1842, E13/1, folio 1-63, HBCA.

"a half fool": Fort Stikine Journal, 1842, from the entry for Monday, June 15, 1840.

"a half-breed and passable": Ibid, entry for June 13, 1840.

"Pressé had been dismissed": McLoughlin Sr., letter to George Simpson, February 1, 1844. According to Foster, Pressé had been "turned out of the Southern Department" of Rupert's Land for trying to shoot a man at Moose Factory, although the exact details were unclear ("Killing Mr. John," 161).

"a smart lad": Fort Stikine Journal, 1842, from the entry for June 12, 1840.

"a good man": Ibid.

"a half fool": Ibid.

"Blackguard . . . who": Cited in Foster, "Killing Mr. John," 161.

"appears to be": Oliver Martineau, deposition before Donald Manson, August 23, 1842.

"the most Criminal": McLoughlin Sr., letter to George Simpson, February 1, 1844.

104 **"Ill Nature and Bad temper":** Ibid.

"getting into difficulties": Ibid.

"the ferocity that": McLean, *Notes of a Twenty-Five Years' Service*, 12.

"they do not pay": Ibid.

"the most uncouth, savage": Ibid., 119, although McLean was not describing the Iroquois of Stikine specifically.

"a good man before": Fort Stikine Journal, 1842, entry for Monday, June 15, 1840.

"Pierre Kanaquassi [*sic*] is": McLoughlin Sr., letter to George Simpson, February 1, 1844.

"a blackguard": Fort Stikine Journal, 1842, entry for Monday, June 15, 1840.

"one of the Greatest villains": McLoughlin Sr., letter to the Governor and London Committee, June 24, 1842, in Rich, *McLoughlin's Fort Vancouver Letters, Second Series*, 74-76.

"appears to have been": From George Simpson, Remarks on the depositions.

"addicted to liquor": Foster, "Killing Mr. John," 161.

105 **"Heroux was tried":** Letter from Dr. John McLoughlin to George Simpson, February 1, 1844.

"He would fly": Ibid.

"savage looks": William Lasserte, deposition before James Douglas, May 8, 1843.

"Heroux's dress was remarkable": William Lasserte, deposition before James Douglas, April 22, 1843.

"a good man": Fort Stikine Journal, 1842, entry for June 13, 1840.

"As a Body the Canadians": McLoughlin Sr., letter to George Simpson, February 1, 1844.

106 **"a very steady pains taking man":** Simpson's Character Book, 199.

"a queer looking fellow": Ibid.

"Work might draw negative": Foster, "Killing Mr. John," 165.

"I shall be obliged": McLoughlin Jr., letter to John Work, February 14, 1842.

Thursday, April 21, 1842—Midnight

109 **Kannaquassé's account** is a compilation of his various statements, including his narrative regarding the murder of John McLoughlin Jr., July, 1842, and his deposition taken at Nisqually, July 15, 1842, with two separate addenda from July 16, 1842. His account is augmented with quotations from eyewitnesses whose version of events corroborate Pierre's testimony.

"elevated": Kannaquassé's narrative.

"made no secret" and **"was heard several times"**: Benoni Fleury, deposition before James Douglas, May 1, 1843, E13/1, folio 226-227, HBCA.

"at the foot of the stairs": Thomas McPherson, deposition before Donald Manson, August 20, 1842.

Lasserte sees Kannaquassé waiting to shoot: William Lasserte, deposition before James Douglas, May 8, 1843.

"McLoughlin would certainly": Ibid.

McPherson provides liquor: Benoni Fleury, deposition before James Douglas, May 1, 1843.

"Mr. John had ordered": Kannaquassé's narrative.

Kannaquassé pours drink down his shirt: Ibid.

110 **"maltreating"**: Benoni Fleury, deposition before James Douglas, May 1, 1843.

"killing Fleury": Louis Leclaire, deposition before Donald Manson, August 19, 1842, with an addendum August 25, 1842.

"struck Urbain in the face": Antoine Kawannassé, deposition before Donald Manson, August 22, 1842, with an addendum from August 26, 1842 (E13/1, folio 1-63, HBCA), and repeated in subsequent depositions.

"I never received a blow": Ibid.

Heroux warns McLoughlin and leaves: Ibid.

"It would be well": Ibid.

"to come down": Joe Lamb, deposition before James Douglas, May 19, 1843, E13/1, folio 236-237, HBCA.

"heard someone jump down": Ibid. Lamb's story was corroborated by Simon Aneuharazie, who "saw someone jump from the gallery to the ground near the end of Urbain's house." It was Urbain Heroux. Simon Aneuharazie, deposition before Donald Manson, August 22, 1842.

111 **"insolent refusal"**: Simon Aneuharazie, deposition before James Douglas, April 22, 1843.

"appeared in a violent rage": Charles Belanger, deposition before James Douglas, May 2, 1843, E13/1, folio 222-225, HBCA.

"gun standing against": George Heron, deposition before Donald Manson, August 19, 1842, with an addendum August 25, 1842.

Heroux hides a gun: Ibid. Heron had found the gun by accident earlier that night. Curious, he had "examined it and found it loaded." Uncertain why it was there, he left it in place.

"saw Urbain taking aim" and **"but the gun appeared"**: Antoine Kawannassé, deposition before Donald Manson, August 22, 1842, with an addendum from August 26, 1842.

Sandwich Islanders asleep in their barracks: Powkow, deposition before Donald Manson, August 24, 1842, E13/1, folio 1-63, HBCA.

"seize Mr. McLoughlin": Kakepé, deposition before James Douglas, May 1, 1843.

McLoughlin orders the Kanakas to shoot Heroux: Powkow, deposition before Donald Manson, August 24, 1842.

"his wife refused": Antoine Kawannassé, deposition before James Douglas, April 22, 1843.

"his shirt was torn": Narrative of Quatkie's daughter.

"Heroux had fired": Antoine Kawannassé, deposition before James Douglas, April 22, 1843.

"continued walking about": Thomas McPherson, deposition before James Douglas, April 22, 1843.

112 **"Urbain wants to kill me"**: Thomas McPherson, deposition before Donald Manson, August 20, 1842.

"I will shoot him": Ibid.

"he would never be happy": Antoine Kawannassé, deposition before James Douglas, April 22, 1843. Although not present in the room, Lasserte testified that he "heard Heroux say if he Mr. John said anything to him, he would shoot him like a dog" (William Lasserte, deposition before Donald Manson, August 11, 1842). Heroux's threats were not the only ones levelled at McLoughlin; Pressé said that the best way to restrain McLoughlin was "to send a ball through his head" (as recounted in Lasserte's deposition before James Douglas, April 22, 1843). Pierre Kannaquassé often said that

McLoughlin "would never die by any hand but his" (also recounted in ibid).

"was aware of everything": Kannaquassé's narrative.

"a demented sort of": Foster, "Killing Mr. John," 163-64.

"kill me if you can": Kannaquassé's narrative.

"does not come soon": Cited in a letter from McLoughlin Sr. to Governor Pelly and the Committee, October 31, 1842 (reprinted in Rich, *McLoughlin's Fort Vancouver Letters, Second Series*, 82-90), and based on John Jr.'s wife's statement, in which she tells of her husband "taking me by the hand [and] said "You will not see me again. I am going to be killed by Urbain Heroux" (Narrative of Quatkie's daughter). In his deposition, Pierre Kannaquassé stated that McLoughlin told his Indian wife "he was to be killed that night." In Kannaquassé's narrative, he stated that Kawannassé told him that McLoughlin said to his wife, "I am going to die tonight.'"

"Never mind": Kannaquassé's narrative.

"that if he wished": Antoine Kawannassé, deposition before James Douglas, April 22, 1843.

Their support made McLoughlin cry: Simon Aneuharazie, deposition before James Douglas, April 22, 1843, in which he stated McLoughlin "was crying bitterly."

113 **"Smith & Simon":** Antoine Kawannassé, deposition before James Douglas, April 22, 1843.

"I must bring": Simon Aneuharazie, deposition before James Douglas, April 22, 1843.

"losing all patience": Antoine Kawannassé, deposition before James Douglas, April 22, 1843.

"as soon as it was loaded": Thomas McPherson, deposition before James Douglas, April 22, 1843.

"a stout bludgeon": Kannaquassé's narrative.

"looking suspicious": Thomas McPherson, deposition before Donald Manson, August 20, 1842.

"were in irons": Ibid.

A non-existent enemy: Francois Pressé, deposition before Donald Manson, August 20, 1842.

"the reports of more than fifteen shots": Kannaquassé's narrative.

"but not finding it": Phillip Smith, deposition before James Douglas, May 22, 1843.

"each a shot, apparently": Captain Cole, deposition before James Douglas, May 7, 1843, E13/1, folio 230-231, HBCA. This is corroborated by Anahi, who watched as Heroux "fired a shot in the air." Anahi watched as McPherson, Kawannassé, Smith, and Martineau did the same thing (Anahi, deposition before James Douglas, May 18, 1843, E13/1, folio 244-245, HBCA).

McLoughlin falls and rifle fires: Simon Aneuharazie, deposition before Donald Manson, August 22, 1842, with an addendum August 24, 1842.

"especially Lesserte [*sic*] and Urbain": Phillip Smith, deposition before James Douglas, May 22, 1843.

114 **On McLoughlin's command:** Ibid.

A dozen shots from the gallery: Phillip Smith, deposition before George Simpson, April 26, 1842, in which he testified that he heard "about 12 shots were fired in all."

"stop, stop, stop": Kannaquassé's narrative.

"walking cautiously": William Lasserte, deposition before James Douglas, April 22, 1843.

"weeping loudly": Thomas McPherson, deposition before James Douglas, April 22, 1843.

"saw Urbain": Antoine Kawannassé, deposition before James Douglas, April 22, 1843.

"Urbain stepped back": Ibid. A number of people saw Heroux fire the fatal round. Lasserte saw Heroux step forward from the corner of the house and discharge his gun at McLoughlin (William Lasserte, deposition before James Douglas, April 22, 1843); Kakepé was positioned at the end of Heroux's house, with a clear view of the platform. He saw Heroux "standing by the front corner of the house and saw him fire off his gun" (Kakepé, deposition before Donald Manson, July 24, 1842); Antoine Kawannassé "saw heroux distinctly when he fired the shot which killed Mr. McLoughlin, he wore a red woollen cap on his head at the time" (Kawannassé, deposition before James Douglas, April 22, 1843). Kawannassé detailed Heroux's second gun (Kawannassé, deposition before Donald Manson, August 22, 1842, with an addendum from August 26, 1842). Thomas McPherson later corroborated the existence of a second, hidden gun in his third and final round of depositions before James Douglas (April 22, 1843): "I saw a gun there that did not belong in that place."

"a very loud report": Phillip Smith, deposition before James Douglas, May 22, 1843. Many men insisted that the fatal shot was unusually loud: "a very loud report" (Thomas McPherson, deposition before James Douglas, April 22, 1843); Nahua also heard a "very loud report" (Nahua, deposition before James Douglas, May 18, 1843); as did Anahi (deposition before James Douglas, May 18, 1843).

"lodging in the Carpenters": Thomas McPherson, deposition before George Simpson, April 26, 1842. The story was corroborated by Charles Belanger in all of his depositions. George Heron claimed "the bullet lodged in the carpentry door after passing through the body" (George Heron, deposition before Donald Manson, August 19, 1842).

"immediately fell forward": William Lasserte, deposition before James Douglas, April 22, 1843.

"noise of a heavy body": Kakepé, deposition before Donald Manson, July 24, 1842.

"quite naked": Captain Cole, deposition before Donald Manson, August 24, 1842, E13/1, folio 1-63, HBCA. Naked might be something of an exaggeration. George Heron saw Captain Cole coming out of his house "with his trousers unbuttoned" (George Heron, deposition before Donald Manson, August 19, 1842).

"Urbain a few paces off": Captain Cole, deposition before James Douglas, May 7, 1843.

"lying wounded": Ibid.

"the murderer walked": William Lasserte, deposition before James Douglas, April 22, 1843.

"retreated a step or two": William Lasserte, deposition before Donald Manson, August 11, 1842, in which he claimed to have been standing between the kitchen and bathhouse "and I being intimidated [by Heroux], retreated behind the bath for a few minutes."

"saw a man laying": George Heron, deposition before Donald Manson, August 19, 1842.

115 **"come on from the corner":** Captain Cole, deposition before Sir George Simpson, April 27, 1842, E13/1, folio 69-81, HBCA.

"and place his foot": Ibid. That Heroux came forward, put his back to the wall, and pressed his foot into McLoughlin's neck comes from Captain Cole's deposition before Donald Manson, August 24, 1842. Others concur: "I saw Heroux with his foot upon the deceaseds neck and on asking him what he was doing with his foot there, he said I am doing nothing and took away his foot" (George Heron, deposition before Donald Manson, August 19, 1842); Powkow also saw Heroux with his foot on McLoughlin's neck (Powkow, deposition before Donald Manson, August 24, 1842); Kannaquassé reported seeing Heroux come forward from the corner and put his foot "savagely on his neck as if to complete the act should the ball have failed in causing death" (Kannaquassé's narrative). Kanakanui testified that Heroux rushed "with vindictive fury upon the victim who was still breathing and extinguished the feeble remains of life by treading upon is neck" (Kanakanui, deposition before James Douglas, May 10, 1843, E13/1, folio 238-239, HBCA).

"as if to finish": Kanakanui, deposition before Donald Manson, August 24, 1842.

"still breathing": Captain Cole, deposition before Donald Manson, July 24, 1842, E13/1 folio 195, HBCA.

"struck him a severe blow": Ibid.

"Get up now": William Lasserte, deposition before Donald Manson, August 11, 1842.

"lying on the left side": Kakepé, deposition before James Douglas, May 1, 1843.

"Mr. John is asleep": Phillip Smith, deposition before Donald Manson, August 11, 1842, with an addendum August 25, 1842, E13/1, folio 1-63, HBCA.

"hurra for my gun": William Lasserte, deposition before Donald Manson, August 11, 1842.

Heroux orders Pressé freed: Ibid.

"I do not know": Captain Cole, deposition before Donald Manson, July 24, 1842.

"I suppose it was": George Heron, deposition before Donald Manson, August 19, 1842.

"it could not have been the Indians": Antoine Kawannassé, deposition before James Douglas, April 22, 1843.

116 **"wrested":** Kanakanui, deposition before James Douglas, May 10, 1843.

"He who killed him": Kannaquassé's narrative.

"He who killed him will not hesitate": Ibid.

"You have killed the master": Captain Cole, deposition before Donald Manson, July 24, 1842.

"No, it was not I": Captain Cole, deposition before Donald Manson, August 24, 1842. Over time, the wording of the exchange evolved. First, Cole swore that Heroux said: "the master is dead, do not say it was me" (Captain Cole, deposition before George Simpson, April 27, 1842). The words cited here are from his second round of depositions. In his third, Cole testified that Heroux "told me not to say that he had killed him" (Captain Cole, deposition before Donald Manson, July 24, 1843). Cole claimed to have been frightened and intimidated by Heroux, who made him promise he "would not divulge the secret" (Captain Cole, deposition before James Douglas, May 7, 1843).

"in a furious manner": Nahua, deposition before James Douglas, May 18, 1843.

"had better take care": Ibid.

Kawannassé in the gallery: In his last deposition, Kawannassé swore that, immediately after Heroux shot McLoughlin, the killer looked at him in the gallery and threatened to "murder me if I informed against him" (Antoine Kawannassé, deposition before James Douglas, April 22, 1843).

"kicked the body": William Lasserte, deposition before Donald Manson, August 11, 1842.

117   **"he would not carry":** Ibid., a translation of the original French: "*Quand on tue un chien on le laisse là.*"

"painted himself with the blood": McLoughlin Sr., letter to Governor Pelly and the Committee, June 24, 1842, in Rich, *McLoughlin's Fort Vancouver Letters, Second Series,* 74-76.

"It was the blood": Ibid.

"some of the men": Charles Belanger, deposition before James Douglas, May 2, 1843.

"the fatal shot had been fired by one Urbain Heroux": Lamb, "Introduction," in Rich, *McLoughlin's Fort Vancouver Letters, First Series,* i. In a later deposition, Antoine Kawannassé told HBC officials: "A good many shots were fired immediately before Mr. John's death, I do not know exactly how many but, the last shot was the one fired by Urbain Heroux," adding adamantly, "on this point I feel satisfied that I am correct" (Antoine Kawannassé, deposition before James Douglas, April 22, 1843).

Chapter Seven: Tight Reins and Loose Women

119   **"Horny Boys' Club":** Newman, *Empire of the Bay,* 13.

"for residence here among": J. Quinn Thornton, "Oregon History," 5.

"took their meals alone": Morrison, *The Eagle & The Fort*, 66.

Infanticide by country wives: Sylvia Van Kirk, "Women and the fur trade," *The Beaver* (Winter 1972): 4-21, reference on page 14.

120 **"were not enlightened":** Galbraith, *The Little Emperor*, x.

"the White Fish diet": George Simpson, letter to John George McTavish, November 12, 1822, reprinted in R. Harvey Fleming, ed., *Minutes of Council, Northern Department of Rupert Land, 1821-31*, vol. 3 (Toronto: Champlain Society for the Hudson's Bay Record Society, 1940).

"She is an unnecessary": Ibid.

"If she is unmarketable": Ibid.

"disgustingly indecent": Simpson's Character Book, 175.

"over intimacy" and **"indiscreet amours":** Simpson's journal entry for March 26, 1825, reprinted in Simpson, *Fur Trade and Empire*, 127.

"off the Ears of an Indian": Simpson's Character Book, 207.

"in the heat of passion": Ibid.

"Almost every difficulty": Simpson's journal entry for March 26, 1825, reprinted in Simpson, *Fur Trade and Empire*, 127.

121 **"short-term, potentially":** Foster, "Killing Mr. John," 178.

"Fourteen or fifteen of the men": Cited in Laura F. Klein, "Demystifying the opposition: The Hudson's Bay Company and the Tlingit," *Arctic Anthropology* 24 (1987): 101-14, quotation on page 111.

"these matrimonial connections" and **"a useful link":** Ibid.

"afforded the Stikine Tlingit": Foster, "Killing Mr. John," 179. Also see Klein, "Demystifying the opposition."

"petty coat politicians": Cited in Newman, *Caesars of the Wilderness*, 262.

"I must beg": George Simpson's letter to Charles Dodd, April 27, 1842.

Abandoned women: Newman, *Caesars of the Wilderness*, 262.

"The Company's practice": Foster, "Killing Mr. John," 180.

Simpson looks for a wife: Raffan, *Emperor of the North*, 165.

122 **"A wife I fear":** Cited in Galbraith, *The Little Emperor*, 5.

"Would you believe it?": George Simpson, letter to John George McTavish, December 26, 1829, B.135/c/2, HBCA.

"I shall settle my bullocks": Ibid.

George's wedding date: Raffan, *Emperor of the North,* 253.

Frances refers to her husband as "Mr. Simpson": Cited in Galbraith, *The Little Emperor,* 107.

"affection-starved": Raffan, *Emperor of the North,* 376.

123 **"a prized but almost inanimate possession":** Newman, *Caesars of the Wilderness,* 270.

"there is no direct evidence": Raffan, *Emperor of the North,* 376.

"overnight, she created": Newman, *Empire of the Bay,* 161.

"Indian wives": James Douglas, letter to James Hargrave, February 26, 1840, Hargrave Papers, Library and Archives Canada.

124 **"his disapproval":** Foster, "Killing Mr. John," 192.

"had fathered": Ibid.

"refused to accept": Williams, *Hudson's Bay Miscellany,* 160.

"mix with their country wives": Cited in ibid., 158.

"old concern": Cited in Van Kirk, "Women and the fur trade," 13.

"Pray keep an Eye": Ibid.

"disposed of": George Simpson, letter to John George McTavish, January 3, 1830, B.135/c/2, HBCA.

"The Govr's little tit bit": William Sinclair, letter to Edward Ermatinger, August 15, 1831, AB 40 Er 62.3, Ermatinger Papers, British Columbia Archives.

"the unmarried men": Kannaquassé's narrative.

125 **"scaling the Picquets"** and **"dusky maidens":** Cited in Lamb, "Introduction," in Rich, *McLoughlin's Fort Vancouver Letters, First Series,* xxxiv.

"the real cause": Cited in John McLoughlin Sr.'s letter to Governor and Committee, November 18, 1843, E13/1, folio 159-178, HBCA.

"All the Ill Will": McLoughlin Sr., letter to George Simpson, February 1, 1844. This policy enforcement led Hamar Foster to wonder whether McLoughlin had refused to allow Kannaquassé and Heroux to bring their women into the fort because "he felt he should exclude all women except his own, or because the Iroquois' marriage had not been approved by Simpson?" (Foster, "Killing Mr. John," 179). The evidence gathered after his death suggests the latter to be true. During his deposition, Kannaquassé was asked: "did you ask permission of the deceased to take wife?" A: "yes, the deceased said you shall not have permission before Sir George Simpson's arrival" (Kannaquassé's deposition). He was also asked: "Did you ever haul up women into the Bastion," to which he replied "no." This claim was refuted by others, including Phillip Smith, who testified that Kannaquassé "disliked me greatly... for having informed against him when attempting to bring women of bad character into the fort by the portholes of the bastions, for which he was punished" (Phillip Smith, deposition before James Douglas, May 22, 1843).

"for giving away his clothes": Francois Pressé, deposition before James Douglas, May 1, 1843, E13/1, folio 228-229, HBCA.

"Mr. McLoughlin summoned": Ibid.

"for allowing his wife": Oliver Martineau, deposition before Donald Manson, August 23, 1842; corroborated in Kakepé's deposition before Donald Manson, August 23, 1842, E13/1, folio 1-63, HBCA.

"brought a woman": Antoine Kawannassé, deposition before James Douglas, April 22, 1843.

"gave the woman 4 yards": Thomas McPherson's deposition before James Douglas, April 22, 1843.

"opened the Fort Gate": Charles Dodd, deposition regarding the murder of John McLoughlin Jr., August 1842, with an addendum November 9, 1842.

126 **"a loose woman":** Thomas McPherson, deposition before James Douglas, April 22, 1843.

"to spend the night": Ibid.

"pilfered from the Store": McLoughlin Sr.'s letter to George Simpson, February 1, 1844.

"Mr. John turn[ed]"; "running after" and **"goods from the":** Antoine Kawannassé, deposition before James Douglas, April 22, 1843.

McPherson suspended: Thomas McPherson, deposition before James Douglas, April 22, 1843.

"McLoughlin did not": Benoni Fleury, deposition before James Douglas, May 1, 1843.

"turning Thomas" and **"dine with the men":** Kannaquassé's deposition.

127 **"was of the fox-hunting type":** Roberts, "Recollections of George B. Roberts," 16.

"a short stout man": Morrison, *The Eagle & the Fort*, 86.

"personal insult" and "too filthy": Ibid.

"a female of notoriously loose character": Ibid., 88

"If Dr. McLaughlin": Roberts, "Recollections of George B. Roberts," 16-17.

"The parson bawled": Ibid.

128 **"employees stand":** Morrison, *The Eagle & the Fort*, 88.

Thursday, April 21, 1842 — Dawn

129 **Rolled the body face up:** George Heron, deposition before Donald Manson, August 19, 1842, with an addendum August 25, 1842.

"carried on a plank": Charles Belanger, deposition before Donald Manson, August 13, 1842, with an addendum from August 25, 1842. The use of planks is noted throughout a number of depositions. The only exception was Phillip Smith, who claimed to have carried McLoughlin by the feet into the house (Phillip Smith, deposition before Donald Manson, August 11, 1842, with an addendum August 25, 1842).

"the body bled": Kannaquassé's narrative.

"was washed away": Ibid.

"hands and front": Antoine Kawannassé, deposition before James Douglas, May 8, 1843, E13/1, folio 234-235, HBCA.

Blood ritual stricken from official record: Ibid.

130 **"washed them in":** Ibid.

Three Kanakas prepare the body: Okaia, deposition before James Douglas, June 2, 1843, E13/1, folio 256-257, HBCA. Okaia claimed he was one of three who washed and dressed the body, although a dozen men claimed to have been in the room at the time.

"stripped, washed clean": George Heron, deposition before Donald Manson, August 19, 1842, with an addendum August 25, 1842. See also Kannaquassé's narrative.

Belanger shaves McLoughlin: Simon Aneuharazie, deposition before Donald Manson, August 22, 1842, with an addendum August 24, 1842, in which he said, "I saw Belanger shave the body." Kannaquassé also noted that "Belanger shaved and assisted to dress it" (Kannaquassé's narrative).

"tore the shirt open": Kanakanui's deposition before Donald Manson, August 24, 1842.

"attempted to tear": Okaia, deposition before James Douglas, June 2, 1843.

"threw the body on": Kanakanui's deposition before Donald Manson, August 24, 1842; corroborated by Okaia, deposition before James Douglas, June 2, 1843.

"saw Pierre strike": Kakululkulu, deposition before Donald Manson, August 23, 1842, E13/1, folio 1-63, HBCA.

"strike it on the face": Powkow, deposition before Donald Manson, August 24, 1842; corroborated by Anahi, deposition before James Douglas, May 18, 1843.

"the head by the hair": Kakepé, deposition before Donald Manson, August 23, 1842. Almost identical testimony was given by Okaia, deposition before Donald Manson, August 23, 1842 (E13/1, folio 1-63, HBCA), and corroborated by Kanakanui, deposition before James Douglas, May 10, 1843.

"While you were living": Simon Aneuharazie, deposition before Donald Manson, August 22, 1842, with an addendum August 24, 1842.

"were all crying": Okaia, deposition before Donald Manson, August 23, 1842.

"white blood": Kanakanui, deposition before Donald Manson, August 24, 1842.

131 **"was customary in Canada":** Kannaquassé's narrative.

"I do not know": Kannaquassé's narrative and deposition.

"till daylight": Oliver Martineau, deposition before Donald Manson, August 23, 1842.

"I was told": Benoni Fleury, deposition before Donald Manson, August 19, 1842, with addenda dated August 23 and 25, 1842.

"to move out" and **"go down stairs":** Narrative of Quatkie's daughter.

"quarrelled about who": Foster, "Killing Mr. John," 182. According to William Lasserte's deposition before James Douglas, May 8, 1843, Heroux "appeared determined to usurp the command of the establishment," and everyone was acting as if they were in command.

Nothing was accomplished: Fort Stikine Journal, 1842. According to the entry for April 21, 1842, written by Thomas McPherson, there was "no trade this day."

"up all night": Ibid.

132 **"I am afraid that":** Thomas McPherson, letter to John Work, April 21, 1842.

"Now Mr. John is dead": Kannaquassé's narrative.

"I see we must": Kannaquassé's deposition.

II: "A Skin for a Skin"
Chapter Eight: Casus Belli

135 **"to be much the best account":** Lamb, "Introduction," in Rich, *McLoughlin's Fort Vancouver Letters, First Series,* xxxiii.

"bored by his captivity": Foster, "Killing Mr. John," 162.

136 **"agreeing to murder":** Kannaquassé's deposition.

"care for killing": Lamb, "Introduction," in Rich, *McLoughlin's Fort Vancouver Letters, First Series,* xxxiv.

"that he had himself": Cited in Foster, "Killing Mr. John," 163, paraphrasing a similar passage from Kannaquassé's narrative.

"dejection of mind": Kannaquassé's narrative.

"put his foot on the neck": McLoughlin Sr., letter to Governor Pelly and Committee, June 24, 1842, in Rich, *McLoughlin's Fort Vancouver Letters, Second Series,* 74-76.

"Cowardly wretch": David McLoughlin, letter to John Fraser, March 19, 1843.

"such a dunce": Ibid.

"there is a mystery": Ibid.

137 **A discrepancy of £10:** McLoughlin Sr., letter to Governor Pelly and the Committee, June 24, 1842 (in Rich, *McLoughlin's Fort Vancouver Letters, Second Series,* 74-76), as well as countless other references in subsequent letters.

Researchers have undertaken audits: Lamb, "Introduction," in Rich, *McLoughlin's Fort Vancouver Letters, First Series,* xxxviii.

"however badly McLoughlin": Foster, "Killing Mr. John," 166.

"almost in the same state": Letter from Dr. McLoughlin to the Governor and the Committee, November 15, 1843, E13/1, folio 134-158, HBCA. In a letter David McLoughlin wrote to John Fraser, dated March 19, 1843, he noted: "The Wine which was sent to him, allowance for the year, was found almost complete."

"whom the men Made believe": McLoughlin Sr., letter to John Fraser, April 12, 1843 (Barker, *The McLoughlin Empire*, 249-51), reiterating prior comments made in his letters to Simpson and the Committee.

"I did not see the deceased": John Rowand, letter to McLoughlin Sr., March 11, 1843.

"having seen Mr. John": As recounted in John O'Brien, statement regarding the death of John McLoughlin Jr., June 4, 1842.

"he never saw Mr. McLoughlin": Ibid.

"without [McLoughlin] tasting a": Ibid.

"Indians do not view": McLoughlin Sr., letter to the Governor and Committee, October 31, 1842.

"to screen the drunkenness": Ibid. McLoughlin Sr. cited numerous other corroborating witness accounts, which are all recounted in a protracted discussion regarding John Jr.'s scant use of liquor in Appendix A in Rich, *McLoughlin's Fort Vancouver Letters, First Series,* 356-58.

138   **"When we Examine":** McLoughlin Sr., letter to George Simpson, February 1, 1844.

"If it is fair": Ibid.

"In consequence of this": McLoughlin Sr., letter to John Fraser, April 12, 1843, in Barker, *The McLoughlin Empire*, 249-51.

"Finlayson saw Mr. McLoughlin": John O'Brien, statement regarding the death of John McLoughlin Jr., June 4, 1842.

"Capt. Cole was flogged": McLoughlin Sr., letter to George Simpson, February 1, 1844.

139   **"every advantage of insulting":** David McLoughlin, letter to John Fraser, March 19, 1843.

"remote from civilization": Galbraith, *The Little Emperor,* 36.

"summary disciplinary action": Ibid.

"all the troublesome characters": McLoughlin Sr., letter to George Simpson, February 1, 1844.

"Is it surprising": McLoughlin Sr., letter to the Governor and Committee, November 18, 1843.

"hearing what kind of Indians" and **"it was not safe":** John Rowand, letter to John McLoughlin, March 11, 1843.

"had full confidence," "he would do well," and **"had found Everything":** John McLoughlin Sr., letter to George Simpson, February 1, 1844. McLoughlin revisited this complaint repeatedly, as in a letter to John Fraser, dated April 12, 1843 (in Barker, *The McLoughlin Empire*, 249-51), in which he groused that Simpson chose to "leave my Son the only Officer at the place Where there is the most Danger on the N W Coast, and which Sir George Simpson would not have done so if my deceased sons Good Conduct had not given us the Utmost confidence in his abilities."

"heard from the Natives": John Work, letter to George Simpson, May 1, 1842.

140 **McLoughlin knew of the plot against him:** In his letter to Simpson (February 1, 1844), McLoughlin Sr. recounted his interview with Saix's son, who claimed to have told John Jr. that "four of his men wanted to Employ him (Saixs Son) to murder the deceased."

"were in the habit": McLoughlin Sr., letter to George Simpson, February 1, 1844.

"had heard Heroux state": Antoine Kawannassé, deposition before James Douglas, May 8, 1843.

"there were three men": McLoughlin Sr., letter to John Fraser, April 12, 1843, in Barker, *The McLoughlin Empire*, 249-51.

"men at the fort": Foster, "Killing Mr. John," 174.

"I destroyed the paper": Thomas McPherson, deposition before Donald Manson, August 20, 1842.

141 **Search of the fort reveals nothing:** Donald Manson, letter to John McLoughlin Sr., September 3, 1842.

"we cannot find the paper": John McLoughlin Sr., letter to George Simpson, February 1, 1844.

"impossible to convict": Lamb, "Introduction," in Rich, *McLoughlin's Fort Vancouver Letters, First Series*, xlii, original emphasis.

"In my opinion": Donald Manson, letter to John McLoughlin Sr., September 3, 1842.

"in order to secure the principal": Ibid.

"and perhaps might be inclined": Ibid.

Manson orders six prisoners sent to Fort Simpson: Ibid.

"distinctly told me": Letter from George Simpson to Deputy Governor and the Committee of the Hudson's Bay Company, January 5, 1843 (B223/b/29, folio 23-28d, HBCA), citing McLoughlin's prior letter.

142 **"had no desire":** Ibid.

"at a British post": Foster, "Killing Mr. John," 149.

Historic Tudor statute: Ibid., 172-73.

Canada Jurisdiction Act: Raffan, *Emperor of the North*, 73.

"other Parts of America": Foster, "Killing Mr. John," 148.

"the sort of case": Ibid., 173-74.

"might prosecute the case": Ibid., 159.

"Instead of conducting": McLoughlin Sr., letter to George Simpson, February 1, 1844, repeating comments made in a letter dated March 20, 1843.

143 **"If the Deceased":** McLoughlin Sr., letter to George Simpson, February 1, 1844.

"the Best proof": Ibid.

"put me off": Kannaquassé's deposition.

"be allowed to make": Simpson's Character Book, 219, entry for Alexander William McKay.

"If you Sir": McLoughlin Sr., letter to George Simpson, February 1, 1844.

"vacillating, unsteady and arbitrary": McLean, *Notes of a Twenty-Five Years' Service*, 333.

"untimely End": McLoughlin Sr., letter to Governor Pelly and the Committee, June 24, 1842, in Rich, *McLoughlin's Fort Vancouver Letters, Second Series*, 74-76.

"insisted, with fanatical perseverance": Lamb, "Introduction," in Rich, *McLoughlin's Fort Vancouver Letters, First Series,* xxxviii. Chief trader John Tod thought the blame was shared equally between Simpson and McLoughlin Jr., saying: "They are to blame, I think, placing the young man in a situation for which his well known propensities rendered him so totally unfit" (from a letter by John Tod to James Hargrave, March 15, 1843, cited in Foster, "Killing Mr. John," 180).

144 **"Simpson's capacity":** Cited in Foster, "Killing Mr. John," 192.

"blood hounds": Simpson's Character Book, 222, entry for Thomas McKay.

"bruisers": Simpson's Character Book; see for example the entry for Antoine Hamel on page 215, or for George Linton, page 216.

"a necessary evil": Simpson's Character Book, 222, entry for Thomas McKay.

"I have, as you know": Originally from a letter by George Simpson to McLoughlin Sr., June 21, 1843; quoted back to him by McLoughlin Sr. in his letter to Simpson, February 1, 1844.

"become all at once": Cited in Foster, "Killing Mr. John," 177.

"I never saw a man": Cited in Galbraith, *The Little Emperor*, 45. The man struck was Thomas Taylor, Simpson's personal servant and the brother of one of Simpson's native mistresses. Taylor was smacked for bringing a "leud [*sic*] woman" into the outpost (ibid., 212).

"on at least two": Cited in Foster, "Killing Mr. John," 177.

"the principles of honour": McLean, *Notes of a Twenty-Five Years' Service*, 335.

"writing for Effect": McLoughlin Sr., letter to George Simpson, February 1, 1844.

"washed his Throat": George Simpson, letter to John George McTavish, August 1831, B.135/c/2, folio 74, HBCA.

145   **"until I gave him such a pounding":** Ibid. Curiously, although Simpson saw alcoholism as an unforgivable sin, he did not consider mental instability to be grounds for dismissal. Chief trader George Barnston, a Scotsman with more than twenty years of service, had a long history of depression, sometimes falling into such "a gloomy desponding turn of mind" that Simpson feared "he would commit suicide in one of those fits" (Simpson's Character Book, 231). Although it was "evident that he is of unsound mind at times," the Governor continued to "feel an interest in him" (ibid), eventually promoting him to the rank of chief factor.

"The Big Doctor": J.E. Harriott, in a letter to James Hargrave, December 2, 1842, reproduced in G.P. De T. Glazebrook, ed., *The Hargrave Correspondence, 1821-1843* (Toronto: The Champlain Society, 1938), 415-16, original emphasis.

"making each new fragment": Lamb, "Introduction," in Rich, *McLoughlin's Fort Vancouver Letters, First Series*, xxxv.

"had lost both his self-control": Barker, *The McLoughlin Empire*, 49.

"a number of new facts": Foster, "Killing Mr. John," 161. Foster also highlighted the irony that "it was the elder McLoughlin who pried most of this information loose, motivated as he was by grief and, possibly, by guilt over not having sent his son an able assistant when Finlayson was transferred."

Chapter Nine: Prior Bad Acts

147 **George Simpson and Thomas Simpson's early years:** Raffan, *Emperor of the North*, 311.

"Perfectly correct": Simpson's Character Book, 228.

"Secty and Confidential Clerk": Ibid., 227.

"considered one of the most finished scholars": Ibid., 228.

148 **"Entre nous, I have":** A. Simpson, *The Life and Travels of Thomas Simpson*, 78.

"when the Governorship": Ibid., 52.

"got the worst of the scuffle": Ibid., 42.

"Simpson was forced": Raffan, *Emperor of the North*, 315.

Thomas Simpson sent to the far north: In *Emperor of the North*, James Raffan argues that such a solution "shows George Simpson at his best" (293), prioritizing continued good relations with aboriginal people over his own well-being. I argue it shows Simpson at his laziest, shipping off troublemakers rather than dealing with the underlying problem.

"not calculated": Simpson's Character Book, 184.

"jealousy of his rising name": A. Simpson, *The Life and Travels of Thomas Simpson*, 338.

149 **"Fame I will have":** Ibid., 340.

Thomas Simpson receives the Royal Geographic Society medal: Raffan, *Emperor of the North*, 318.

Thomas Simpson's cause of death: Ibid., 319.

"committed suicide": Marjory Harper, *Thomas Simpson: Dingwall's Arctic Explorer* (Dingwall, Scotland: Ross & Cromarty, no date), 5.

"if Simpson had wanted": Raffan, *Emperor of the North*, 322.

Thomas Simpson buried in a pauper's grave: Ibid.

150 **Three researchers question Simpson's culpability:** Marjory Harper in *Thomas Simpson: Dingwall's Arctic Explorer*, Vilhjalmur Stefansson in *Unsolved Mysteries of the Arctic* (New York: Macmillan, 1942), and James

Raffan in *Emperor of the North* have openly questioned whether George Simpson orchestrated the attack on Thomas from afar. It is not only historians who feel this way. At the time of the murder, the victim's brother held George Simpson accountable for the death. He claimed the Governor had driven the victim from HBC service through his "callous disregard for his welfare and sneers at his superior education and intelligence" (quotation from Galbraith, *The Little Emperor,* 150, although he is referencing A. Simpson, *The Life and Travels of Thomas Simpson,* 21-22).

"Mr. Dease's name": McLean, *Notes of a Twenty-Five Years' Service,* 240.

George Simpson represses Thomas Simpson's achievements: Raffan, *Emperor of the North,* 323.

Thomas Simpson's Fame: Ibid.

Simpson knighted: Ibid., 4.

"fed by their wings": Ibid., 354. Newman (*Caesars of the Wilderness,* 217) translates it as "I am fed by birds."

"It is sometimes pleasant": Attributed to Baron Modar Neznanich, cited in Raffan, *Emperor of the North,* 354.

"The bauble perishes": McLean, *Notes of a Twenty-Five Years' Service,* 388.

151   **Simpson's investiture envisioned:** Raffan, *Emperor of the North,* 331.

Queen Victoria's height: Christopher Hibbert, *Queen Victoria: A Personal History* (London: HarperCollins, 2000), 61-62.

"Sir George owes his ribbon": McLean, *Notes of a Twenty-Five Years' Service,* 387-88.

Chapter Ten: An Irresistible Force, an Immovable Object

153   **The war between Simpson and McLoughlin Sr.:** Viewing the skirmish from a safe distance, historians have trivialized the duel with lopsided analogies that paint Simpson as the "pawky little bantam" to Dr. McLoughlin's "grizzled giant" (Raffan, *Emperor of the North,* 171, paraphrasing Galbraith's "cocky bantam" versus "proud giant" [Galbraith, *The Little Emperor,* 77]) or — taking the literal measure of each man — the "Big Doctor" versus the "Little Emperor" (Foster, "Killing Mr. John," 169, who in turn was paraphrasing from Lamb, "Introduction," in Rich, *McLoughlin's Fort Vancouver Letters, First Series*).

"McLoughlin's loyalty": Foster, "Killing Mr. John," 176.

"the pill without daring to complain": McLean, *Notes of a Twenty-Five Years' Service,* 387.

"ludicrously unrealistic": Galbraith, *The Little Emperor,* 48.

"You are pleased to jest": McLean, *Notes of a Twenty-Five Years' Service,* 336.

"the prepossessing manners" and **"his cold and callous heart":** Ibid., 383.

154 **"Simpson expected to rule":** Galbraith, *The Little Emperor,* 77.

"It is evident Mr. McLoughlin" and **"difficult and troublesome":** George Simpson's letter to Deputy Governor and the Committee of the Hudson's Bay Company, January 5, 1843.

"I had no power": Ibid.

"many worthless characters": Ibid. Simpson went on to defend his assessment of each man, writing: "Phillip Smith...was described to me...as a steady well conducted man and...I had every reason to believe that he merited the character that was given of him.... Of Fleuri [*sic*] I have not so good an opinion, and should not be disposed to place much reliance on his testimony if any advantage could arise to him by withholding the truth; but in the present case, I do not see that there is any good reason for doubting his statements.... Of George Heron's character I know but little, but I have never heard anything to his prejudice; on the contrary, there was an impression on my mind that he was a well conducted man, and he gave his evidence with much clearness. On a close comparison of the evidence of some of these people, it is possible that inconsistencies may be found; but I have no hesitation in again repeating my belief, that the main features are correct.... some of those Whites were anxious to fasten the charge upon an Iroquois named Antoine, who, however, appeared to me perfectly innocent of it."

155 **"became slothful and insolent":** Cited in Galbraith, *The Little Emperor,* 36.

"the very dross": Ibid.

"If humoured with trifles": George Simpson, letter to Duncan Finlayson, September 29, 1820, reprinted in E.E. Rich, ed., *Journal of Occurrences in Athabasca Department by George Simpson, 1820 and 1821 and Report* (Toronto: Champlain Society for the Hudson's Bay Record Society, 1938), 63-64.

"to find it is better": George Simpson's letter to Deputy Governor and the Committee of the Hudson's Bay Company, January 5, 1843.

"led [him] to suppose": Ibid.

"From what Mr. McLoughlin knew": Ibid.

"informed by their servant La Graise": Ibid.

"which I afterwards found": Ibid.

156   "at Least as much": McLoughlin Sr., letter to George Simpson, February 1, 1844, in which he cited Simpson back to himself.

"Simpson was indispensable": Foster, "Killing Mr. John," 182.

"crime was clearly" and "the charges of habitual intoxication": Foster, "Killing Mr. John," 168, who was in turn citing Lamb, "Introduction" in Rich, *McLoughlin's Fort Vancouver Letters, First Series*, xli.

157   "[The] evidence taken": Archibald Barclay, letter to George Simpson, September 4, 1843, reprinted in Lamb, "Introduction," in Rich, *McLoughlin's Fort Vancouver Letters, Second Series*, xli-xlii.

"has not been allowed to triumph": Ibid.

"the persons placed there": Governor Pelly and the Committee, letter to McLoughlin Sr., September 27, 1843, reprinted in Rich, *McLoughlin's Fort Vancouver Letters, Second Series*, 300-310.

"You have thus": Ibid.

Lamb feels McLoughlin Sr. was too personal in his attacks: Lamb, "Introduction," in Rich, *McLoughlin's Fort Vancouver Letters, First Series*, xliii.

"already damned himself," "saved," and "lost all sense": Galbraith, *The Little Emperor*, 146.

158   "may be the fabrications": Governor Pelly and the Committee, letter to McLoughlin Sr., September 27, 1843.

"that such scenes": Ibid.

"Is murder not to be punished": McLoughlin Sr., letter to George Simpson, February 1, 1844. As letters spent months in transit, it was not uncommon for the timing of correspondence to be wildly out of sync.

"I presume there is no place": Ibid.

159   "cold brave man": Quotation attributed to John Sebastian Helmcken, cited in Barry M. Gough, "Sir James Douglas as seen by his contemporaries: A preliminary list," *BC Studies* 44 (Winter 1979-80): 32-50, quotation on page 47.

"Old Square-Toes": Newman, *Caesars of the Wilderness,* 302; see also John D. Adams, *Old Square-Toes and His Lady* (Victoria, BC: Horsdal and Schubart, 2002).

"get on by dint": Margaret A. Ormsby, "Douglas, Sir James," in *Dictionary of Canadian Biography,* vol. 10 (Toronto/Quebec City: University of Toronto Press/Université Laval, 2003), www.biographi.ca/en/bio/douglas_james_10E.html.

"imperious, penny pinching": Newman, *Caesars of the Wilderness,* 301.

160 **"gentleman of the interior":** Adams, *Old Square-Toes and His Lady,* 43.

"mulatto of elegant mien": Newman, *Caesars of the Wilderness,* 301.

"furiously violent": Cited in Ormsby, "Douglas, Sir James."

"under watch and ward": Cited in Foster, "Killing Mr. John," 168.

"to be a man": Adolph Etoline, letter to McLoughlin Sr., September 1, 1843, translation from original French in Rich, *McLoughlin's Fort Vancouver Letters, Second Series,* 329.

161 **"I am going":** Kannaquassé's narrative.

Men remanded to McLoughlin Sr.: John Henry Pelly, letter to George Simpson, November 3, 1843, cited in Lamb, "Introduction," in Rich, *McLoughlin's Fort Vancouver Letters, First Series,* xlv.

Wrangel informs Pelly the Russians had no jurisdiction: Foster, "Killing Mr. John," 172.

"more fudge alleged": Archibald Barclay, letter to George Simpson, November 18, 1843, cited in ibid.

"If these men cannot be tried": Ibid.

"money was the real reason": Foster, "Killing Mr. John," 170.

"the expense involved": Ibid., 172.

"worth the trouble": Ibid.

162 **"I am no Lawyer But":** McLoughlin Sr.'s letter to Governor Pelly and the Committee, November 10, 1844, cited in Foster, "Killing Mr. John," 171.

"the Warrant of a Magistrate" and **"until instructions come":** McLoughlin Sr., letter to Governor Pelly and the Committee, November 18, 1843.

Sent to Canada for trial: According to McLoughlin Sr.'s letter to the Governor and Committee, November 20, 1844, Pressé had been injured and could not make the trip. McLoughlin sent Kannaquassé, Heroux, Lasserte, Kawannassé, Belanger, Captain Cole, Kakepé, Aneuharazie,

Fleury, Heron, Leclaire, Smith, Martineau, and McPherson to York Factory as either perpetrators or witnesses. William Spencer accompanied the group, serving as an interpreter (see also endnote 107 in Foster, "Killing Mr. John," 190).

Dr. McLoughlin would prosecute the killers himself: Foster, "Killing Mr. John," 170.

"[If] the prisoners either escape unpunished": George Simpson, letter to Governor Pelly and the Committee, June 21, 1844.

"to make up a statement": Ibid.

"simply cut off": Raffan, *Emperor of the North,* 349. McLoughlin Sr. wrote of incurring Simpson's wrath, "for which my salary of five hundred pound p annum is stopped."

Simpson pays the accused men: Foster, "Killing Mr. John," 180.

163 **"pile upon pile of":** Archibald McDonald, letter to George Simpson, April 27, 1843, quoted in Lamb, "Introduction," in Rich, *McLoughlin's Fort Vancouver Letters, First Series,* xliv.

"I fear the Dr.": John Tod, letter to Edward Ermatinger, March 10, 1845, cited in ibid.

"even McLoughlin ran out": Foster, "Killing Mr. John," 171.

"About that time": Harvey, "The Life of John McLoughlin," 22.

"Douglas was 17": Ibid., 24. She also noted that her father "was not so pompous as Sir James Douglas" (ibid., 23).

164 **Hopkins's instructions:** Galbraith, *The Little Emperor,* 126; see also the accession notes for Simpson's Remarks on the depositions in the HBC Archive finding guide.

"We shall not quote": George Simpson, Remarks on the depositions.

"From the forgained": Ibid.

Chapter Eleven: Putting Flesh to Bone

165 **"a fascinating, if somewhat pathetic":** Foster, "Killing Mr. John," 149.

"The dispute between the two": Newman, *Empire of the Bay,* 142. In *Caesars of the Wilderness,* 294-95, Newman dedicated several paragraphs to the event.

166 **"In all fairness":** Willard E. Ireland, "McLoughlin's letters, 1839-1844," *The Beaver* 24, no. 2 (1944): 45-46.

169 **"a bullet which"**: Benoni Fleury, deposition before George Blenkinsop and Sir George Simpson, June 26, 1842, E13/1, folio 69-81, HBCA. Phillip Smith tells an identical story: "the ball entering between the shoulders near the spine and exiting through the throat above the breast bone" (Phillip Smith, deposition before Sir George Simpson, April 26, 1842).

"having broken the spine": Pierre Kannaquassé's narrative. A similar description is found in the depositions taken by James Douglas of Antoine Kawannassé, William Lasserte, and Okaia. Regarding the gunshot wound, the only dissenting voices belonged to Kannaquassé and McPherson, men whose involvement in the crime casts some suspicion on the credibility of their accounts. Even so, both men described the exact same injury. In his later deposition, Kannaquassé simply reversed the trajectory of the bullet, suggesting "the ball [had] entered at the upper part of the breast a little below the gullet and came out a little below the shoulders" (Kannaquassé's deposition). McPherson reported the same wound but was uncertain as to the direction of fire: "a Ball having passed through his Body either ent'ring between the Shoulders near the Spine and coming out at the Throat or entring at the Throat and coming out between the Shoulders" (Thomas McPherson, deposition before George Simpson, April 26, 1842).

"the wounds made by the ball": Kannaquassé's narrative.

"Indian trade" or fuke: The fuke or Indian trade gun used is described in detail in Charles E. Hanson, *Northwest Guns* (Lincoln, NE: Bison Press, 1956), and S. James Gooding, *Trade Guns of the Hudson's Bay Company, 1670-1970*, Historical Arms New Series No. 2 (West Hill, ON: Museum Restoration Service, 2003).

"the Deceased was about": McLoughlin Sr., letter to John Fraser, February 17, 1844, reprinted in Barker, *The McLoughlin Empire*, 251.

Both men of similar stature: Although McLoughlin Sr.'s height was recorded for posterity, his son's and Heroux's were not. Both men were described as "big." At the time that meant near or above six feet in height.

170 **Lasserte's location:** Lasserte would later claim (in his deposition before James Douglas, April 22, 1843) that he was hiding in the blacksmith shop when the murder occurred, but Louis Leclaire—who was hiding in the smithy and whose story never changed over time—did not corroborate that claim. Furthermore, Lasserte repeatedly stated he had actually witnessed the murder, impossible for a man hiding in a closed workshop. In the same deposition, Lasserte also revised his account, saying he was unarmed at the time of the murder, which contradicted his prior statements. Kannaquassé saw Lasserte and noted "the back end of his gun resting on the top rail . . . in readiness to fire" (from Kannaquassé's narrative).

"The night was clear": Charles Belanger, deposition before James Douglas, May 2, 1843. Lasserte claimed he knew Heroux by his "red worsted cap, which he had on" (William Lasserte, deposition before James Douglas, April 22, 1843).

"in a stooping position": Kannaquassé's narrative.

171 **"Look where the balls"**: Louis Leclaire, deposition before Donald Manson, August 19, 1842, with an addendum August 25, 1842.

172 **"I examined his arm"**: Charles Belanger, deposition before James Douglas, May 2, 1843.

"I heard no report": Antoine Kawannassé, deposition before James Douglas, April 22, 1843.

"I saw no blood": Thomas McPherson, deposition before James Douglas, April 22, 1843.

McLoughlin exaggerates injury: Lasserte testified: "I saw Mr. McL after Fleury had torn his shirt sleeve & he complained of having been wounded in the arm by a ball, but there was no appearance of any wound on his arm" (William Lasserte, deposition before James Douglas, April 22, 1843). See also Charles Belanger, deposition before James Douglas, May 2, 1843.

"I saw him tear": Simon Aneuharazie, deposition before James Douglas, April 22, 1843.

No bullet wound to arm: Kawannassé stated: "The deceased had no other wound except the gunshot in the back and the cut on the forehead" (Antoine Kawannassé, deposition before James Douglas, April 22, 1843). His testimony was corroborated by Okaia: "I saw every part of the body while washing it and could discover no injury except a cut on the forehead, and a gunshot wound in the upper part of the breast bone near the gullet. Every other part of the body appeared sound and uninjured" (Okaia, deposition before James Douglas, June 2, 1843).

"one of his hands": Antoine Kawannassé, deposition before James Douglas, April 22, 1843. McPherson concurred: "One of his hands was also a little swelled" (Thomas McPherson, deposition before James Douglas, April 22, 1843).

"had hurt it": Thomas McPherson, deposition before James Douglas, April 22, 1843.

173 **"a large gash"**: Antoine Kawannassé, deposition before James Douglas, April 22, 1843. Belanger also mentioned "a deep cut on the forehead" (Charles Belanger, deposition before James Douglas, May 2, 1843), as did George Heron: "a severe cut in the forehead as if inflicted with some heavy

weapon" (George Heron, deposition before Donald Manson, August 19, 1842, with an addendum August 25, 1842).

"a perpendicular cut": Kannaquassé's narrative.

"from an Indian with": Recounted in Kannaquassé's narrative.

"lying on his side": Captain Cole, deposition before Donald Manson, July 24, 1843. Belanger corroborated the story; immediately after the shot, he saw the body lying on its face "with the rifle under it" (Charles Belanger, deposition before James Douglas, May 2, 1843). George Heron concurred (George Heron, deposition before Donald Manson, August 19, 1842).

"and with one hand": Kannaquassé's narrative. At times, the narrative was written in the third person by the recording officer.

"did not appear to be": Powkow, deposition before James Douglas, May 18, 1843. A similar report can also be seen in Kanakanui, deposition before James Douglas, May 10, 1843.

McLoughlin's breath laboured: Captain Cole, depositions before Manson and Douglas; and Nahua, deposition before Manson (August 26, 1842, E13/1, folio 1-63, HBCA). Okaia noted that the deceased "was still breathing" in his deposition before Donald Manson, August 23, 1842.

"writhing in the Agonies": McLoughlin Sr., letter to John Fraser, April 12, 1843, in Barker, *The McLoughlin Empire*, 249-51.

"made an attempt to rise": Captain Cole, deposition before James Douglas, May 7, 1843.

"to prevent his rising": Kakepé, deposition before Donald Manson, August 23, 1842.

"as if determined": Okaia, deposition before Donald Manson, August 23, 1842.

"upon it with his whole force": Captain Cole, deposition before James Douglas, May 7, 1843.

174 **"Urbain had no gun":** Kannaquassé's narrative.

"seized the deceased's rifle": Charles Belanger, deposition before Donald Manson, July 24, 1842, E13/1, folio 194, HBCA.

"broke the rifle": Captain Cole, deposition before Donald Manson, July 24, 1843. In an earlier deposition, Cole claimed that Heroux had picked up McLoughlin's gun and tried to strike him in the head with it but hit the railing instead, breaking the stock (Captain Cole, deposition before Donald Manson, August 24, 1842).

"the door of the men's house": Kakepé, deposition before Sir George Simpson, April 27, 1842, E13/1, folio 69-81, HBCA.

"a noise as if a musket": George Heron, deposition before Donald Manson, August 19, 1842.

"saw Mr. John's rifle": Ibid.

175 **"Was his rifle loaded":** See, for example, George Heron, deposition before Donald Manson, August 19, 1842.

"heard it was": Louis Leclaire, deposition before Donald Manson, August 19, 1842, with an addendum August 25, 1842.

"When he first came out": Antoine Kawannassé, deposition before Donald Manson, August 22, 1842, with an addendum from August 26, 1842.

Chapter Twelve: The Judas Goat

177 **"attempted to use a dirk"** and **"prevented by snatching":** Benoni Fleury, deposition before George Blenkinsop and Sir George Simpson, June 26, 1842.

"because I told the other Kanakas": Joe Lamb, deposition before Donald Manson, July 26, 1843, E13/1, folio 196, HBCA.

178 **"Fleury began soon afterwards":** Kakepé, deposition before James Douglas, May 1, 1843. Powkow concurred: "Fleury who was very drunk beating his wife severely" (Powkow, deposition before James Douglas, May 18, 1843).

"been a very wasteful expenditure": John McLoughlin Sr., letter to the Governor and Committee, September 1, 1843, E13/1, folio 131-133, HBCA.

"Deliver the following goods": List of goods given to Fleury's wife by John McLoughlin, 1842, E13/1, folio 198, HBCA.

"If their [*sic*] is no Blue Regatta": Ibid.

179 **"goods given to Fleury's wife":** Ibid.

"habits": Attributed to Finlayson, cited in Foster, "Killing Mr. John," 165.

"an extremely proper young man": Foster, "Killing Mr. John," 165.

"The only thing": Roderick Finlayson, letter to John McKenzie, May 1843, B.134/c/55, folio 348-351, HBCA.

"the deceased's attachment to women": Ibid.

"in having sexual relations": Foster, "Killing Mr. John," 165.

"troubled me": Finlayson's letter to John McKenzie, May 1843.

"Mr. McLoughlin, tho' he was my master": Ibid.

"the deceased's good Conduct": Ibid.

180 **"All hands in the Fort":** Ibid.

"the general opinion": Ibid.

"appetite for women": Foster, "Killing Mr. John," 166.

"allegations surfaced": Ibid., 165. Such allegations were not restricted to the Heroux household. Pierre Kannaquassé said, "Lasserte was excited against Mr. John on account of a suspected intrigue which he carried on with his wife" (Kannaquassé's narrative).

"met Mr. John near the door": Phillip Smith, deposition before James Douglas, May 22, 1843.

"On seeing me": Ibid.

181 **"wife or Antoine's wife":** Thomas McPherson, deposition before James Douglas, April 22, 1843.

"I think Urbain's hatred": Antoine Kawannassé, deposition before James Douglas, April 22, 1843.

"put him with the men": Kannaquassé's deposition.

182 **"The reason he gave":** Antoine Kawannassé, deposition before James Douglas, May 8, 1843.

"Can any man Blame my son": McLoughlin Sr.'s letter to George Simpson, February 1, 1844.

"men were not hung in Canada": Joe Lamb, deposition before James Douglas, May 19, 1843.

"that we had nothing to fear": Ibid.

183 **"as the life of the people":** Okaia, deposition before James Douglas, June 2, 1843.

"that Mr. John's Father": Phillip Smith, deposition before James Douglas, May 22, 1843.

"was never punished": Ibid.

"that he thought": Ibid.

McPherson launches second phase of his scheme: Thomas McPherson, second deposition before Donald Manson, August 23, 1842, E13/1, folio 1-63, HBCA.

"prepare the paper": Ibid.

"it was a good paper":: Nahua, deposition before James Douglas, May 18, 1843.

"the paper contained": Joe Lamb, deposition before James Douglas, May 19, 1843.

"merely to please him": Anahi, deposition before James Douglas, May 18, 1843.

"[I] cannot read": William Lasserte, deposition before James Douglas, April 22, 1843.

184 **"kill McL":** Kannaquassé's deposition.

"Mr. McLoughlin then took": Ibid.

McPherson reinstated: Thomas McPherson, deposition before James Douglas, April 22, 1843.

"McPherson destroyed the petition": Benoni Fleury, deposition before James Douglas, May 1, 1843.

"room in the night": Thomas McPherson, deposition before James Douglas, April 22, 1843. Although this specific quote referred to a similar instance with Charles Dodd, McPherson was describing a pattern of behaviour he began with McLoughlin.

Between 9:00 and 9:30 p.m.: Benoni Fleury, deposition before James Douglas, May 1, 1843.

"Every Canadian and Iroquois": John McLoughlin Sr., letter to John Fraser, April 12, 1843, in Barker, *The McLoughlin Empire*, 249-51.

"told Sir George": Ibid.

"did it of my own accord": Thomas McPherson, deposition before James Douglas, April 22, 1843.

185 **"highly unusual":** George Heron, deposition before James Douglas, April 22, 1843, E13/1, folio 206-209, HBCA.

"[He had] never gave us rum": William Lasserte, deposition before James Douglas, April 22, 1843.

"There was a light": Ibid.

"The porch was dark": Charles Belanger, deposition before James Douglas, May 2, 1843.

"the men would drink": Thomas McPherson, deposition before James Douglas, April 22, 1843.

"gave Heroux any rum": Charles Belanger, deposition before James Douglas, May 2, 1843.

McPherson enacts his plan: Had McPherson actually wanted to save McLoughlin that night, he could have. "Smith saw Heroux Load his Gun to kill the deceased and that he (Smith) never told the deceased of it" (McLoughlin Sr.'s letter to George Simpson, February 1, 1844). Smith did tell McPherson to warn McLoughlin to stay in his room, but McPherson did not relay the warning (Thomas McPherson, second deposition before Donald Manson, August 23, 1842).

"who carried a lantern": Powkow, deposition before James Douglas, May 18, 1843; corroborated by Okaia, deposition before James Douglas, June 2, 1843.

186 **"to fire two blank shots":** Oliver Martineau, deposition before James Douglas, May 18, 1843, E13/1, folio 240-241, HBCA. That Martineau had two guns loaded with blanks suggests some degree of premeditation.

"I saw Heroux": Antoine Kawannassé, deposition before James Douglas, May 8, 1843.

McPherson continues to break into the chief trader's room: Thomas McPherson, deposition before James Douglas, April 22, 1843.

McPherson's possible forgery: Although handwriting samples are available for both McLoughlin and McPherson, a handwriting analysis of this note is not possible as the document contained in the HBC archive is a copy, handwritten by another man and included in the packet of depositions sent by Simpson to McLoughlin Sr.

187 **"If ever men deserved":** Foster, "Killing Mr. John," 168, citing Lamb, "Introduction," in Rich, *McLoughlin's Fort Vancouver Letters, First Series,* xli, who in turn was citing Archibald Barclay's letter to Simpson, with original emphasis.

"Thomas McPherson...I firmly believe": George Simpson, letter to Deputy Governor and the Committee of the Hudson's Bay Company, January 5, 1843.

Thursday, April 21, 1842 — Midday

189 **LeClaire makes the coffin:** Fort Stikine Journal, 1842 — entry for April 22, 1842.

"My friends, pray do not": Charles Belanger, deposition before James Douglas, May 2, 1843.

"McPherson gave the men": Foster, "Killing Mr. John," 182

The weather on April 23: Fort Stikine Journal, 1842, entry for April 23, 1842.

"The men were employed" and **"the corpse was carried":** Ibid.

"the salute of a gun": Ibid.

"the men drank another dram": Kannaquassé's deposition.

McLoughlin's wife returns to her village: Narrative of Quatkie's daughter.

190 **"five black bear skins"** and **"Several canoes arrived":** Fort Stikine Journal, 1842, entry for April 23, 1842.

Chapter Thirteen: Endgames

191 **"divine Service"** and **"on the rising ground":** Entry S2, of Harriet Duncan Munnick, *Catholic Church Records of the Pacific Northwest*, vol. I & II: *Vancouver (1838-1856) and Stellamaris Mission (1848-1860)* (St. Paul, OR: French Prairie Press, 1972), 25; see also Foster, "Killing Mr. John," 193, and Bryn Thomas and Linda Freidenburg, *A Review of Data Pertaining to Cemeteries, Human Remains, Burials and Grave Markers Associated with Fort Vancouver and Vancouver Barracks, Clark County, Washington,* Short Report 543, Archeological and Historical Services, Eastern Washington University, January 1997 (revised August 17, 1998).

Paul Fraser was a trader at the McLeod Lake outpost from 1845 to 1848 (see "McLeod Lake Post, 1845-1848," M-1530, Hudson's Bay Company Posts fonds, Glenbow Museum). Despite repeated searches, I could find no biographical data to show any familial relationship between Paul Fraser and Dr. Simon Fraser. However, his presence at McLoughlin Jr.'s funeral suggests some familial tie.

"Stikine remained open": Foster, "Killing Mr. John," 180-81.

"beavered out": Newman, *Empire of the Bay*, 14.

"the posts were not remunerative": Roberts, "Recollections of George B. Roberts," 7.

192 **"a very fine"** and **"quite a Mechanical Genius":** Simpson's Character Book, 225.

"from constant Desk Work" and **"a rising man":** Ibid.

"a wretched place": Cited in Morrison, *The Eagle & the Fort*, 112.

"shot himself": Roberts, "Recollections of George B. Roberts," 42.

"indulged in a torrid affair": Newman, *Caesars of the Wilderness*, 256.

McLoughlin Sr. blames Simpson for everything: McLoughlin Sr.'s letter to the Governor and Committee, November 10, 1844, cited in Foster, "Killing Mr. John," 171.

"collapsed under the strain": Cited in Foster, "Killing Mr. John," 181.

"glass-covered coffin": Newman, *Caesars of the Wilderness*, 257 (footnote).

"Sir George Simpson's visit": McLoughlin Sr.'s letter to Governor Pelly, July 12, 1846, cited in Rich, *McLoughlin's Fort Vancouver Letters, First Series*, 171.

193 **"he would no longer":** Foster, "Killing Mr. John," 181.

"I found women & children": McLoughlin Sr., quoted in Thornton, "Oregon History," 6.

"Dr. McLoughlin furnished": Thornton, "Oregon History," 6.

"generous treatment": Ibid., 8.

"to destroy" and **"every effort be made":** McLean, *Notes of a Twenty-Five Years' Service*, 351.

194 **"overawing the natives"** and **"a travelling circus":** Newman, *Caesars of the Wilderness*, 292.

"rebuked him sharply": Thornton, "Oregon History," 6.

"Gentlemen, I have served": Ibid.

"threw up his commission": Ibid., 7. McLoughlin did not share his turmoil with his adult children. As his daughter Eloisa later recalled: "Towards the last something happened, I do not know what; I could not learn what it was. [Simpson] was against my father in something and my father was very angry about it. It was just about the time my father left; he got angry and left the company.... I know it was something my father was angry about that he left the company for the time" (Harvey, "The Life of John McLoughlin," 24).

"I have Drunk": Cited in Raffan, *Emperor of the North*, 349.

195 **Simpson wanted McLoughlin Sr. to pay outstanding debt:** Thornton, "Oregon History," 6-8.

McLoughlin Sr. never paid the debt: Morrison, *The Eagle & the Fort*, 149.

"a very generous pension": Raffan, *Emperor of the North*, 445 (endnote).

"his word was no longer law": Barker, *The McLoughlin Empire*, 50.

"fairly crushed": Roberts, "Recollections of George B. Roberts," 39.

"caused American citizens": Attributed to Dr. McLoughlin, cited in Newman, *Caesars of the Wilderness*, 296.

"saved all I could": Ibid.

"Father of Oregon" and "a continuous protest": Barker, *The McLoughlin Empire*, 50. Newman called him "Oregon Country's king" (*Caesars of the Wilderness*, 305).

"I might better": Cited in Lamb, "Introduction," in Rich, *McLoughlin's Fort Vancouver Letters, First Series*, lxii.

"prized most": Barker, *The McLoughlin Empire*, 318.

Knights of St. Gregory the Great: McLoughlin's knighthood was the lowest of the four classes in the civil order. Fellow recipients include Walter Annenberg, creator of *TV Guide*, and actor Ricardo Montalban, star of the 70s TV drama *Fantasy Island*.

196 "at the breast": From the Apostolic brief, reproduced in the appendix of Barker, *The McLoughlin Empire*, 319.

"in a sort of agony": Attributed to the "Chronicles of St. Mary's Academy in Portland" and cited in Barker, *The McLoughlin Empire*, 52.

"wilderness administrator" and "a diplomat": Newman, *Empire of the Bay*, 157.

"harassing service": Cited in Galbraith, *The Little Emperor*, 117.

"into theatrical productions": Newman, *Empire of the Bay*, 163.

"swath of absolute power": Ibid.

"a very valuable piece": McLean, *Notes of a Twenty-Five Years' Service*, 383.

197 "well knowing": Ibid., 387.

"pontifical sternness": Williams, *Hudson's Bay Miscellany*, 154.

"determination of blood": Cited in Galbraith, *The Little Emperor*, 101.

"my old complaint": George Simpson, letter to John George McTavish, no date, B.135/c/2 folio 57, HBCA.

"affections of the lungs": George Simpson, letter to Donald Ross, December 20, 1831, B.C.M. 432, Ross Correspondence Collection, British Columbia Archives.

"fagged Night & Day": George Simpson, letter to John George McTavish, August 1830, B.135/c/2, folio 73, HBCA.

"arm bared up": William Todd, letter to George Simpson, 1849, D.5/25, folio 390d, HBCA.

Duncan Finlayson and wife ordered to care for Simpson: Raffan, *Emperor of the North*, 366.

"enforced intimacy with": Cited in Galbraith, *The Little Emperor*, 127.

198 **Details of Frances Simpson's death:** Raffan, *Emperor of the North*, 377.

"Our old Chief": Edward Ermatinger, letter to James Hargrave, November 8, 1853, cited in Galbraith, *The Little Emperor*, 189.

"some suspected": Galbraith, *The Little Emperor*, 189.

Canadians thought the land was theirs: Ibid., 192.

199 **"I do not think"**: From an exchange between Simpson and parliamentary committee chair Henry Labouchere, cited in Douglas MacKay, *The Honourable Company: A History of the Hudson's Bay Company*, rev. ed., ed. Alice MacKay (Toronto: McClelland and Stewart, 1949), 246.

"quite disgusted": George Simpson, letter to John George McTavish, cited in Williams, *Hudson's Bay Miscellany*, 160.

"wretched expedition": Lord Selkirk, letter to George Bryce, January 20, 1882, MG 14 C15, Bryce Papers, Archives of Manitoba.

"deficient in sound judgement" and **"his nerves"**: Ibid. Galbraith defended Simpson's poor showing, saying Simpson had grown accustomed to the deference of politicians and had never before encountered such openly hostile opposition to his ideas (Galbraith, *The Little Emperor*, 197).

"'Tis high time": See Simpson's Character Book, 188, for example.

"I have never been": Cited in Galbraith, *The Little Emperor*, 203.

200 **"for the Indian Country"**: McLean, *Notes of a Twenty-Five Years' Service*, 351.

"dash, vivacity and song": Cited in Galbraith, *The Little Emperor*, 204.

"a social triumph": Ibid., 209.

Simpson delusions: Ibid., 206; see also Newman, *Empire of the Bay*, 166.

201 **Simpson issues bonus cheques:** The tale of Simpson's bonus cheques and the legal debate surrounding his state of mind is detailed in the Montreal Superior Court case file *The Rev. John Flanagan, Plaintiff vs Duncan Finlayson et al., Defendants,* which is discussed in the *American Journal of Insanity* 19, no. 3 (January 1863): 249-316.

"a fellow whom nothing will kill": Cited in Newman, *Caesars of the Wilderness*, 220.

Tertiary syphilis theory: Frits Pannekoek, "The historiography of the Red River Settlement 1830-1868," *Prairie Forum* 6, no. 1 (1981): 75.

"the Caughnawaga Indians": George Simpson's obituary, *Evening Pilot* [Montreal], September 12, 1860.

"The Little Emperor's light": Cited in Galbraith, "The little emperor," in *The Beaver* 40, no. 3 (1960): 28.

"his own friends will admit": McLean, *Notes of a Twenty-Five Years' Service*, 388.

Canada purchases Rupert's Land: Newman, *Empire of the Bay*, 169.

202 **"as if drawn by a dead horse":** Cited in ibid., 16.

Additional Sources

Beattie, Judith Hudson, and Helen M. Bass, eds. *Undelivered Letters to Hudson's Bay Company Men in the Northwest Coast of America, 1830-1857.* Vancouver: UBC Press, 2003.

Fogdall, Alberta Brooks. *Royal Family of the Columbia: Dr. John McLoughlin and His Family.* Portland, OR: Binford and Mat Publishers, 1982.

Montgomery, Richard Gill. *The White-Headed Eagle: John McLoughlin, Builder of an Empire.* New York: Macmillan, 1934.

Morrison, Dorothy Nafus. *Outpost: John McLoughlin and the Far Northwest.* Portland, OR: Oregon Historical Society Press, 1999.

Payne, Michael. *The Most Respectable Place in the Territory: Everyday Life in the Hudson's Bay Company Service, York Factory, 1788 to 1870.* Ottawa: National Historical Parks and Sites, Canadian Parks Service, 1989.

Wilcocke, Samuel Hull, Simon McGillivray, and Edward Elice. *A Narrative of Occurrences in the Indian Countries of North America, since the connexion of the Right Hon. The Earl of Selkirk with the Hudson's Bay Company, and his attempt to establish a colony on the Red River: with a detailed account of His Lordship's military expedition to, and subsequent proceedings at Fort William, in Upper Canada.* Montreal: Nahum Mower, 1818. Reprinted from the London edition.

Index